CW00345298

GERMAN
AIR ATTACHÉ

GERMAN AIR ATTACHÉ

The Thrilling Story of the German Ace Pilot and Wartime Diplomat *Peter Riedel*

MARTIN SIMONS

Airlife
England

Copyright © 1997 Martin Simons

First published in the UK in 1997
by Airlife Publishing Ltd

British Library Cataloguing-in-Publication Data
A catalogue record for this book
is available from the British Library

ISBN 1 85310 879 0

All rights reserved. No part of this book may be reproduced or transmitted
in any form or by any means, electronic or mechanical including photocopying,
recording or by any information storage and retrieval system,
without permission from the Publisher in writing.

Typeset by Hewer Text Composition Services, Edinburgh
Printed and bound in Great Britain by MPG Books Ltd, Bodmin, Cornwall

Airlife Publishing Ltd

101 Longden Road, Shrewsbury SY3 9EB, England

Contents

Introduction: How this book came to be written   7
Chapter 1 Interview with the General   9
Chapter 2 And Now the Admiral   18
Chapter 3 Cloud Flying to Washington   26
Chapter 4 The Führer Calls the Tune   38
Chapter 5 Gaining Intelligence   48
Chapter 6 The Crossing of Watersheds   59
Chapter 7 All the News that's Fit to File   71
Chapter 8 The Sleeper Wakes to Nightmare   82
Chapter 9 Invasion of the USSR   94
Chapter 10 Honeymoon With the FBI   103
Chapter 11 Winter of Discontent, Greenbriar Spring   112
Chapter 12 Return to Germany   122
Chapter 13 Defeatism   131
Chapter 14 Old Friends, New Despair   141
Chapter 15 Heinkel's Mankiller   151
Chapter 16 Stockholm Spies   164
Chapter 17 The Final Solution   176
Chapter 18 A Letter to America   186
Chapter 19 Hanna Amidst the Ruins   197
Chapter 20 Treachery   204
Chapter 21 Boat People   216
Chapter 22 Casablanca Interrogation   227
Chapter 23 Guilty Until Proved Guilty   237
Chapter 24 The *Gracie Blue*   245
Epilogue   264
Index   269

List of Maps and Diagrams

Area of the American National Soaring Competitions
   in 1937 & 38   31
Place names in the South West USA   55
Central Europe in September 1939   68
Some Significant Place Names   69
Central Europe After 1945   215
Map Showing the position of Nordviksstrand   217
Voyage of the *Elvie*   223
Voyage of the *Gracie Blue*   264

Introduction: how this book came to be written

In April 1970, having been involved in the sport of gliding since childhood, I was the editor of the small magazine, *Australian Gliding*. I had been appointed to this honorary post in 1969, a year after arriving in Australia from England. I was also working on a book, *The World's Vintage Sailplanes*, and wrote, care of the Soaring Society of America, to Peter Riedel, who I knew had flown several of the early aircraft in which I was interested. Within a few months the arising correspondence led to Peter visiting Australia to fly modern sailplanes at Waikerie (South Australia) and Tocumwal (New South Wales). He stayed at my home for a few days and during the evening conversations some of his extraordinary life story began to emerge. I strongly urged him to write his autobiography. He replied that it was on his agenda but he had other things to do first.

Among these was writing his three volume history of gliding and soaring on the Wasserkuppe, where as a schoolboy he began flying in 1920. Our correspondence continued with other occasional meetings in Germany and the USA but the autobiography was constantly postponed as he involved himself in other projects. By about 1985 it became clear that he would never write his own story. I suggested that we might co-operate and with his encouragement and that of Helen, his wife, began to go through the very large quantity of scattered notes and unfinished text which he had accumulated. There were some lengthy sessions with a tape recorder later. It proved impossible in one volume of reasonable size to write the whole life but the ten year period from 1938 to 1948, covering his experiences immediately before, during and just after the Second World War, seemed especially interesting and we decided to concentrate on this. The following text is the outcome. It is based chiefly on a typescript which Peter began to write under very difficult circumstances in Casablanca, but this has been greatly expanded and re-written to include other material from notes, taped interviews, Helen's own reminiscences and a very few previously published short articles.

Although the writing is mine, it is Peter Riedel's narrative and for this reason the first person has been used throughout. This also has imposed on the writer a certain discipline. The temptation to add a personal commentary has been very strong, especially since I am, by the standards of the SS, half Jewish.

There remain some obscurities where memory has failed and no written records can be found, and there are some events of which Peter still finds it difficult to speak. There are a small number of passages where he disputes in minor detail what has been written here. In these I have relied on notes he made at the time or very soon after the events, rather than on his interpretations fifty and more years later. All the footnotes, except for those in Chapter 18, which is an unedited and uncorrected letter of Peter's own, are mine, as are all the maps and the epilogue.

Martin Simons
Adelaide, November 1996

1

Interview with the General

The General took me on one side for a private conversation. He seemed a pleasant enough man aged in his late fifties, fitting my notion of a bishop rather than an old Prussian soldier; about average height, on the plump side with a round head, jovial, kind, smiling but quite serious now and there was a shrewd gleam in his eyes. It was 11 July 1937. We were in the Mark Twain Hotel in Elmira, New York State. I had just won the American Eighth Annual National Soaring Competitions, although as a German I could not receive the official title of National Champion. I was feeling very pleased with myself all the same. I had had a wonderful time, despite some bad weather, flying the special *Sperber Senior* glider that had been sent over from Germany for me. Before the competition started I had soared in it for seven hours over Manhattan, looking down on all the skyscrapers and attracting quite a lot of publicity. I had made many new friends and enjoyed some excellent competitive cross-country flying. Now all the celebrations were over and I was expecting to return soon to my airline job in Colombia.

After some conversation General Bötticher, to my puzzlement, began to ask penetrating questions.

'Let's see now. You are 32 years old?'

'Yes, almost. My birthday is in August.'

'Are you married?'

'No.'

What was this old soldier with the whiskers after? I knew he was the Military Attaché at the German Embassy in Washington, DC.

'How long have you been flying?'

It sounded as if he were interviewing me for a job! I didn't need one but decided that I should answer.

'Well, I started with a little biplane glider that I built myself at home. That was in 1919, I was thirteen. It didn't last long! I built another glider and took it to the first gliding competition on the Wasserkuppe in 1920. I was the youngest person there. That's when I started learning to fly.' This meant very little to him.

'Yes, yes, but never mind the gliding. When did you get your commercial pilot's licence?'

9

'In 1928. I was at the DVS, *Deutsche Verkehrsfliegerschule*, at Braunsch-weig and Schleissheim.'

'And after that you worked for *Lufthansa*?'

'Not immediately. I had a spell as a student co-pilot to complete my training and I gained my commercial pilot's licence but airline jobs were impossible to find. Because of my gliding experience Professor Georgii took me onto his staff at Darmstadt, working for the Soaring Research Institute there. We worked out safe methods for aeroplane towing of gliders and I did a lot of soaring too. I won the Hindenburg Cup in the Wasserkuppe competitions in 1933. I didn't join *Lufthansa* until '34 and then only for a couple of years. At present I am flying Ford Tri-motors and Boeing 247s in Colombia, for SCADTA.'

'What's SCADTA?'

'*Sociedad Colombo – Alemana de Transportes Aeros*. The Colombian-German airline. We work our schedules to connect with Pan American and we have a mail carrying contract with the Colombian government. I joined them in 1936.'

He nodded. 'And I am told you are a qualified aeronautical engineer?'

'Yes. I graduated from Darmstadt Technical University.' He apologised for this probing but said he had good reasons. The General had arrived earlier in the day at the gliding site on Harris Hill above Elmira town, introduced himself to the competition officials and been among the international crowd that greeted me on my return, by road, from the cross-country flight which confirmed my place at the top of the score sheet. I had not taken much notice of him.

'Hmm. That all seems satisfactory. Have you any military training?'

I almost laughed, but did not want to annoy him. During the winter of 1934-35 I had been included twice in 'voluntary' four-week special service training camps. *Lufthansa* was compelled by the Nazi govern-ment to send all pilots to these thinly disguised military courses. They were run by regular army officers and sergeants whose job it was to transform, in a few weeks, a group of reluctant and ill-disciplined civilian pilots into proper Prussian soldiers. We were all totally unenthusiastic about it.

You might be a good pilot, Riedel, but you'll never be a good soldier, was the sergeant's final comment when the course ended.

I admitted to Bötticher that I had, after all, become a *Gefreiter*[1], after my eight weeks of drilling on the barrack square. Nominally I suppose I still held that rank in the reserve but it was meaningless.

'Well, it's better than nothing. It would be enough. Your family?'

---

[1] Equivalent to Aircraftsman 1st class, AC1, in the RAF

10

'Father was a Lutheran minister, in Dehlitz. That's a small village, not far from Halle in Saxony.' I didn't tell him how wretched a minister father had been, how wracked with doubts, how he became mentally ill. Nor did I say that my mother had committed suicide when I was nine. I rarely could talk to anyone about that for it still brought me to tears when I thought of it. At the time we four children, Felix, Annchen, Beate and myself were told only that she had died suddenly of a heart attack. That she had shot herself with a small pistol, unable to face life with a deranged husband, was revealed to us only years later.

'My grandfather, on mother's side, was Professor of Theology in Halle.' I was proud of that. Halle had absorbed the University of Wittenberg in 1817, so Grandfather Herring was in direct line of succession, academically, from Martin Luther himself!

'My father's father, Grandpa Riedel, was an industrialist. He died in 1916.'

'Old German family, then. Well off, were you?'

'No one was wealthy for long after 1918. The money all melted away in the inflation.'

The General grunted.

'Are you a member of the National Socialist Party?'

'I, er, well, no, not really.'

'Are you or aren't you?'

'I did apply for membership, in '33. A friend of mine in Darmstadt persuaded me. I had voted for Hitler in the elections, like so many others. I thought that was enough. My friend said I ought to have the courage of my convictions and he said it would help me to get on. I didn't go through with it. I never joined.'

'What changed your mind?'

'Dr Goebbels.'

'What? How could that be?'

'Goebbels made one of his speeches soon after the Führer came to power. He said, now the Party was in government lots of hypocrites and self-seekers were rushing to join in the hope of advancing their careers. That certainly was not how I saw myself. I thought, damn it, if that's what they think they can do without me and I shall get on well enough without political friends. So I never actually signed up.'

'I see! But you approve of the Führer's policies?'

'I did at that time. I couldn't see much choice. The Republic seemed so weak and helpless. It was obvious the so called democratic government had failed, members in the Reichstag abusing each other instead of rational debating, while the country was going to hell, people starving. You remember! Huge unemployment, lists every day in the papers of people

11

who had killed themselves in despair. The choice for us was either the Reds or the Nazis. I didn't know much about it. Someone said to me, the National Socialist Party stood for comradeship, patriotism and the performance of one's duty. That sounded good. It seemed to me that the *Führerprinzip*, strong leadership, was what Germany needed. Things were very bad with the communists talking about revolution all the time. I thought the Nazis had some good ideas. I don't think I really understood their policies,'

'What do you think now?' I hesitated. The truth was, I had not given such things much thought.

'I've seen more of the world since those days.'

'So what does that mean?'

'Things look different when you get away from your own country. I had four months living in Latin America when I was with Georgii's soaring expedition to Brazil.[2] When I got back home in '34 and got the *Lufthansa* job, Hitler seemed to be carrying everyone along with him. The economy was booming, the unemployment problem had almost disappeared, the country was becoming strong again after all those years of hopelessness. I thought Hitler must be the right man . . . for Germany.'

'But still, you left the country in '36!'

'It just didn't suit me any more. As a matter of fact when I left *Lufthansa* that's exactly what Baron von Gablenz, my boss, said. *Riedel, you are the sort of person who is otherwise perfectly all right but you do not fit into the Third Reich. You are too restless, an individualist.* I suppose that was true. That's why I am in Colombia now.'[3]

I didn't mention the other reason, the real reason. My fellow pilots at Tempelhof Airport in Berlin had been amazed when I resigned from a secure and well paid job and asked why I had decided to run away to join what they saw as a sort of foreign legion. Had some girl upset me? Was I suffering from a broken heart? I was, though I didn't let them know about it. I wasn't running off for the purpose of forgetting Doris, quite the other way round, I was running towards her. I had met her on board the ship which took us with our sailplanes from Santos to Buenos Aires. She was Argentinian but of German origin. We had loved each other immediately

[2] This expedition to Brazil and Argentina was organised by Professor Walter Georgii, director of the DFS (*Deutsche Versuchsanstalt für Segelflug*, German Research Institute for Soaring Flight). It extended from 5 January to 8 May 1934. Led by Georgii four sailplane pilots, Wolf Hirth, Hanna Reitsch, Peter Riedel and Heini Dittmar with Wilhelm Harth as meteorologist and Richard Mihm as tug pilot took four sailplanes, *Moazagotl*, *Grunau Baby*, *Fafnir*, *Condor*, and a Messerschmit *M 23* tug aeroplane. Dittmar broke the world height record in his *Condor* by soaring to 14,108 ft in a thunderstorm and Riedel himself made several long cross-country flights in the *Fafnir*.

[3] Freiherr von Gablenz later became Chief Equipment Officer of the *Luftwaffe*.

and been very passionate. Our shipboard romance continued on shore with even greater delight, but she was already married with a husband and small son. When our expedition ended I had to return to Germany with Georgii and the others. Colombia was far from Argentina but a lot closer than Europe. I hoped to persuade Doris to join me there and I was sure she would do so. I wanted her to leave her husband but bring her child with her.

Von Gablenz had been quite irritated at my decision. He said he had me in mind for a future position as an administrative engineer in the technical department of *Lufthansa*. I did not enjoy paperwork and wanted to continue flying. My time as a student at Darmstadt, in the mid-1920s, had become a dim memory of heavy bookwork. After getting my diploma I had sworn to myself that I would never return to such tedious stuff if I could avoid it. I loved gliding and I had enjoyed flying for the German national airline, but the life seemed narrow and limited under an increasingly militaristic regime. I yearned for wider horizons. I tried to persuade *Lufthansa* to post me abroad, even to China perhaps, but nothing had come of it. When I succeeded in getting a two-year contract to fly for SCADTA I signed immediately. I had sailed from Cuxhaven late in 1936 for New York, thence going by rail to Miami and Pan American Clipper flying boat to Barranquilla. I privately resolved never to return to live in Germany.

Von Bötticher hummed and hawed a moment.

'Well, I am not a Party man either. Army men do not have to be, it makes no difference,' he said, finally. 'I know you speak English quite well. I expect you've got some Spanish now too?'

'Yes.' He seemed satisfied.

Bötticher now explained himself. He was an artillery man who had been Military Attaché in Washington since 1933. He knew little about aeronautics.[4] The Air Ministry in Berlin recognised that Attachés in various important embassies around the world, almost all soldiers, needed technical advice on aviation. Assistants to the embassies in Japan, Britain, France, Italy and the USA, were appointed. He thought I would be very well fitted for the post as his assistant in Washington. I had made a good impression in America already, I was a qualified engineer as well as a pilot and he assured me the pay would be better than I was getting from SCADTA. The lack of an army officer's rank was a nuisance but would not necessarily be an insuperable difficulty. If I agreed he would put my name up to the people in Berlin.

---

[4] Bötticher was not altogether ignorant about aviation and was quite far-sighted. He had already sent several reports to Berlin about the rocket experiments being conducted by Goddard in the USA. This was at a time when Goddard's work was hardly taken seriously by anyone except, perhaps, those who were working in the same direction in Germany.

Such an idea had never entered my head and my first reaction was to dismiss it immediately, too quickly. I had only the vaguest idea about what such a job would be. I thought a military attaché was a sort of diplomat, concerned mainly with going to swell parties and sitting on chairs behind the saluting podium at army parades. I could just see this fine fellow doing that, in full dress uniform with a helmet on and medals all over his chest. I suppose he would go to witness army exercises sometimes, which might be exciting but what would an *assistant* to an attaché have to do? Probably while the boss had all the fun the assistant would be stuck in a dusty office doing his work for him! Wasn't there a sinister and dishonourable side to it all, as well? Weren't military attachés also spies?

I was still feeling elated by my recent success in the soaring contest and the idea of changing from active flying to paperwork did not appeal at all. I hated the thought of myself as a bureaucrat keeping masses of documents in order, which is what I supposed Bötticher had in mind for me. I turned him down on the spot and that, I supposed, would be the end of it. I enjoyed myself for a few more days, visiting the President of the Soaring Society of America, Richard du Pont, and his wife, Allaire, in Wilmington. This delightful interlude soon ended and by 16 July I was waiting in a Miami hotel for the Pan Am Clipper on my way back to Colombia.

Now I was alone and depressed. All my new friends had been left behind and Colombia suddenly did not seem so attractive after all, Things between me and Doris had not gone as I had dreamed they might. She knew that her husband would never let her take their child away, even if he would agree to a divorce. That in any case was very unlikely. She could not bear to part from her little boy and what prospects had I, as a pilot working for a small company with out-of-date aircraft? Doris considered an airline pilot would not make a good husband. The risks with the equipment we had then were quite high and we were always flying off somewhere or were grounded by bad weather at some distant tropical airfield, rarely able to spend long at home. I had been forced to recognise that it was hopeless for me to linger in Colombia waiting for her to come to me.

On the other hand now I had seen America's brightest side, feeling absolutely at home in the society of men and women who were so easy going. For the last few weeks I had often been the centre of polite interest and attention so perhaps my impression was somewhat coloured by this, but I made allowances for it. One of the things that had impressed me most was the behaviour of Richard du Pont. He came from a fabulously wealthy family and lived, as we in Europe would have said, like a lord. But he dressed no differently from the men who worked for him, and spoke to them as friends and equals, so unlike the ways in which aristocrats treated their servants in Germany. It had been a revelation to me. Certainly I had seen poverty and discontent in the USA, but nothing like what I saw in Colombia or, for that matter, in Germany.

I thought again. I did not wish to return to Germany. I had sampled a new sort of life, loved it, and here was an offer of a job which would allow me to live in America! How stupid to turn it down. What a fool I was! In the hotel room that evening I wrote to General Bötticher telling him I had changed my mind and would take the job if it was still open. I posted the letter before leaving Miami.

Nothing happened for months and I imagined I had missed this chance. I reconciled myself to continuing with SCADTA at least until my contract ran out. Flying over the forest and the high Andean cordilleras was still interesting and at times exciting. Also I arranged for a sailplane, a new Kranich two-seater, to be sent out from Germany and I was able to do some soaring. I toured the country with it, giving joyrides to all kinds of people.

Then in the middle of December a letter came from Berlin signed by my old friend Ernst Udet. In 1935 we had both flown sailplanes from the high, snow-bound slopes of the Jungfraujoch in the first International Alpine Soaring Competition. Later, he and I with Hanna Reitsch had performed displays of sailplane aerobatics at the winter Olympic Games at Garmisch in early 1936. That was fun, landing and taking off from the same frozen lake where Sonja Henie performed her fantastic figure skating! Ernst was unquestionably the most brilliant display pilot in Europe and probably the world. Now he was a colonel in the *Luftwaffe*, chief of the technical department in the Air Ministry, responsible for supply and procurement. Even more than I, Udet was devoted to flying but there he was in a desk job! If he could stomach it, why not I?

He now asked me formally if I was willing to take the position Bötticher had offered, Technical Assistant, Air, to the Military Attaché in Washington. He added that, if I accepted, SCADTA had already agreed to free me from my contract as soon as a replacement pilot could be found. Ernst had been working behind the scenes on my behalf! I wrote immediately to accept the job.

My replacement, another German pilot, took a couple of months to arrive in Bogotá. Ponderous telegrams came bearing heavy signatures from *Attaché Gruppe* and *Reichsluftfahrtministerium* (RLM, Air Ministry.) In formal military style they required my presence in Berlin and asked for my earliest possible arrival date. As soon as I was free I responded to this pressure, cancelled an arrangement to spend a holiday in the Bahamas and left Colombia on 24 February 1938, flew to Miami and thence by rail to call on General Bötticher in Washington.

I was still not very clear about what my duties would be. He explained easily enough. I was to gather intelligence about American air power, military aircraft, performance, armament and production.

'What is the difference, then, between being an adviser to a military attaché, and being a spy?' I asked.

'The difference lies in the methods used. An attaché is allowed to use all *legal* means, such as newspapers, magazines, published statistics and so on. The whole thing works on a principle of reciprocity. Sometimes you may be permitted, or invited, by the American military authorities to observe manoeuvres or visit industrial establishments. If you are given the chance to visit a factory, the American Air Attaché in Berlin will expect similar opportunities. When their man in Berlin visits a *Luftwaffe* squadron you are entitled to see the American equivalent. On the other hand, espionage is illegal. What that means is quite clear. No spying, no secret meetings, invisible inks, stolen plans or any of that nonsense. You will recognise and accept the legal limitations.' I nodded.

'You will have me to reckon with first if you forget this.' Bötticher gave me a stern warning. 'You will certainly be approached by Canaris's people, the *Abwehr* (The military intelligence and counter-espionage service of the German General Staff, headed by Rear-Admiral Wilhelm Canaris). On no account whatsoever will you have anything to do with them. I have been in Washington six years and I am in very good standing with the American War Department. I shall not tolerate any conduct that casts even the slightest shadow on my reputation.'[5]

I understood him well enough.

'You are not really a military man, I know,' he went on. 'You are a civilian as far as I am concerned, your army rank is purely nominal.'

I was relieved, for I hated uniforms. We parted temporarily, for I was expected in Berlin to be initiated into my new role. I took a ship from New York.

Six days later we docked briefly in Southampton. During a short spell on shore I was suddenly made aware of the great political tension that had arisen in Europe. While living for the past fifteen months in the Americas I had hardly been aware of it.

While we were at sea, on 11 March 1938, German troops had marched into Austria, so forestalling a national plebiscite intended to test popular support for the country's independence. The *Anschluss*, long expected, had

---

[5] Bötticher was notable for his dislike and distrust of the *Abwehr*. Not only did he insist on his staff giving them no direct assistance, he also opposed Canaris's attempts to introduce agents into the USA. Other military attachés in other embassies were not so strict on either count. Apart from his desire to remain *persona grata* in Washington, Bötticher might have had other reasons for being wary of the *Abwehr*. In 1938 Canaris himself set up the so-called *Schwarze Kapelle* or Black Orchestra (so named by the Nazi *Sicherheitsdienst*), an under-cover conspiracy using the *Abwehr* itself as cover. It was intended to undermine and eventually overthrow Hitler. Bötticher was not involved in this but was well known in the Army as an opponent of Hitler. See further comments in the epilogue.

taken place by force and Austria was now simply a part of the greater German Reich. Press photographs showed thousands of people in the streets of Vienna waving Nazi flags and cheering delightedly. Opposition to the move, if there had been any, was suppressed. Headlines in the English newspapers and the faces of people in the streets expressed gloom and foreboding. All this worried me a great deal too. I had an uneasy feeling that I had made a mistake after all but it was too late. I could hardly change my mind again. We docked at Cuxhaven on 16 March. As I left the ship I was comforted by the prospect of soon returning to the USA.

2

And Now The Admiral

I presented myself at the RLM (Air Ministry) in Berlin expecting to be chided for my delayed arrival. I imagined that I should, after some sort of brief course on the duties of an Attaché, be sent back as soon as possible across the Atlantic. It did not work like that.

My first call was on Udet, now playing the role of Chief of the Technical Office. He had been elevated to the rank of Major-General! As I entered his big room I could see that despite his glittering uniform he was depressed. He rose from behind his huge desk and greeted me with his old friendly smile, though looking a little weary. How strange to see him in such a situation. I wondered if some sergeant had, on some occasion, said to Private Udet what had been said to me: *You'll never be a good soldier!* He and I had much in common, including a dislike of military pomp. In Germany at this time such feelings were rare. He was in the midst of a massive re-organisation of his department and only our long-standing friendship got me in to see him. Generals, I discovered, were having to wait for weeks sometimes!

'You lucky bugger,' Ernst said after we had shaken hands. 'To be able to go to the USA! To live there! I envy you, I really do.' He had flown in the Cleveland Air Races, had gone barnstorming and won aerobatic contests in the USA before 1933. He had made flying films for the extraordinary woman director, Leni Riefenstal, and the cosmopolitan Bohemian style parties he had held in his Berlin apartment were still remembered. Wherever he went he made friends at every level of society, was immensely popular with the crowds but equally with some of the most influential people in the aircraft industry on both sides of the Atlantic.

We caught up on our personal news and I told him about the soaring championship in Elmira. When chatting about our flying adventures he brightened up a good deal, though I still sensed an underlying gloom. He was no longer the light-hearted, humorous man I had known. Now all was serious business; he was a high officer in the mighty *Luftwaffe*. When we turned to the present I asked about the best way to prepare for my new job. He was rather vague. He suggested I might visit the different departments of the Air Ministry and maybe have a look at some of the aircraft factories.

There came a pause while he looked out of the window, giving me time again to think how much older he looked. He turned back and grinned slightly.

'Peter Riedel, you don't look much like a Major in the Engineer Corps to me. Most of our full Air Attachés have the rank of Major, you know, professional military men. I could pull you in at *Oberleutnant*, but I know you, you worry too much, you won't fit in. Don't join the Corps. Remain as a civilian employee of the RLM. They won't pay you as much but it will be enough. You will appear on the books as an assistant to the Military Attaché, not Air Attaché. Not yet, anyway.'

Finally came an echo of General Bötticher, 'One more thing, Peter. Stay away from the *Abwehr*. Espionage is totally out of place in the United States. You will find they are quite open in every respect. I know from my own experience over there, they are careless about military matters to an extent which Europeans can hardly understand. It is natural in a way. The Americans have no one to fear in their own hemisphere. Europe is far away. They have no intention of starting a war against anybody and they feel quite safe from attack. You will be able to find out all you want quite easily, so leave the *Abwehr* alone.'[1]

Bötticher had warned, however, that they were not likely to leave me alone.

I left Udet and went as he suggested first to see a friendly giant, Engineer-General Rulof Lucht.[2] He told me the same as Udet. No formal training existed for Air Attaché. I should make the rounds of all the departments in the Air Ministry, paying duty visits to departmental chiefs and their deputies and noting their requirements concerning my work in the USA. In addition it would be a good idea to get a clear overview of the German aircraft industry by visiting the main factories and spending a few days at Rechlin, the testing centre for the *Luftwaffe*. Rechlin corresponded to Wright Field, the experimental base for the US Army Air Force.

---

[1] Before joining the air force Udet was frequently consulted by the senior Luftwaffe staff, including Göring, although he and Hitler's deputy did not get on well. Udet first saw dive bombers in the USA when he was invited by Glenn L. Curtiss to visit the Curtiss-Wright plant in Buffalo, NY. No secret was made of the fact that the US Navy was experimenting successfully with dive-bombing. Udet had, therefore, some genuine insight into the kind of thing that Riedel would find. His enthusiasm for the dive-bomber was in large measure responsible for the adoption of this type of aircraft by the Luftwaffe high command. Udet became chief of the Luftwaffe Technical Office on 9 June 1936. Previously he had been Inspector of Fighters and Dive-Bombers, which, since it involved flying, suited him very well. It is generally recognised that Udet, though a brilliant pilot, was quite unsuited to his technical role. (See H Molloy Mason, *The Rise of the Luftwaffe*, Cassell, 1973, p. 199, and Matthew Cooper, *The German Airforce 1933-45*, Janes, 1981.)

[2] According to Cooper *op cit*, 'Leading Chief Engineer Rulof Lucht, at thirty four, was quite incapable of making an independent evaluation of technical problems. (Even Udet's understanding was regarded as more profound.)'

Finally Lucht gave me the name of an official in the Air Ministry who would, he said, take care of my formal registration as Assistant to the Military Attaché in Washington and organise such things as salary, pension funds and the rest. I hastened to find him, *Regierungsrat* Dr Genthe, and made an appointment for a few days hence. He greeted me politely but lost no time in saying that I had come to the wrong person. His only duty was enrolling members into the Engineer Corps. This organisation was only for serving members of the *Luftwaffe*. I should, Genthe said, go to the department for hiring civilian employees.

Another appointment, another delay. In this office the official shook his head in baffled amusement. There were no arrangements for me at all, it was completely out of his sphere. I was directed to the *Attaché Gruppe*.

At the *Attaché Gruppe*, Major von Cramon, when I managed to get to see him, was dismissive. Attaché positions were for serving officers, never for civilians with the comical rank of *Gefreiter* in the reserves. He declared he could and would do nothing until I was *angestellt*, that is, until I had a contract of employment from the Air Ministry. That would be something new in his experience.

Who could deal with me in the RLM? No one seemed to have the faintest idea what to do. I was back at the beginning. I did not fit into the system.

I felt altogether deflated. No one gave the impression of having waited impatiently for my arrival. On the contrary they knew nothing about me and didn't want to know. For this I had rushed home and abandoned my holiday in the Bahamas. I spent two or three weeks chasing through the long corridors of the Air Ministry, making appointments with people who didn't have time for me, flattering dragon-like women secretaries, speaking for ages on the phone to bored petty officials, adjutants, registrars and clerks, trying to find someone prepared to begin thinking about my case and with the authority to do something. I began to lose more illusions. Previously I had believed in a special German talent for efficient organisation. Now I discovered that a lot of it was over-organisation and departmentalisation which lacked flexibility.

One morning during my hunt for the right man I ran, apparently by chance, into Fritz Grosskopf, an old acquaintance whose rank was now *Flieger Oberstabs Ingenieur* (Chief flight engineer). Ten years before we had been together in the DVS, Transport Pilot's School. He showed great interest in my new appointment and, he said, since he had nothing much to do just then and knew his way around, he would accompany me on my wanderings from anteroom to anteroom to see if he couldn't smooth my path. I was feeling fed up and lonely, having lost touch with most of my old friends, and was very frustrated. Fritz, an entertaining, jolly sort of man came to my rescue and apart from his knowing which sensitive points to touch when tackling the bureaucracy, we spent many evenings together. He was well up-to-date with all the gossip and knew about all the intrigues behind the scenes in the RLM.

As I listened to Fritz I began to understand Udet's unhappiness more clearly. Regarded by all in Germany as the epitome of the gallant, swashbuckling aviator, he had known and learned to dislike Göring during the war but as the Nazi party rose to prominence and eventually to government, Göring was anxious to gain his overt support for the new air arm. The *Reichsmarschall*'s powers by now were vast. He used every device possible to win over Udet, inviting him to private hunting parties where Göring begged for his friendship, poured out his soul, treated him like a brother. Göring flattered him endlessly and offered a brilliant career flying the most advanced aircraft, which was like a promise of immortality to Udet.

On the other hand, the fat man had the power to ruin him if he chose. Udet was too easy-going and too politically naïve to resist for very long. He had finally agreed to join the *Luftwaffe*. It was for him a catastrophic error. He never overcame his fundamental dislike of the man who was now his supreme commander. The professional career officers, suddenly his subordinates, regarded his instant promotion from barnstorming aerial showman to Colonel and then to Major-General, to be disgracefully unfair.

And, Grosskopf continued, there was head of the RLM, Field Marshal Erhard Milch. He, Grosskopf pointed out, was also a civilian at heart. He had been a successful administrator when he was running *Lufthansa*, before von Gablenz's time, but had been jerked out of that into the top military job by Göring. Milch was bitterly jealous of Udet's popularity and of his piloting skills, for Milch himself had been an aircrew observer of no special reputation during the 1914–18 war. Udet had been second only to von Richthofen, winning the 'Blue Max' for sixty-two victories in air fighting. So Milch detested Udet, the professional officers in the lower ranks resented both of them and while Milch was Göring's pet, fat Hermann and Udet were always on the edge of a bust up. Grosskopf did seem remarkably well informed.

I began again to feel oppressed by the sense of having made a mistake. If my new job meant I should have to survive in a world of such underlying tensions and personal enmities, I should hate it and inevitably offend everyone before long. Flying an old Ford Tri-motor through Andean storms would be much simpler and cleaner. I tried to bury my doubts. My new work, when eventually I was allowed to begin it, would be far away from all this and surely it would be fascinating. I was envied by many and I would probably never again get the chance to see America from such an interesting angle. After talking to myself in this vein I felt more comfortable.

I began to wonder about Fritz. How did he, a mere flight engineer, know so much and how was it that he had so much time to spare for me, tramping round all day, lingering over lunch, talking about this and that? Did this man spend all his time gathering gossip? The truth emerged.

'There's someone I think you ought to meet,' he said, one day.

'Who's that?'

'My boss. He's *Abwehr.*'

I suppose I should have expected this. Grosskopf was an *Abwehr* man. That explained a great deal. I realised I had told him a lot about myself, my experiences and my political views too. He had been cleverly drawing me out all the time.

I told him about the orders from Bötticher and Udet but he persisted in asking me as a personal favour to meet his chief. There would be no obligation but I should at least see him. The boss would not take 'no' for an answer. I became curious and felt there could really be no harm in meeting this man providing it went no further than a meeting. I had a brief vision, drawn from popular fiction, of mysterious agents wearing dark glasses and false beards, of secret rendezvous with slender beautiful women in dark veils. It might be a bit of an adventure just to meet some of these shadowy people!

The next day Fritz and I entered the door of a sober, ponderous building, 72-76 Tirpitz-Ufer, just along from the War Department. Two floors up we came to a name plate on a door: *Amts Chef* Admiral Canaris. The big cheese himself! Surely not for me! A moment later I was introduced, not to the Admiral but to a rather insignificant man in civilian clothes, a colonel who said he had met me before at the gliding school on the Wasserkuppe though I did not remember him. After a little casual conversation he said we were expected for lunch at Horcher's, one of Berlin's most fashionable restaurants, so we'd better get along. At the restaurant we were shown to a private room. A round table was set elaborately for eight persons, no improvised luncheon. It looked like a special occasion. Who could the guest of honour be?

Five men soon joined us, among them a short, kind-looking elderly gentleman: Admiral Canaris himself! So I did meet the big cheese and all this was apparently arranged for my benefit. Someone was taking an interest in me at last. Perhaps I was important after all! A splendid meal was served with excellent wines. When the coffee and cognac arrived the assault was launched.

They said they understood my resolution to stick to my orders but such orders should be taken with a pinch of salt. Most if not all my colleagues in corresponding positions around the globe were *Abwehr* men. It was accepted that my superior in Washington, Bötticher, would certainly have to keep his hands clean. The General must not be compromised. But it would be a little different for me. I should not be asked to crawl round military airfields at night or to play with secret codes. There would be very little extra work and the General need never know anything about it. All I should have to do would be to note people possibly sympathetic to the German cause among those I met in America and mention them to my contact in the *Abwehr*. They would take care of everything after that. Naturally a special fund would be set up for me to allow for entertaining these people. A little extra money would always prove useful, would enable me to keep up appearances, present a confident exterior in Washington. They would not be too scrupulous about book-keeping.

I found myself in unknown territory. I did not want to make enemies of these powerful men but I must keep the rules. I told them I had heard of how Bötticher had already rejected one man who had been suggested as his assistant before myself. He had said something which gave the General a bad impression.

'If you already have such notions about your future work, then we need not go any further,' Bötticher had said brusquely, and that was that. Neither the *Abwehr* nor I would gain if the General pronounced such a sentence on me a few months after I had started in Washington. Canaris smiled. I could see that I was telling him nothing about Bötticher that he did not already know. As tactfully as I could I thanked the assembled gentlemen for the excellent meal, but my answer was still *NO*. We parted apparently on polite terms.

Yet as the little party broke up, one of the officers drew me aside. If I changed my mind, the offer remained open. They would talk to me again during my next visit to Germany, which they expected would be in about a year's time. I said it would be a waste of effort on their part.

Now at last the bureaucratic jungle seemed to clear. The petty clerks began to recognise me and were all charm. Their bosses began to smile. Had they all been waiting deliberately until the *Abwehr* had had a chance to look me over? I never knew for sure but everything that had been vague and doubtful before was now clarified. My plans became concrete. I made a round trip by air to get a general idea of the size and production methods of the German aircraft industry. I visited Junkers, Fieseler, Klemm, Dornier and Messerschmitt and the BMW engine works. Everywhere I went I met old friends and acquaintances from the early gliding and soaring days and many whom I had known as students at Darmstadt. A few further days at Rechlin and my initiation was completed. I was cleared now to go to Washington.

A short trip to England made a melancholy impression. I seemed to be the last German admitted to Britain without a visa in my passport. The very next day they became compulsory. It had been two years since I was in London and during that time relations between the two countries had deteriorated greatly. Fortunately the friends I stayed with, the Burberry family who made the famous rainwear, did not let this interfere with our long established relationships.

Then it was back to Berlin to wind up my affairs and pack my suitcases. When I had left in 1936 I had cleared my furniture and some other possessions out of my bachelor apartment. A Jewish neighbour, Frau Lintz, agreed to let me store the heavier things in her cellar, though I did not know when I should return for them. Now I visited her again to tell her about my new job and to see that everything was still safe with her. All was well but as we sat over a cup of coffee she shook her head at me.

'Herr Riedel, you will see. The Nazis are going to make war. They are spending so much money, the nation is in debt again up to here. Before the economy breaks down they will go to war. Mark my words. What else are all the huge armaments for?'

I heard her but tried to convince her otherwise. Naturally, I thought, she would fear the Nazis. Anti-Jewish propaganda was appearing everywhere, many Jews were leaving Germany. She made me think, all the same.

I had never really sorted out my own ideas on what the Party called 'The Jewish Question'. Could there really be a vast international Jewish conspiracy preparing to destroy Germany and take control of the world? Talking to Frau Lintz seemed to make nonsense of the idea. Yet that was what Goebbels and the Party machine insisted on the street corners, on the hoardings, in the radio broadcasts. The outpouring of hate was never-ending.

I had special reason to admire and like Jewish people. I owed almost everything to one in particular, Dr Kotzenberg. Dr Kotzenberg was a Frankfurt businessman who had made his fortune in haberdashery. Shortish, plump with a bristling moustache, he had poured huge sums of money into the University of Frankfurt, helping it to rise to a very prominent position in the academic world. Then, in the very hard economic times after 1918, he made a habit of supporting promising young men whose families had run out of money by awarding what amounted to informal scholarships. He had in this way seen me through university and flying school and had never even asked me about my own religion or racial origins. Far from being a Jewish plutocrat now, he had in the end impoverished himself and had to depend on a pension granted him by the city of Frankfurt. A conspirator? Not he. Then there was Senhor Moses, a leading newspaper proprietor in Rio de Janeiro who had done everything in his power to give our soaring expedition favourable publicity in 1933 and 1934, despite the swastikas on all the sailplane's tails and the fact that we represented the new anti-Semitic Reich. I could not believe that such people as he were working to destroy my country.

I began to realise that there was no Jewish question. There were only questions about individual people.

The material promises made by Hitler had been realised in an impressive way, or so it appeared to the ordinary citizens. Everyone believed that Herr Schacht was a financial wizard. We knew nothing of any vast international debts. As to armaments, Germany, they said, was under constant and terrible threat from outside with the Russian communists on one side, the French, British and perhaps the Americans all bought by Jewish money on the other, preparing war against Germany.

Was it true that vast armaments were being created by these other countries? Well, I reassured myself, at least I was on my way now to see about that. I was glad, at last, to step aboard the *Europa*. It was early June 1938.

3

Cloud Flying to Washington

The voyage was a quiet interlude of several days, sailing peacefully towards America but I was not quite free from worry. On board I met Commander Vihlein, the President of the well known Schlitz brewing company of Milwaukee. As a young US naval officer he had been an Attaché in Japan during the Russo–Japanese war and observed the battle of Tsushima in 1905 where the Russian fleet had been almost totally destroyed. Now, a very refined and cultured man, he buttonholed me one day as we strolled around the promenade deck. We spent many hours afterwards talking about his experiences and the world at large. Most of the time I just listened. He was so much older than I and carried such an air of authority that I felt unable to argue with him beyond a few words here and there, when he turned to Germany.

'Mr Riedel, I am profoundly concerned about developments in Germany. What is this man Hitler trying to do? Why is he taking such an aggressive posture? I have friends in Germany and England so I know what they are thinking. The British believe there will be a new war. Another war would be disastrous, the end of European culture.'

'They are alarmists,' I said. 'You should not be so pessimistic.' I reminded him that in his book, *Mein Kampf*, Hitler had said that Britain and Germany were natural allies. On every possible occasion since, he had promised peace. We should trust him.

'You trust him, do you?' I nodded. I could not believe that a man in Hitler's position could deliberately set out to deceive the world.

'You're too naïve. But even if you are right about his intentions, he is taking far too many risks. The man is forcing the pace. If he took a more reasonable attitude I expect many of his claims would be recognised before long, if they can be justified. The Versailles treaty was unfair in some ways. Many people are admitting that now, in retrospect. The frontiers, with German-speaking peoples in Czechoslovakia and Alsace-Lorraine, the Danzig corridor dividing your country into two parts and so on; I can understand that those things rankle. But, given a few years, people will come to see where wrongs have been done and put them right peacefully. Time is on Germany's side. Hitler can afford to wait. All he seems to be doing now is stirring things up, forcing opinion to harden against him. Did you know the English are going to spend more than thirty million dollars on propaganda in the USA? My British friends, some of them mighty influential people, see themselves threatened and they are looking for an alliance with us. What do you suppose will happen to Germany if America is drawn into another great war, like last time?'

This made me uneasy but I reassured myself and him as best I could. I could not accept that Hitler intended war and I said so again. He went off, shaking his head.

A worse shock awaited me. On disembarking in the midst of a New York heatwave I saw a newspaper headline: GERMAN SPY RING SMASHED. I could hardly believe the front page story but it turned out to be true. An obscure medical doctor, of German origin, had organised a spy ring, paying some layabout fellows to go to work at the Brewster Aircraft Corporation on Long Island and report back to him on the plant. The results of their espionage were passed to Fraülein Hofmann, a hairdresser on the *Europa*, the very ship from which my baggage was being unloaded as I stood there reading. The woman had handed over the papers in Germany to the *Abwehr*, Canaris's men.[1]

The whole enterprise had been utterly stupid and unnecessary. The repercussions continued for months. I soon found out that the Brewster Company was one of the least important aircraft factories in the USA and, as Udet had said, everything one wanted to know about it could be discovered simply by reading the aviation magazines, but this scandal did great damage to German-American relations at a sensitive time. The British hardly needed to spend millions on propaganda when these idiotic amateur spies gave the American newspapers such a story. They continued rehashing it for weeks, adding details and making scathing editorial comments. It was never mentioned in the German press. Goebbels made sure of that!

I had arranged to stay a couple of days in New York before going on to Washington. I imagined that all my American friends would now see me as an agent sent out hastily to replace those who had been arrested: as soon as one spy master has been caught, the substitute arrives to start another ring!

---

[1] A fuller account of this affair from the German side is given in Paul Leverkühn's book, *German Military Intelligence*, Weidenfeld & Nicolson, 1954. It was evidently not an *Abwehr* operation but an attempt by rank amateurs to set up a spy ring. The *Abwehr* became involved unwillingly. The hairdresser was temporarily standing in as courier for a regular *Abwehr* man who happened to be on leave at the critical time. Nonetheless, 'The whole episode assumed enormous proportions and eighteen people, among them the German officers Colonel Busch, Lieut-Commander Menzel, Captain von Bonin and Captain Pheiffer were charged. The case has been described in a book written by an FBI officer, Leon G. Turrou.'

Something occurred now which years later was to influence my life in a totally unexpected way. I had a cousin, Renate, a few months older than myself, who was by the standards of the times a very wild young woman. After my own family had broken up in my teens I had lived in her parents' home for a while and knew her well. I did not find her very attractive but other men obviously did. She married a Berlin lawyer called Paul Leverkühn who had been a member of the international Mixed Claims Commission which worked during 1924 to 1928 on various war damage issues. Renate and Paul, who was now aged forty-five, were living in New York at present and I telephoned as soon as I could to let them know I had arrived.

A friend of Renate, whom I also knew well, was Bertha von Kalkreuth, a most unusual character. She was from a family of well known artists and had become a sculptor with quite a good reputation. I had gone out with Bertha a few times in Berlin and although no serious attachment developed we remained friendly. She too had lived in New York for several years where, finding it difficult to make a living with her sculpture, she had earned some money by playing, of all things, a hand saw. By holding and flexing a saw in a certain way, bending it to create tension, it can be scraped rather like a fiddle and will make a most peculiar ringing, whining sound. With skill, melodies can be produced and her ability was sufficient for Bertha to become a professional performer in night-clubs, until audiences became tired of the trick. One way and another after this, and assisted by her aristocratic title, she became well known in New York society. Through Renate and her husband, Bertha met and became much more than friendly with an older man, a lawyer called Donovan who had been on the Mixed Claims Commission with Leverkühn. Their affair nearly broke Donovan's marriage and created a scandal. He had a position to maintain and there had never been any likelihood of them settling down together. After Bertha's sorrowful return to Germany she kept a small bust of him which I had seen in her apartment. What more natural than that a sculptor should use her man friend as a model? She was obviously still fond of him.

Hearing I was off to the USA, Bertha was among the small group of friends who had come to the docks in Hamburg to see me depart on the *Europa*. She insisted that on arrival in New York I must get in touch with the man and give him her best wishes. It meant nothing to me but I remembered. After my dutiful call to the Leverkühns I rang the number Bertha had given me.

At once I realised this Donovan was no small figure. His office was at Number 2, Wall Street and he was head of the firm. When I got through the barriers of secretaries and underlings, insisting that I had a personal message for him, he was at first very reluctant to speak but when I said I brought greetings from Bertha von Kalkreuth he changed immediately.

'When did you see her? How is she? How do you come to know her?' I explained.

'Come and have breakfast with me tomorrow morning,' he said. He gave the name of a breakfast place in the city and I went there by subway at the agreed time, 8.30 am. He was a large, energetic and forthright man who was delighted to have Bertha's message and seemed anxious for news. He spoke little of himself but enquired about her and then myself, my new position, my flying adventures and so on. He became my host for much of the day.

It was some time afterwards that I made the connection. That was 'Wild Bill' Donovan, a great American hero of the First World War, now a wealthy lawyer who at one time was even considered a possible presidential candidate for the Republican Party. He never became President but he was to become very important not only to the USA but to me.

Next day I went to see C. B. Allen the aviation editor of the *New York Herald Tribune*. I had met him originally at the Elmira gliding championships in 1937. He did his best to reassure me about suspicions of espionage.

'No one who knows you will believe it, Peter,' he said, laughing. All the same, I wondered about people who didn't know me. The *Europa* hairdresser spy scandal, I feared, was going to make my job more difficult in the months ahead.

'You will be at Elmira again this year, they tell me,' said my journalist friend, and we talked more cheerfully about the prospects. As before, I was sponsored by the German Aero Club, with Udet, Professor Georgii and other members of the German gliding establishment behind me. A Kranich two-seater like the one I had flown in Colombia was shipped over on loan. It would eventually have to be returned to Germany.

The only crew man I had been able to arrange for myself was a German-born but naturalised US citizen who lived in New York. I was put in touch with him through Alfred Bayer, founder in 1927 of a German–American Aviators club in New York. Alfred too would compete in the championships and had imported for himself another Kranich. However, an additional crew of young American fellows had been found. At Elmira there was an aviation ground school and some of the youngsters from there had volunteered to help with the soaring contest. There were to be some Lithuanian pilots this year who would also need crews and the workshop of the school would be available if repairs to any of the aircraft were needed.

A few days later I was soaring again over Harris Hill. I met all my friends from the previous year and made many new ones. The Kranich carried the national markings, a swastika, each side of the vertical tail. This had been true the previous year with the Sperber also and no one had commented

29

then. The other competing sailplanes, including Alfred's, were free of such political emblems. It hardly occurred to me to bother about it at first but now I was forced to realise that the political atmosphere had changed a good deal in the past twelve months. My German-speaking crew man, without asking me, hoisted a swastika flag over the wooden cabin provided for us on Harris Hill. This was just the kind of brash display I wanted to avoid. I made sure the flag was quickly removed but it drew unfavourable attention and the marking on the glider's tail now did become an embarrassment. To paint over the swastika would get me into trouble. I explained to everyone who would listen that the sailplane was necessarily registered and marked like all other German aircraft that might be seen at international airports. Its owners were in Germany and it could only be imported temporarily if it were clearly marked so. Otherwise, like Alfred's Kranich, import duty would have to be paid on it. The explanations did not convince everyone, especially when it became generally known that I was now attached to the German Embassy. By some people, now, I was regarded as a dedicated Nazi.

There were only twenty aircraft competing. The Soaring Society of America had decided to restrict entry to more experienced pilots. Thus, the number of competitors was greatly reduced compared with 1937 but they were of a much higher standard. The best of them, like Emil Lehecka, Chet Decker and Richard du Pont were flying imported German aircraft, a Rhönsperber and two Minimoas. Alfred Bayer, was flying his own Kranich. The Kranich was a two-seater but we flew it solo from the front seat. In this configuration it was considered at least as good as the others. I did not expect to beat them all so easily this time. The attractive American-designed Ross-Stevens to be flown by Bob Stanley would also be capable of good performances.

The weather for soaring was good on most days during the fortnight. The points were scored for flights to distant pre-declared goals. Before take off the sailplane pilot had to state in writing his intended destination, usually an airfield. If he reached it he would achieve a high score based on the distance flown and a large percentage bonus for reaching the goal. The choice was difficult, requiring a good understanding of the weather pattern along the proposed direction and an accurate forecast of the expected average cross-country speed. If the selected target was too far away one would fail to get there, landing in a field somewhere. One might then be beaten easily by someone who had nominated a less ambitious target and managed to reach it and score the bonus. On the other hand, if one was too cautious one might arrive at the goal early in the afternoon with several hours of good weather remaining. Other pilots then would sail much further to arrive safely at more distant nominated destinations. The perfect flight was one of large distance which just managed to get to a distant goal in a long final glide after the last thermals for the day died.

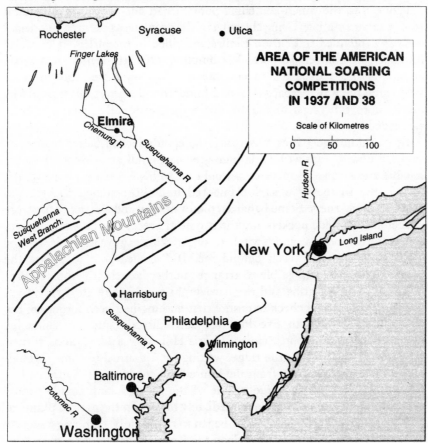

I achieved two successful goal flights early in the competition, one to Harrisburg, Pennsylvania and the other to the du Pont Airport at Wilmington, Delaware. These flights, of about 209 km (130 miles) and 286 km (178 miles) respectively, were considered very good in those days and I scored well.

My position on the list was already at the top but the real adventure was still to come. The National Fiduciary Council had offered a thousand dollar prize to the first glider pilot who could fly from Elmira to Washington DC. All the leading competitors were hoping to achieve this, not so much for the prize but because of the personal prestige and the favourable publicity that would result for the sport of soaring.

When I awoke on the morning of 3 July I saw at once that conditions were going to be favourable for the attempt on Washington. Small, puffy cumulus clouds were already forming and drifting with the north-westerly breeze. We had breakfast hastily and hurried to get the Kranich ready, dragging it to the winch-launching point. I had only a road map, bought from a service station. Using the wing of the sailplane as a temporary desk I drew my intended track from Elmira and filled in the official declaration form. Goal: Hoover Airport, Washington, DC. It seemed hopelessly ambitious and I expected to end the day looking rather silly in some field along the way, perhaps fifty or a hundred miles short but it would be much more ridiculous to fail by not trying, especially if another pilot succeeded.

By the time everything was ready the clouds looked better than ever, sunlit, billowing tops with dark, blue-grey bases indicating where the most reliable and strongest upcurrents would be. 'This is what we have waited for!' I said to the crew as I clambered into the cramped cockpit and fastened my harness. Some bananas, pieces of cake and a drink bottle were pushed into the side pockets and the two height recording barographs were set, officially sealed and switched on, ticking away in their special compartment out of reach behind me. If I landed somewhere on the way it would not be possible to arrange another launch or aeroplane tow. That would be cheating and the barographs would show it.

After a quick final check to ensure that nothing had been forgotten, the winch kited me up to five hundred feet, directly into the slope lift upcurrent above the north face of Harris Hill. It was 10.30 am. I turned the Kranich to fly along the ridge, waiting for a thermal to come through and allow me to get away from the limited hill soaring beat. Within a few minutes I felt a strong surge as one of the good-looking clouds passed overhead and I began to circle immediately to keep in the narrow plume of rising air. Having centred the lift I began to rise rapidly, climbing at nearly 10 feet per second. I was away! Soon the Kranich, banked over steeply in the thermalling circles, was at cloud base, the hill slopes now looking insignificant, almost flat far below with a few tiny sailplanes down there still waiting for their launch and some others circling as I had done to get up. I must not linger for they would soon reach my height if I waited. I turned on course away from Elmira to glide onwards, heading for the next good looking cloud on track southwards, slightly across the wind direction.

Washington lay impossibly far away on the other side of the Allegheny mountain ranges. By circling to regain lost height when I found a thermal, and gliding fast and down on track after reaching the top of it, in only half an hour after setting course I was approaching the high ridges which reached 3,000 feet in many places while the bases of the cumulus clouds were at 4,000. It would not be wise to try to cross the ranges too low. In the mountains it would be easy to get caught and forced down into some narrow valley with nowhere much to land safely if the necessary upcurrent was not found. I decided to take the next thermal as high as possible to give myself plenty of clearance above the ridges. This necessitated entering the cloud and flying blind. The thermal itself was responsible for forming the cloud as the water vapour in the rising air condensed. As the Kranich circled up we should be sucked into the dark belly of the cumulus, losing sight of the ground and the sky, surrounded entirely by dense fog with nothing to see outside the narrow cockpit except the wings disappearing into mist on either side, and nothing to hear but the hum and whistle of the airflow.

Sailplanes in 1938 rarely carried artificial horizons. There was no electrical power and no radio. Apart from the indispensable sensitive variometer to indicate rates of climb and descent my panel had an altimeter, magnetic compass, airspeed indicator (ASI) and a single gyroscopic instrument, the turn and slip indicator which was driven by a suction venturi. This instrument had two needles, the upper one indicating whether the sailplane was turning, the lower one showing if there was any slip or skid. Ideally the lower needle should always stay in the middle, indicating accurate and efficient flight. The turn needle above moved to left or right depending on the direction and rate of the turn. If I flew clumsily the airspeed would begin to rise and fall. I might stall and spin out of the cloud or, more dangerous, allow the airspeed to rise too high with the risk of overstressing the aircraft and, possibly, breaking up. This had happened to several people in Germany but I was after all a qualified airline pilot. A good, strong thermal in cloud is usually quite smooth if one has found the centre properly. Flying blind in a continuous series of circles with only the turn and slip indicator and ASI was not too difficult for me.

I checked that my parachute harness was done up correctly and tightened the seat straps. With the gyro running I established a steady rate of turn while still in the clear air before the thermal carried me up to the cloud. Soon the grey base of the cumulus was immediately above, wisps of mist whipped past the wings, the ground below became indistinct, faded and was gone. The Kranich rose into the chilly gloom. My world shrank to a little plywood compartment with those five very basic instruments in front of me. All I had to do was keep everything steady: the turn needle not too far over to one side, the slip indicator centred, the airspeed constant. The compass spun round erratically, as always when circling, quite useless. I climbed. The altimeter moved nicely upwards. In their compartment the barograph needles would be tracing out a steep climb on the charts. At 6,000 feet, with 3,000 feet between me and the ridges, I was now high enough.

It was time to level out and set a course to make some distance. Straightening out at the top of a spiralling climb in cloud is not easy even for an experienced pilot. As the turn needle comes back to the middle, indicating straight flight, the blind pilot gets the strongest possible impression that the aircraft is entering a steep turn the other way. There is no external reference and all human instincts contradict the gyroscope. It requires the utmost concentration to keep the needles in the middle and prevent oneself from steering the glider into a steady turn again. It is very easy at this moment to convince oneself that the instruments have suddenly gone wrong, to ignore them and to fly, as they say, by the seat of the pants. This can be fatal, for the almost certain result is that the glider will enter a spiral dive. A spiral dive is not a spin. Spinning comes from trying to fly too slowly. It is not dangerous if one is high enough to straighten up and regain control. In a spiral dive the airspeed will rise and rise, and the 'g' forces will multiply until something breaks.

The instruments must be believed. If they do actually fail, of course, the pilot is in real trouble! Fortunately, once settled on track the misleading sensations fade after a minute or two, the compass steadies and begins to make sense at last and then it becomes fairly easy to maintain a good heading and ride out the turbulence that often occurs around the edges of an upcurrent.

Suddenly we broke out of the cloud into clear sunlight. All around, the cumulus formed brilliant aerial mountains, canyons and valleys with a landscape darkly visible in the depths. The exhilaration of such a moment is tremendous. I saw the silvery glint of the Susquehanna River winding southwards, showing me the way. So the Kranich and I pushed on, using more thermals and clouds to gain height, and gliding on after each climb to make distance. At Harrisburg where I had landed just a few days before, I crossed the last ridge of the Alleghenies, three and a half hours after leaving Elmira. If this continued I ought to reach Washington at six o'clock in the evening. If it continued! I couldn't expect it to do so.

On this side of the mountains the base of the clouds was much higher, 7,000 feet, and I pressed on making good time, circling up, gliding along and down, circling up again, until shortly before 4 pm. I discerned a grey mass of housing and the smoke haze of a large city directly ahead. It could only be Baltimore!

Eating my last banana I looked at the map and considered my situation. The north-west wind had drifted me a little off course to the east but that could be easily corrected. More worrying, the sun was lower now, the rays striking the ground at a more oblique angle, warming the land less and allowing the air to cool. The thermals were going to die soon and still I had far to go. Distantly, on the horizon, I could just make out the waters of Chesapeake Bay. The clouds on the way to my goal were looking weaker and dissolving, wispy and ragged instead of bright, rounded sunlit tops.

At 5 pm I was directly over the centre of Baltimore, circling in what proved to be the last good thermal of the day. Once more I climbed to 7,000 feet but slowly this time. The hours were running out! I set a course. Sixty kilometres, about forty miles to go and conditions were fading fast. Instead of the strong surges I had felt earlier, upcurrents were soft and feeble, each weaker than the last. Despite using every trick I knew, circling and gaining a few hundred feet here and there, the Kranich was gradually losing the battle, two steps down in the glides, only one up in the next thermal, gliding on again, following the main highway towards Washington. Progress seemed dreadfully slow and I was using up my precious height.

Mental arithmetic. So many thousand feet up and my gliding ratio was, I supposed, about 20 to 1. That meant from about 5,300 feet, a mile high, I ought to travel twenty miles but that would bring me right down to the ground. For safety I must have a margin to find a suitable landing field. The map said I wouldn't reach Hoover Airport by miles. Also I had to reckon with the chance of running into sinking air. Where some air goes up, some must come down to take its place! Glide on, see the altimeter slowly unwinding.

What was that? A tall, slender object sticking up in the haze. The Washington Monument! Dimly visible beyond it, the dome of the Capitol! But, so far away, and I so low! One more thermal, only one, only one more climb, just a weak one, please, please . . . and I might get there! I prayed, let there be just one little puff of warm air from below!

And there it was! Circle, gently, gently. The tired thermal struggled to carry me upwards. The altimeter showed 2,500 feet as it gave its final gasp. Not enough, not enough! Over ten miles to go. The huge sprawl of the city was before me with nowhere to land in sight except, just over there, a small airport which I knew quite well, College Park near the University of Maryland. Should I surrender and land at once rather than attempting to cross the city? No, keep on, hope. The University buildings silently drifted past. Soon College Park was out of reach and I still needed one more little thermal. If this continued I was not going to make the last few miles but surely there must be a park or sports field I could get down in without damage.

Just when I needed it least, I ran into sinking air. The variometer needle sagged, the altimeter moved down more rapidly. My heart sank with the glider. This was it! Find a field or I should crash ignominiously among the avenues of the national capital. Which would be worst, to go through someone's roof, to crash into the traffic on a street, or to flop into trees? It would have to be the trees, smashing the wings and probably dropping through the branches to break my legs on the ground, or worse. Find a golf course, a ball park, anything!

But I thought I knew what was happening. The more open country of the suburbs of Washington had chilled in the late afternoon more rapidly than the city centre. Air would sink over the cool area but it must rise above the hot, paved streets, the tiled rooftops and walls which had been baking all day. Where there is sink, I told myself, there must be lift not far away. At least, I hoped so. I glided on. My height was melting away but sure enough the sink did not continue. The variometer needle eased gradually, returned to normal, nudged up a little more and remained poised on zero. The lift was just sufficient to cancel out the natural sinking rate of the Kranich. We floated on, breathlessly, neither losing nor gaining height. Getting nearer!

If I ran into more sink now, I should be done for! But I held on, the monument coming closer, beckoning me forward.

And at last we were approaching the Mall. There was open space within reach but I could not land for there were scores of people all over the place! It was the eve of the great national holiday and Washington was full of visitors. Since I was so silent, none of them was aware of the eighteen-metre (58 feet) wings whispering over their heads. The Capitol at one end, the Lincoln Memorial at the other and now almost immediately below, the huge obelisk. Still I was not losing height and could continue with my delicate glide. The column was 550 feet tall and the Kranich was two hundred feet above its pointed tip when I reached it. I could not see the airport but I knew exactly where it was, on the other side of the Potomac River. From this height I thought I should just make the distance and, by the thickness of the steel plate on my skid, scrape over the fence into Hoover Airport!

Ironically, at this moment when I no longer needed it, I felt the strong surge of a last good thermal. The variometer showed six feet per second rate of climb, then seven. Immediately I banked the Kranich over and circled. As the sharp point of the monumental needle began to recede at last someone on the ground happened to glance up. Perhaps they heard the faint, flute like song of the glider passing through the air, stared about in puzzlement, caught sight of the sailplane and, I suppose, shouted and pointed. I could not hear the crowd over the sound of the rushing airflow over the wings and fuselage but I saw what looked like hundreds of little flowers suddenly appearing to blossom below me as faces turned in my direction. Is it a bird? Is it a plane? I felt like shouting with joy, 'No it's Peter Riedel and I have flown without an engine all the way from Elmira!' The great bird circled, gaining height smoothly to 3,000 feet.

There was no difficulty now in gliding across the river to the airport and I had sufficient height to do some aerobatics, Immelmann turns and loops, before landing. The skid touched the runway near the administration building at 6.20 pm. I had been in the air for nearly eight hours.

The distance was 365 km (227 miles), a new world best for soaring to a pre-declared goal and qualifying for part of the international Gold badge for soaring.[2] No one else from Elmira reached Washington although Bob Stanley almost repeated my exploit next day. Where I had found that gentle lift over the city, tempting me on, he missed it and landed a few miles short.

The day after this I reached Roosevelt Field on Long Island, 315 km (196 miles). I had flown by sailplane from Elmira both to Washington and New York airports now! By the end of the contest I was again at the head of the list with Emil Lehecka 200 points behind. As before, a German could not be declared U.S. National Champion. The title went to Emil. Alfred Bayer damaged his Kranich in a field landing, but it was repaired in the Elmira school to fly again a couple of days later. Unfortunately it was completely destroyed on its road trailer in a traffic accident after the championships ended.

From the diplomatic viewpoint I could hardly have done better. After the competition ended, at Richard du Pont's behest, I took the Kranich to Wilmington for a couple of days and flew it from the du Pont airfield, giving joy rides to as many influential people as possible. They included Igor Sikorsky, the great Russian pioneer of flight who had settled in the USA and was famous for his flying boats and airliners. He must, at the time I met him, have been working on his helicopter ideas. In the following year he flew his VS-300 which soon led to the development of a whole new industry. Sikorsky's chief designer, Michael Gluhareff, was with him. Others who flew with me at this time included Henry du Pont, Colonel Olds and E. J. Noble of the Civil Aviation Authority. All these people were impressed with soaring flight and I enjoyed demonstrating the beautiful sailplane to them. From the point of view of General Bötticher, I was making the kind of contacts he would have wished. I suppose he was pleased with me but he let me see that he did not take this aspect of my activity very seriously.

---

[2] The flight was also recognised, many years later, for a Diamond was added to the Gold badge, for a flight of more than 300 km to a pre-declared goal. This award did not exist in 1938 but was awarded retrospectively.

4

The Führer Calls the Tune

Playtime was over! General Bötticher, unsmiling, left me no room for doubt about that as soon as I arrived in his office on a hot, humid July morning after driving back from Wilmington. I had just come from the exhilarating world of gliding in good soaring weather and the company of friends to enter the dark, ugly rooms in the annexe of the Embassy surrounded by the stale smell of old papers, files, ink and the clatter of typewriters. I reconciled myself to it somehow. This was my chance to live in America and I resolved to put up with the work.

The General soon proved to be a very different man from the affable and friendly old fellow I had thought. He was a sober, solemn, rigid old Prussian soldier, moody, often unreasonable, humourless, disagreeable and pompous. He seemed unable to discriminate between important matters and trivia. Every problem was serious to him, whether it really mattered or not, and he expected his underlings to have the same attitude. He would often leave me boiling internally with fury. In the next few months there were many occasions when I felt like walking out on the whole situation as I found it. Had I done so, by using the many friendly contacts I had made, I might have been allowed to stay in the USA. My engineering and flying qualifications would have enabled me to find a job. I did not do so but continued along the path I had chosen until it was much too late to change. I had somehow acquired a strong sense of patriotic duty.

I hung on and got down to work. Most of what I had to do was simple, though at first very boring. The Embassy subscribed to all the aviation journals and newspapers. I scanned them carefully for military news and clipped out all the items of interest for filing. Each week I had to summarise these in writing for presentation to the General who might question me further about anything that caught his eye. He then incorporated what he thought worthy of official attention into his own reports to Berlin. I did not see his reports at this time, for I was only an assistant.

After a while I suggested to Bötticher that it might be useful for me to visit some of the larger American aircraft factories in an official capacity to see directly how they were organised. He turned this down. He regarded my request as merely an excuse for a paid holiday, junketing round the country with my pals and escaping from the routine. I cannot deny that I should have enjoyed myself but I thought there was good sense in my proposal from his viewpoint too.

At the request of the Soaring Society of America I did manage one or two short excursions. The General could hardly refuse permission when the invitations came from members of influential and wealthy families like the du Ponts. One such occasion was at Frankfort in Michigan where there was an Open Soaring Meet. I took the Kranich and put on an aerobatics display. I used to specialise in doing successive loops, each one nearer to the ground until the spectators were sure I was going to kill myself but, having practised this sort of thing for years, I knew exactly when the last loop had to be made, finishing with the Kranich skimming the ground by only a few feet before using the excess speed to climb, turn and land on the chosen spot before the crowd. I asked Stephen du Pont to capture my display on his cine-camera but he admitted that at the last moment he had been so sure I was going to crash that he forgot the camera and just stood frozen in alarm. Afterwards I gave some joy rides before motoring back to Washington with the glider de-rigged on its trailer behind me.

A more exciting and important occasion was the 1938 Cleveland Air Races in early September. A German presence at this Ohio meeting was considered important enough to justify sending several pilots and aircraft from Europe. Ernst Udet himself, such a superb showman pilot, would have been the obvious choice. He had been a star attraction at previous Cleveland meetings but his elevated position in the *Luftwaffe* hierarchy now made it impossible for him to attend. I suggested to Cliff Henderson, organiser and promoter of the Air Races, that Hanna Reitsch, the outstanding woman sailplane pilot and a friend of mine from our Latin American trip in 1934 and the Winter Olympic displays, would be an excellent contributor to his programme. She had recently flown the Focke Achgelis, the first successful helicopter, actually inside the huge Berlin Deutschlandhalle Sports Hall, watched by a large crowd. She was invited to Cleveland.

It was decided that she should bring with her one of the specially built aerobatic Habicht sailplanes which she and others had demonstrated over the Berlin Olympic Games stadium in 1936. Rather than the helicopter, which was still regarded as experimental, Emil Kropf came to demonstrate the Fieseler Storch. The Storch, designed for army observation and field communications, was capable of extraordinarily slow flight. It could take off and land in very small spaces and, at this stage of its development, was considered more useful than the Achgelis helicopter. In addition Graf Hagenburg, second only to Udet in aerobatics and who had also been to Cleveland before, was to put on a display in his Bücker Jungmeister aerobatic biplane.

I met the party off the liner *Bremen* as they disembarked in New York. It was a delight to see Hanna again for she was like a sister to me. Such a small woman yet so very full of sparkling energy, she was as lively and enthusiastic as ever and made herself very popular with the assembled crowd in the hall where the official reception was staged. Her English, though not perfect, was much better than either of the other two pilots so she was pushed forward to make a short speech to thank the organisers.

At Cleveland, Hanna's display was very impressive. Cleverly, she asked the organisers to ensure that there was complete silence. All aero-engines and music had to be stopped so the crowd could hear the varying organ notes made by the airflow as the Habicht went though a fabulous routine of spins, rolls, stall turns, inverted flight, chandelles, high speed passes and loops before the mandatory perfect spot landing in front of the spectators. The crowd applauded her wildly and, for once, the clapping and cheering was not drowned by the roar of aero-engines. Unfortunately when his turn came, von Hagenburg, caught by turbulence when flying upside down near the ground, crashed. He was unhurt, but went home in disgrace.

I was still furious about the hairdresser spy scandal and knew that General Bötticher agreed with me, though he had not written any official complaint. In the diplomatic service one did not publicly criticise the *Abwehr*, this sinister but powerful branch of the army. He said he meant to take the matter up privately with the Foreign Office in Berlin on his next routine visit there. I decided to speak to Hanna about it too so that she could pass the word to Udet, whom she knew as well as I did. I thought he might be able to prevent the secret service from blundering about in the USA any more. I doubt if she ever did say anything to him about it. Had she done so, I never heard that Udet managed to change anything.

What should have been a happy occasion was spoilt. I had hoped to entertain the group with Hanna in Washington for a few days. Instead, immediately after the Cleveland meeting the entire German team were ordered by telegram back to Germany. The crisis of the Sudetenland was upon us and even I began to see there was a real danger of war.

The Sudeten question arose, at least as it was presented by the official Nazi ideology, because of the failure of those who drafted the Versailles Treaty to recognise genuine ethnic and linguistic divisions. Few of us realised that Hitler was cleverly using this familiar issue merely as a cloak for his own imperialism. It was not difficult to unite the German people behind him at this time because there was a good deal of justification for the limited claims he made. It was an old problem going back to the dissolution of the ancient 'Holy Roman Empire', which as they said in Napoleon's time, had been neither holy, nor Roman, nor an empire.

Czechoslovakia was created at Versailles in 1919. The negotiators at Versailles recognised the strengthening of nationalistic feelings in central Europe after centuries of oppression under the dynastic rule of the German-speaking Hapsburgs from Vienna. The US President Wilson spoke grandly of the principle of self determination for national minorities but in this case at least the treaty makers blundered. Four old provinces, Bohemia, Moravia, Slovakia and Ruthenia were pulled together in the hope that, somehow, a new nation would form despite the very different cultural traditions of the diverse peoples within the new boundary.

The diamond-shaped Bohemian basin is enclosed on three sides, south-east, south-west and north-west, by mountain ranges which separate it from Germany and Austria. Under the old empire this region had been inhabited by two different peoples. The Czechs occupied most of the central plateaux and lowlands around Prague. The people in the surrounding mountainous margin, the Sudetenland, were almost entirely German, about three million of a total Bohemian population of about seven million. That these Sudeten German folk should be considered Czechoslovakians was, in the view of most Germans, including myself at the time, an example of the injustice of the Versailles Treaty imposed upon us after the First World War. Still it was not something that many people felt like fighting about. As my acquaintance, Commander Vihlein, on the *Europa* had said, given time the anomaly might have been corrected peacefully. Meanwhile in Prague there was a good deal of resentment and dislike of Germans and the German language, while in the Sudetenland there was equal resentment of the Czechs. At times there were violent incidents on both sides.

The existing tensions were deliberately magnified by Hitler. This was one of those occasions when the power of his oratory worked on his audiences to bring them into a kind of euphoric passion, a feeling that Germans united and powerful were capable of achieving anything, insisting upon rights, demanding justice, prepared in the end even for war. In the Embassy we listened attentively to a radio broadcast of Hitler speaking to a vast audience. There was a kind of harsh rhythm which had an almost hypnotic effect. People around me would become transfixed. I saw eyes brighten, faces become tense, the listeners began to feel that they were there in the audience with the masses. I could feel it happening to me, too, but I was suddenly reminded of the *Schnitzelbank* song. I was introduced to this at Elmira in 1937. One wet day when there was no flying all the pilots and crews gathered in a small restaurant, talking and laughing. Suddenly someone took my arm.

'Come on, Peter. We are going to sing *Schnitzelbank!*'

'What? What's that? *Schnitzelbank?*'

'It's German. You must know it.'

'Never heard of it! That isn't a German word at all!'

'Isn't it? Anyway, you'll enjoy it.'

I wondered what was coming. The restaurant had a small band of musicians. They unrolled a large sheet, something like a wall map, on which a number of objects were crudely drawn: a sausage, a man with a long nose, a rabbit, a glass of beer, some sticks, a vase of flowers and so on. There was no theme, just a random collection of about thirty objects that had occurred to the person who had sketched them. Evidently the musicians took this chart with them wherever they went and unrolled it when the occasion arose. The master of ceremonies raised his baton and the music began with a lively tune. He pointed to one of the items on the screen, a carpenter's bench.

'Ist das ein Schnitzelbank?' he called.

Fifty American voices responded in unison: 'Ja, das ist ein Schnitzelbank!'

'Ist das nicht ein Kurz und Lang?'

'Ja, das ist ein Kurz und Lang! Schnitzelbank, Kurz und Lang, ei du schöne, ei du schöne, ei du schöne SCHNITZELBANK!' they sang.

Then our leader pointed to another item. It might have been a sausage.

'Ist das ein Schnitzelbank?'

'Ja, das ist ein Schnitzelbank!'

'Ist das nicht ein Leberwurst?'

'Ja, das ist ein Leberwurst, Kurz und Lang, ei du schöne, ei du schöne, ei du schöne SCHNITZELBANK!'

It went on, each time round a new item was added to the nonsensical list, the figure on the stage directing us and all responding, 'Kurz und Lang, Leberwurst, grosser Durst, lange Nase, Blumenvase, Rosenmund, schwarzer Hund, Schnitzelbank, ei du schöne, ei du schöne, ei du schöne SCHNITZELBANK!'

Once the rhythm was established it tended to take over with a kind of hypnotic effect. Everyone joined in the repetition, joyfully chanting the nonsense, having a fine time. We stamped our feet, hammered on the tables, waved our arms and raised our voices in the last cheerful shout, 'SCHNITZELBANK! SCHNITZELBANK!'

We were all such good fellows singing together, obedient to the baton waving character on the stage, following his direction, following the leader, all friends united, we didn't need to think. If we slipped up anywhere he would correct us and everyone laughed but the rhythm was maintained . . . Such nonsense! We would sing anything for him!

And now in Germany, Adolf Hitler was singing a grimmer song, listing the wrongs done to Germany and adding something extra every time round. The enormous power of this simple technique made itself felt even as we, in the Washington office, listened to that grating, rough voice on the radio. He had the rhythm, the list of questions calling for the required responses. Now he was pointing to a new item on the chart, the map of Czechoslovakia.

'German folk, you have rights!'

'We have rights.'

'This is a great injustice!'

'We have rights, this is a great injustice.'

'The Sudeten lands are part of the Reich!'

'We have rights, great injustice, part of the Reich.'

'One race, one state, one Führer. Sieg Heil!'

'SIEG HEIL, SIEG HEIL, SIEG HEIL!'

Such good fellows, so strong, united following the leader on the podium. Sing anything for him. Stamp your feet, thump the tables, wave your arms and shout together to terrify the world. If you hesitated, made a slip or got the words wrong, no one laughed.

Chamberlain flew to Bad Godesberg, returned to London and went back again to Munich. We waited anxiously. When the settlement was announced I was carried away by relief and hope. My faith in Hitler's honesty was justified, I thought. He had achieved a great success by peaceful negotiation. A wrong had been righted, a justice done. In my delight I sent a telegram to my friends the Burberrys in England, convinced that Chamberlain and Hitler had indeed assured 'peace in our time'. I was saddened when the considered, cool reply came by mail a few days later: 'Many people in this country begin to think like Anthony Eden.' Eden had resigned from the foreign ministry over the Italian invasion of Abyssinia and he, like Winston Churchill, opposed the Chamberlain policy of appeasement.

The German army moved into the Sudetenland and was undoubtedly welcomed by the population. Newsreels showed smiling, flag-waving multitudes in the streets of the villages and small towns. How easy it was to relax again.

I had become stale from sitting in my office sifting through papers. This was what I had dreaded. I decided I must get some regular exercise and heard of a small riding club in Rock Creek Park not far from the apartment where I was living. I went along there and found it to be very simple with no competitive pressures and very tame horses. I had done no riding before and had to learn how to sit, how to avoid falling off and how to get the horse to obey me. When the weather was bad or cold, or it was after dark, we trotted round and round in a large shed which had at one time housed streetcars. There was a good layer of sand mixed with sawdust on the floor. The horse they gave me was not at all dangerous but I was not good at getting him to obey me. Sometimes he would not move at all but I discovered that if I gave him a lump of sugar he would go. I soon learned to carry some with me every time I went riding and when the old fellow had had enough he would stop, turn round and look at me as if to say, *Come on, sugar time!* I would reach into my pocket, give him a lump and off he would trot again until the next time. I did not realise that I was actually teaching him not to move unless he had the sugar first! It was a bad way of learning to ride and a bad way to train a horse! One day when I reached into my pocket the sugar had all gone and I was stuck. A young woman rode by.

'Do you have any sugar lumps?' I asked her. She came alongside and gave me some. My mount got himself into gear again and off we went. That was how Helen and I first met. Afterwards I spoke again to her. She was a very lovely girl, responded cheerfully and we went to supper together. We met again the following week and soon were seeing each other regularly, becoming very fond of one another.

A few weeks after the Munich crisis we in the Embassy were told to expect another important speech from Hitler in Saarbrücken. Eagerly, we listened to the radio. I was sure we had passed a great turning point. All the important issues had been settled and the less important ones would be cleared up now without much trouble. Hitler had achieved so much. Germany was strong again, industries were flourishing. We could once more be a proud member of the European family of nations and this was the time for reconciliation. After the triumph of the Sudetenland the Führer would surely make some convincing gesture to soothe and reassure the British and French governments. Perhaps he would propose a new disarmament conference, demonstrating his peaceful intentions and giving the lie to Eden and Churchill and their friends. This is what the speech would be about.

When it came my euphoria dissolved, doubts which I had suppressed and forgotten surfaced again with increased strength although I still could not entirely shake myself free of my wishful thinking. Instead of offering concessions, Hitler made what seemed to me a most obvious and arrogant blunder. He savagely criticised for their weakness, the very same men who had yielded to him in Munich. Why did the British and French governments allow critics to speak so loudly against this agreement? Why did they not silence the people who opposed it? Why were these outspoken persons not restrained? All the menace, the threats, the rough demands were there as before. The song was not ended, the list of demands was no shorter. There was not a word calculated to help the cause of peace, nothing to relieve tension, no hint of disarmament or restraint. Everything the man screamed tended to confirm what Churchill had been saying all along. No wonder, I thought, that Britain was re-arming. The hopes that I had nurtured began to fade. That Saarbrücken speech shook me profoundly, causing me at last to begin questioning Hitler's good sense. I had to conceal my doubts not only from my colleagues in the Embassy but also from myself.

Yet international tension seemed to relax. I convinced myself I was too inexperienced, too far from the centre of affairs to make sound judgements. I began to forget that stupid Saarbrücken speech and hoped that one day Adolf would prove to be a real statesman.

Then came *Kristallnacht*, 10–11 November. During my visit to Berlin earlier in the year I had seen Jewish shops and businesses flourishing on Kurfürstendamm and Tauentzierstrasse. The big Café Wien was packed with German-Jewish clientele. To a three-month visitor, as I was on this occasion, these signs seemed to point to a moderation of the Nazi spirit. Despite the vitriolic outpourings of little Dr Goebbels, ordinary Jewish folk seemed to be doing quite well.

Then a young Zionist shot a German diplomat in Paris. It presented the Nazis with the excuse they had wanted. The reaction of Heinrich Himmler and Josef Goebbels made me ashamed for the first time of being German and I hated them and their brutal, organised bullies. The American newspapers published detailed reports of the barbaric behaviour in Berlin, the smashed windows that gave the night its infamous name, the innocent people beaten and tormented, businesses ruined, synagogues burned, people driven from their homes, as bad as any medieval pogrom.

A few days previously I had accepted an invitation to 'Wild Bill' Donovan's home at Beekman Place for a dinner party. It was part of his daughter Patricia's twenty-first birthday celebrations. Now I was reluctant to go, sure that on my arrival there would be a deadly hush, people would whisper, *Here comes one of them, a Nazi, a Jew baiter! How disgusting that he should be here!* I should be treated like a leper, no one would wish to speak to me and I should be compelled to crawl away. But cousin Renate and Paul Leverkühn were to be there too, for they were the Donovan's house guests and not to attend would also be offensive to them. It would be cowardly to withdraw without a good excuse, so, when the time came, as quietly as I could I slipped into the room where the people were gathered. American guests were standing in groups and Mrs Donovan welcomed me and drew me forward to be introduced. For a few seconds I wished myself far away but the moment passed and I was greeted with perfect naturalness and goodwill. All the confusions and conflicts of feeling in myself were quite unrecognised by these apparently untroubled souls. They did not think of me as a rotten German but as myself, Peter, a friend.

Donovan and Leverkühn had both been to Germany recently because of some joint business there. There was no doubt that Donovan and

Leverkühn had become very good friends. Apart from knowing each other on the Mixed Claims Commission years before, they had done some legal work concerned with the Russian Czar's supposed family fortune. It seemed a strange business to me since it involved the supposed Anastasia claimant and I could not form any concrete idea of what it was expected to achieve. Renate, I could see, was no tamer than she had ever been and I wondered how a sobersides like Paul could put up with her.

Patricia Donovan and I got along well together that evening and we made a date to meet again. When the time came she took me to a party which went on until the small hours. It was a much livelier affair than the rather ponderous dinner party at her parents' home. I was a good deal older than most of the youngsters there and felt out of place. Patricia, I suppose, saw that I did not quite belong in her youthful set and we did not meet again.

In February 1939 General von Bötticher took his annual trip to Germany. By this time I had settled into my job and the General seemed content with me during the weeks before his departure. Yet I was still not allowed to use my own initiative. He insisted on keeping all decisions in his own hands. For example, two young engineers arrived at the embassy during the General's absence. They came from Rechlin, the *Luftwaffe* testing centre, and wanted me to accompany them on visits to some American aircraft engine factories. I had to use the trans-Atlantic telegraph to get Bötticher's permission before arranging to join them in visiting the Wright Aeronautical Corporation in Paterson, NJ and the United Aircraft Corporation in Hartford, Conn. The US War Department's consent to these visits was readily given. We were even permitted to inspect the testing facilities for motors and propellers at Wright Field, Dayton, Ohio because the two visitors were especially interested in such technical devices. This was all I had seen at first hand of the American aircraft industry by the spring of 1939. Whatever my doubts about Hitler I did not want to lose my position now. I was feeling very much at home in Washington and wished to stay, not least because of Helen.

Helen Klug came from the town of Terre Haute, Indiana. In French, Terre Haute means high ground. The town was first established by French colonists clear of flood land by the Wabash river. For Helen in Washington now, home on the banks of the Wabash was far away, as the popular song said! She had been lonely and so was I until we met.

She was the eldest of seven brothers and sisters, her mother having had two sets of twins. Her grandparents were Catholics who, three generations before, had emigrated from Alsace-Lorraine. Their language had been German although technically they were French. Her maternal grandparents farmed a 250-acre property near the river about ten miles south of the town. Helen herself grew up in Terre Haute but spent holidays at the farm. Loving the scenery there Helen became fascinated by painting and discovered she had talent. She attended Saint Mary's of the Woods High School run by the Sisters of Providence. After winning a small scholarship she went to art school in Indianapolis but had to work in a department store on Saturdays at a $1.50 per day to stretch her very meagre funds.

In 1933, during the depression, the store had to cut even part-time staff and she lost her Saturday job but managed to complete the school year and graduate. Then there was no demand for artists. For a while she worked with a friend as an independent art teacher, taking a few paying pupils in their homes, but it proved barely possible to make a living this way. Fortunately, recommended by one of her former teachers, she was able to find a more secure post in a small elementary convent school in Washington and so she moved there by herself. Pay was meagre and convent living conditions spartan but before very long she was able to transfer into the public education system. In the summers she attended Columbia University in New York where she completed her Masters degree. When I met her she was one of four art supervisors for the elementary schools in Washington. At home Helen had never picked up any German except for a few songs at Christmas. My English by now was quite good enough for this not to bother either of us. We got along famously and began to think of marriage. We knew there would be difficulties.

5

Gaining Intelligence

Bötticher returned from his Berlin trip clearly in a state of great excitement. He was full of himself and his own importance, pompous and bombastic as ever but driven now by a sort of inner zeal which I had not seen in him before. The reason appeared quickly. He had met the Führer face to face!

Here stood the General who, for all his obvious faults, was nevertheless an educated man with a good understanding of history, a shrewd thinker far above average and, because of his puritanical upbringing, strictly adherent to severe principles in both his private and his public life. Before 1933 he had been known as a convinced anti-Nazi and had been saved from premature retirement then only by his friendship with General von Fritsch.[1] A single meeting with Hitler found him carried away almost as if hypnotised. I did not like Bötticher but I could not remain unaffected by his outpouring of enthusiasm.

'My dear Herr Riedel, I have come to understand a great deal. In Germany, I was kept hard at work every day from morning till night but the outstanding event, unforgettable for the rest of my life, was when I was called to the Führer and stood face to face with this extraordinary man! I wish you could have had this chance to look into his eyes and feel the magnetic power of his person. Now, he has given us special orders!'

A clever psychologist, Bötticher, to say 'us' and so seem to bring me into his orbit as an equal! Suddenly I was more than a mere assistant attaché, a glorified office boy. I was Herr Riedel, the man who works alongside a man who knows the Führer! As Bötticher intended, I was awe-struck and flattered. I had seen other friends, over the years, coming under the spell

---

[1] Colonel-General Werner von Fritsch, Commander-in-Chief of the Army under the Chief of Staff, Blomberg, had attempted to isolate the Wehrmacht from the Nazi party, submitting only to the direction of the Führer, who was nominally above politics. In 1938, Blomberg married a woman who was proved to be a prostitute by the Gestapo and he was forced to resign. The Gestapo attempted at the same time to discredit Fritsch by accusing him of being homosexual. Fritsch retired, although eventually proved innocent of all charges. Two important effects of the affair were the replacement of Fritsch by Brauschitsch and the alienation of Admiral Canaris from Hitler, leading Canaris to start plotting against Hitler.

and now I was feeling it myself. In me, as in others, the longing for a saviour was always there and finally one did not want to see Hitler in any other way. The feeling did not last long but it was there at that moment.

The crash came immediately.

'This is the question we are required now to answer. *If war should break out in 1939, how long will it be before the United States is able send decisive help to Europe?*'

I was chilled, my sudden rush of fervour was gone, leaving me shocked and weak. Was Hitler really planning war after all? Had I been wrong from the beginning?

Bötticher may have detected my reaction despite my trying to remain impassive. Did he himself have some doubts after all? No decision had been made. He commented more fully, telling me what he himself believed, softening the shock and convincing me as well as himself yet again that Hitler would stop short of final confrontation. What we reported would help policy to be framed, we were in a position to influence events in favour of peace.

Hitler certainly wished to continue righting the wrongs inflicted on Germany at Versailles and there was now only one problem left, a comparatively small matter of the Danzig Corridor which divided German East Prussia from the rest of the nation. Some other minor readjustments of the Polish frontier might be needed. There was no need to fear that war would really break out over these small territories, especially if it could be shown to the world that they were inhabited predominantly by Germans. Right and justice were on our side. These areas were not even as important as the Sudetenland and the matter would be solved the same way with forceful diplomacy. But the Führer needed to know how far he could go. If American aid was unlikely to appear quickly, those opposing his moves would know their weakness and be less likely to challenge him with force. War would not result if the American help was doubtful or if it would come too late. This was what we must establish. We knew already in outline what kind of answer we should give but we must provide precision and evidence.

I believed. There would be no explosion.

Now, the General said, we must co-operate on preparing our report. He would apply himself to the military arm, tanks and guns. I must produce a full picture of the present and future production capacity of the American aircraft industry. We must take care and avoid rushing ourselves but nevertheless there was some urgency in the matter. I told him I thought it would take me at least a week of hard work. He accepted this. I left his office feeling uneasy. Away from his presence my worries increased. I had given myself a deadline.

The entire secretarial staff of the Military and Air Attaché in the German Embassy in Washington consisted of two women, one of whom, the younger, was allowed to help me. Fortunately I knew what needed to be done. From my first day in the embassy I had collected all newspaper articles on aviation, all information possible from aviation magazines, congressional hearings and other legal, readily available sources. I had classified the material in alphabetical order of the various aircraft factories. For each plant I had a number of clippings and notes. I had never yet tried to bring all the fragments together to make a complete picture but as I began to evaluate what I had, I gained assurance. It was all there, in the files.

We took out the file on one of the big companies, the Glenn L. Martin Corporation in Baltimore. I spread the heap of papers across my desk. Where to begin? News clippings, little scraps of paper, the occasional photograph, this, that or the other company executive doing something or other, a new type of aeroplane, an old one, an article by some journalist who might know something but more likely had padded out a story from almost nothing. I had wondered whether there was any point in collecting all this stuff but now knew I had been wise to do so.

There were financial statements, which had come from the commercial sections of the larger newspapers, chairmen's reports, statements of profits, dollar figures of output and turnover. Interested men in Wall Street knew that the Glenn Martin Company had an output worth $3,452,645 in 1938. The firm made a net profit of $477,652 and paid a dividend of six cents in the dollar. These were hard facts. (The figures given here are fictitious and are intended only to illustrate the methods I used.)

In elementary school arithmetic problems if a farmer sells an unknown number of eggs for five dollars and one knows the price of an egg it is easy to work out how many eggs he sells. Eggs or aeroplanes, there isn't much difference.

It was comparatively easy to find out the exact prices for the different aircraft types in the USA. The American War and Navy Departments used to publish every order they gave to the aircraft industry with all the important data: the number of each type, their prices, lists of spare parts, more dollar figures. Among the news clippings I had many of these official statements which had been given out freely to the press. There was no attempt to hide or falsify the figures. From these I was able to calculate the prices for a number of bombing, pursuit, transport and training aircraft.

Then there was the American Aviation yearbook which could be picked up in any bookshop. It contained a scrupulously correct and detailed list of all aircraft ordered and delivered to the US Army, Navy, Marine Corps and

Coastguard during the corresponding year. Number, equipment and price, everything of military significance was listed for whoever wanted such information. I wanted it, now! I worked my way through these yearbooks beginning with the issue of 1933, which was the year General Bötticher had come to Washington. I formed a clear picture of the strength of the American navy and army air forces.

From a study of publicity emanating from the Company itself I knew that Glenn L. Martin had delivered only twin-engined bombers during 1938 and that the outstanding orders not yet completed included a number of Martin 167 Maryland bombers for France, twenty twin-engined Martin 162 Mariner flying boats for the US Navy and one big four-engined flying boat for Pan American Airways. If I divided the sum of output, $3,452,654 by the price of one-twin engined bomber, $118,000, I found that this Company could by no means have delivered more than about thirty bombers during 1938. That was a maximum.

I had developed my system and went through the lists of American aircraft manufacturers to discover how many planes each had produced during 1938 and the first quarter of 1939. If my results were not perfectly accurate they showed at least the upper limit of present production capacity for each organisation, which was what I needed to answer the first part of the important question: what was available immediately. The answer was, as I had already guessed, nothing.

The second problem concerned the future capacity of the industry. What could the factories produce in the next six months, the next year, two years, or longer, to feed any possible European war? Thanks to the unlimited publicity given out from the various organisations I was able to compile a list of all the important factories, plant by plant. I recorded the present size of the production elements, space required in square feet of shop floor and number of workers. When an expansion was planned the Company would publish all details of it, the intended output, the expected number of workers to be taken on and the time necessary for the increased production to appear. It was no secret at all that some limited growth of American aircraft production was already underway in 1939 but how far had it progressed? I found enough in the various periodicals and in the business sections of the major newspapers to inform myself about bottle-necks which must slow down any accelerated, large scale further expansion. Being an engineer myself and having heard enough about the corresponding bottlenecks in Germany, I could estimate the time necessary for the American industry to reach a size that would make possible the delivery of aircraft to Europe on a large scale.

What was the result? The entire American military aircraft industry in early 1939 employed about 40,000 workers with an output of about 150 military planes per month.[2] Of these I estimated some thirty were bombers, forty pursuit planes (fighters) and the rest training aircraft. The engine factories had about 4,000 workers including a few hundred in propeller plants. These totals were very small indeed compared with what I knew of the corresponding German figures. The prestige of the American aviation industry was so great and surrounded by such 'ballyhoo' that a newcomer lacking the files I had assembled would have guessed much higher all round. My estimates were based on reports prepared for Wall Street where solid financial facts, not guesses, were required and I was convinced of their accuracy. This was start of the statistical system on which I based this first important report to Bötticher and through him, to Berlin. As I elaborated the method further in the following months it became thoroughly reliable and I used it in compiling all my subsequent reports.

A little more than a week of intensive work had been done before I was ready to show the outcome to Bötticher. He made no enquiry as to how I had arrived at my figures and declined my suggestion that I should explain it all to him, expressing full confidence in me. From this time on my position on his staff became much stronger. He began to rely on me more. I continued on good terms with him though he frequently irritated me enormously and I was often forced to conceal my true feelings. After several days of discussion, which continued over the Easter long weekend, we formulated our final telegraphic answer: IF A EUROPEAN WAR SHOULD BREAK OUT IN MID 1939 IT WILL BE TWO YEARS BEFORE AMERICA COULD SEND AIRCRAFT IN SUCH NUMBERS THAT THEY MIGHT INFLUENCE THE TREND OF EVENTS IN A DECISIVE WAY.

As things turned out this was a very accurate prediction. People wondered why General von Bötticher was awarded the Knights Cross by the Führer himself in June 1942. This telegram might have been one of the reasons. Doubtless it strengthened Hitler's resolve to risk war, if he needed any such reassurance. He believed it would all be over before the USA could intervene in any material way. It was the autumn of 1941 before American deliveries of war planes to the Allies became significant, a full two years after we sent our message.

Now German troops marched into Prague, overwhelming the small Czech nation. I was very upset and said to Helen that it did seem like the first step on the way to a major war. For several days I saw things clearly

---

[2] Lockheeds for example had a low point of 332 workers in 1934, by 1940 increased to 7,000, reached 16,898 in 1942 and 94,329 in mid-1943. The original contract for the Curtiss P-36 Fighter was $4,113,550 for 210 aircraft. The Curtiss P-40 prototype, already out of date by European standards, had flown by October 1938 but did not enter production until 1940 and cost about $51,538 per aircraft. (Figures from René. J. Francillon, *Lockheed Aircraft since 1913*, Putnams 1982).

and did not fool myself about Hitler's policies. But one can get used to anything. The United States was not directly involved, the embassy routines continued, work engaged my mind and the soothing propaganda by radio from Berlin with supporting bulletins on my desk every day, calmed me. The British and French apparently were going to do nothing. After a few weeks the world at large had apparently accepted Hitler's action. There had been diplomatic protests but I was able to convince myself again what I desperately wanted to believe, that there would be no war.

During those months of 1939 I had ambitious plans to take my mind off politics. On one wall of my office I put up special aviation maps of the entire USA from the Californian coast to the Atlantic. Often I looked up from my desk and was immediately far away, soaring in my sailplane in imagination over the Rocky Mountains, or climbing rapidly somewhere over Texas or Nebraska. In my dreams a larger plan began to take shape.

During the Elmira contest of 1938 I had flown a total distance of nearly 1,600 kilometres (994 miles) in the two weeks. I thought with a month's free time available and some good luck I ought to be able to make a whole series of cross-country soaring flights and accumulate a much greater distance. It would be a sort of soaring safari, a connected string, launching early each day, making as much distance as possible using thermals or slope winds before landing, then taking off again from the landing place and heading off. If I started on the west coast, say at San Francisco or Los Angeles, I might be able to fly a sailplane in stages across the entire continent to New York, 4,600 kilometres (2,870 miles). The idea was not so fantastic as it might have sounded.[3]

The General gave his approval for a four-week vacation and at my suggestion allowed an extension of two weeks to enable me to visit aircraft factories in California and others in the mid-west. Two friends volunteered to drive my car from Washington to San Francisco with the trailer containing the Kranich. I would fly as a passenger with American Airlines ahead of them and do some work before they arrived. Helen helped me to get things ready and used her sign writing abilities on the trailer.

On arrival in Los Angeles I met Hans Wolfram, a lively and cheerful man who was the local representative of the German news syndicate, Deutches Nachrichten Bureau. He introduced me to a bewildering number of his contacts and I gained a confused, but in its way inspiring, impression of the city and of Hollywood. I quickly began my official visits to the

---

[3] The idea of transcontinental sailplane soaring was revived in 1972. The Smirnoff Derby in May 1972 was organised as a race undertaken by six leading glider pilots in seven stages from Los Angeles to Baltimore. All completed the trip, the winner being Wally Scott. The event was repeated several years running.

aircraft companies. I was shown around the great sheds of the Consolidated Aircraft Corporation on San Diego Airport. Hardly anything was happening. A few lonely PBY flying boats could be seen outside. Here there were no preparations for war; the sheds were mostly empty. Ryan's small plant on the same base was turning out a few training planes for export to Guatemala. That was all.

I visited the factories of Douglas, Lockheed, North American and Convair-Vultee (a subsidiary of Consolidated). At Vultee, which was a small factory, the main products were training aircraft for the army. I was permitted to see everything except one small experimental shop. The North American plant was medium in size compared with the German factories I knew. They were turning out aircraft in substantial numbers but they were only advanced trainers. Two of their production lines were working on a contract for Britain building the NA-16, called the Harvard by the RAF. A third line was working for the US Army Air Corps.[4] The Douglas and Lockheed works were also, by my standards, medium sized but I was shown only the divisions producing transport and commercial aircraft, the famous Douglas DC-3 of course, and at Lockheeds there was a wooden mock up of a four-engined transatlantic airliner.[5] I had hoped to visit the Boeing plant at Seattle but although the US War Department had granted permission, Boeings never replied to my letter asking for a visit.

The fact that I was not allowed to see the main military production lines in these three factories might be explained in two different ways. It could have meant that they were secretly producing war planes on a large scale. Or it might have been that they did not want me to see how little was really going on. I was no longer naïve and remembered the information I had collected about each company.

Douglas, I deduced, was mainly occupied with modifications to some 200 B-18s, the army's standard front line bomber at this time. The B-18 was a military version of the DC-2 airliner and had been found lacking in some respects by the Army and required alterations. Such work is not very satisfying or profitable to the manufacturers and I could understand their reluctance to let me see it in progress. The type was approaching obsolescence anyway and that was all they were doing.

It was just as easy to work out what was occupying Boeings. This plant had outstanding orders for a limited number of four-engined Boeing B-17 B and C bombers, so called Flying Fortresses, for the Army. They were building five Clipper flying boats and a single airliner prototype, the Stratoliner, which would have a pressure cabin. It was a commercial version of the B-17. Each

[4] The NA-73, which was to become the P-51 Mustang fighter, did not yet exist even in prototype form.
[5] This would have been the C-69, later known as the Constellation.

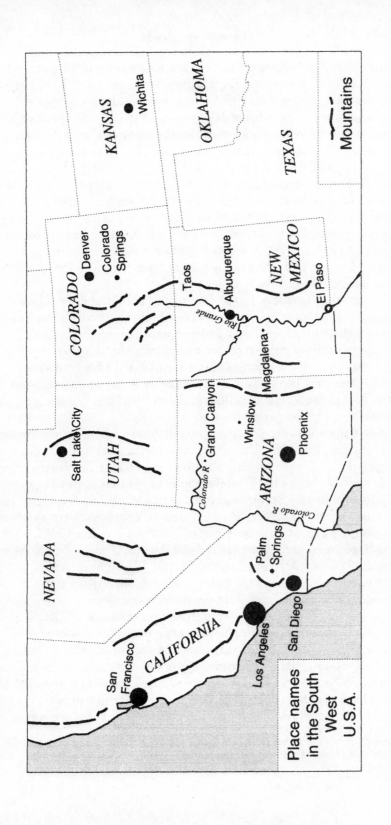

Place names in the South West U.S.A.

delivery of Flying Fortresses had been attended by so much publicity that I knew exactly how many had left the factory. It was not many! I also knew the length of their further order lists because details had been published by the War Department. The value of deliveries so far in 1939 had appeared in the press. The work force was larger than could be accounted for by these facts but it was not difficult to guess that the plant was fully occupied producing parts and sub-assemblies which would be used later for assembly of the next series of B-17s. It was no great disappointment to me that I was not taken round the Boeing works for I had a very exact idea of what was being done there. They would not be able to fill big orders from Europe within the next few months. The same was true of Lockheeds. Between July 1938 and the early part of '39 Britain had ordered 200 Lockheed Hudson reconnaissance bombers, the design developed from the small Model 14 Electra airliner. These, I already knew, were in production.

During these few days I saw almost one half of the entire US aircraft industry. My previous conclusions were solidly reinforced. It was business as usual, no new buildings were under construction and everywhere I went the development of new transport aircraft was the chief activity. I even began to wonder if my estimate of two years should have been stretched to three! There was not the slightest indication of preparation for war. So what was to be made of Hitler's claims that the Jewish-dominated plutocracies were preparing to attack Germany?

Didn't the orders for American aircraft from England prove this case? The tensions before the Munich agreement had awakened the European democracies and forced them to realise their lack of air power. Later it transpired that, on the day Chamberlain went to Munich, Britain possessed only six of the early Spitfire fighters.[6] Germany already had six or seven hundred fighters in service. France's state of unpreparedness was worse. Between July 1938 and the early part of 1939 Britain ordered 200 Lockheed Hudson reconnaissance bombers and 400 Harvard trainers. France ordered between 150 and 200 twin-engined Martin 167 bombers and about the same number of Curtiss P-36 fighters. How could anyone assert that the democracies had been preparing for an aggressive war?

A weekend offered a welcome interruption from my official visits and Hans Wolfram suggested a sight-seeing trip to the beautiful surroundings of Los Angeles which, he said, could be combined with a diplomatic courtesy call on Fritz Wiedemann, the newly-appointed German Consul General in San Francisco. He happened to be spending a few days at a place not far from Los Angeles. Captain Wiedemann had been Corporal Adolf Hitler's commanding officer during World War One and was said to

[6] Production of the Hawker Hurricane fighter had begun earlier than the Spitfire. By the end of 1938 about 200 had been delivered.

be a great favourite. He had been the Führer's adjutant until recently and hence in frequent contact with him.[7] The American newspapers had described him as a sinister mystery man sent out especially to cause trouble. I suppose they were hinting that he was a master of spies. I was curious to meet him.

The day came and we were speeding along in Wolfram's car on the road to see Wiedemann. Hans had confidence in me now.

'Before you meet Wiedemann I think you should know something about him, Herr Riedel, but before I say more you must promise to say nothing whatever about it to anybody at all.'

Usually so cheerful and easy going, Wolfram was obviously very serious. I gave him my promise.

'Hitler, you know, dragged Wiedemann out of semi-retirement in 1934, to serve on his staff. Wiedemann himself would have been happy to stay in retirement on his farm in Bavaria but that wouldn't do. It would raise too many strange questions. He knew Hitler well. If he did not appear openly in support of him it would look very odd.

'Wiedemann and I are very good friends. There were times, he says, when Hitler seemed almost frightened by his own position and responsibilities. Well, you have read the newspapers. What they say about Wiedemann is very far from the truth. He is no longer Hitler's favourite. Only Hitler's reluctance to harm an old comrade has allowed him to take up his post here. He warns me to be as happy as I can, while I am here, to make the most of things while there is still a chance because there won't be a chance much longer. Things are going to be very bad. He assures me, Hitler is definitely planning war.'

I can still remember exactly where we were on the road as Wolfram told me this. The news made me strangely observant of the surrounding details.

'Wiedemann tried his best, with a few other reasonable people, to convince him that he should not go to war. Sometimes when the Führer was in a quiet mood they would get him on one side and describe to him in detail the huge resources of men and material which would oppose Germany if he started serious trouble, the enormous potential strength of the USA. But instead of paying attention he would at some point turn to Hess or some other old pal and say "Oh, let's talk of something else, the good old days of struggle when we beat the communists out of our beer halls in Munich. Those were happy times!" It was no use talking to him.

---

[7] Fritz Wiedemann, according to Höhne, was approached in 1937 by Johannes von Dohnanyi, adviser to the Reich Minister of Justice, with a plan to assassinate Hitler. He replied 'A revolver is the only way out, I grant you, but who's to do it? I can't help to murder someone who trusts me.' That is, he did not object in principle but declined to do the deed himself. (Heinz Höhne, *Canaris*, Doubleday & Co 1979, p. 266)

They might reduce him almost to tears but there would suddenly be a complete change of mood, he would work himself into a rage and accept no contradiction or even the hint of it.

'Hitler believes there is a vast conspiracy of plutocratic powers who will attack him soon. He talks always about getting in the first blow, forestalling the attack which, he insists, the conspirators are preparing against him. He rages against Roosevelt and even poor old Chamberlain. At last, one day Wiedemann expressed himself too forcibly and Hitler showed him the door. He was in disgrace. After a few days the Foreign Office passed the word. He must take a minor diplomatic post far, far away from Berlin, out of Germany. To remain within easy reach would be extremely dangerous. They shipped him quietly out of the way. That is how Wiedemann comes to be here now! Master spy, rubbish; he is practically a refugee.'

Wiedemann, when we reached him, seemed an easy-going type of man, best described as a kind of South German country squire, perhaps not intellectually brilliant but full of common sense. Through the prestige he had gained via his long-standing friendship with Hitler, his voice, had it been raised loudly enough and soon enough, might have warned the world in time and roused conservative forces in Germany itself. He had remained silent, I supposed out of some misguided sense of loyalty, and he still remained so in public.

I cannot answer for Wiedemann but I must try to answer for myself. Why did I not see where all this was leading? I think what restrained me was a complex mixture of tradition, fear and resignation. Official authority at that period always seemed sacred to a German. Duty and obedience were drummed into us by our schooling and became instinctive. Duty and obedience, and duty to one's country, now meant following the leader.

There was also the reaction to be expected from my closest friends. Later, when the war was in its first year, I did think seriously of deserting from the Embassy in Washington. I did not do so. It was not because I gave much weight to the more or less obligatory oaths which bound me. It was because I dreaded what my old friends, people like Hanna Reitsch and Ernst Udet, would think of me. As a last defence against taking personal responsibility for oneself one surrenders to a dark fatalism. One shrugs one's shoulders, sighs, ignores the signals, sees only Obedience, Duty, Fatherland and Honour . . . thinking stops. From that moment one feels much better.

6

The Crossing of Watersheds

My ambitious soaring expedition did not go well at the beginning. It was my own fault. The first leg of the flight, starting on a Friday, was intended to take me from Tracy Airport near San Francisco to Los Angeles. There had been some advanced publicity and the Soaring Society of Southern California had scheduled a public aerobatic exhibition for me to perform at Glendale Airport on the Sunday. The press had advertised the event and cine photographers from 20th Century Fox News were expected to be there. I thought it would require two days to be sure of reaching Glendale in soaring flight from Tracy, a distance of about 500 km (300 miles). Given very good weather I might do it in one flight but if not I could land somewhere and be re-launched. There were no rules against it for the kind of flying I wanted to do.

In too much of a hurry I took off on the Friday. The two seat Kranich was a big and heavy sailplane for its time which, as before, I was flying solo from the front cockpit. It had no wheels. Landings were made on a simple rubber-sprung skid. With the method of car-towed launching we used there was not enough power to overcome the initial friction of the skid on the ground. The Kranich had provision for a two-wheeled dolly to be attached under the fuselage and the pilot was supposed to drop this from a height of a few feet after becoming airborne. Through absent mindedness and nerves I forgot to release the dolly until I was at about 300 feet, kiting up steeply during the launch. I suddenly remembered and pulled the handle to release the dolly because it would be likely to come loose and damage the Kranich if I tried to land with it still in place. After releasing the launching wire I didn't make contact with a thermal and had to land within a few minutes back on the airfield. When we went to find the dolly we discovered it in pieces. Falling from 300 feet it had been smashed. I could not take off again that day.

Fortunately glider pilot friends enlisted the help of an expert welder and it was possible to repair the damage overnight. Next day I was off again but more trouble followed. The weather was not good and I was forced to land only a short distance out in a farmer's field. It was about midday. The property owner, looking precisely like Charles Laughton playing the role of beachcomber, arose from his bed and offered me a drink from his whisky bottle.

My crew arrived quickly and the car towed me off from the large field. This time I released the wheels too soon and they bounced up and made a bad hole in the plywood skin of the fuselage. I had to land at once. Discouraged, I was forced to give up the attempt to reach Los Angeles by air. I telegraphed from the farmer's home to the president of the Californian Soaring Society asking if the damage to the sailplane could be repaired with some help from the gliding fraternity in Los Angeles. The president was none other than Dr Wolfgang Klemperer. I had met him in 1920 when I was a schoolboy and he was the winner of the very first gliding competition held on the Wasserkuppe in the Rhön mountains. From an old Jewish family in Dresden he had left Germany in 1925 and now was an American citizen with a high position in the aircraft industry. We packed the Kranich into its trailer, said farewell to the merry beachcomber and drove to LA, reaching the suburbs before midnight and arriving at Van Nuys Airport where Klemperer had arranged everything we needed. Glider pilots had sacrificed their rest to help us and in a small workshop they were ready with sleeves rolled up and equipment: sheets of aircraft plywood, saws, chisels, scrapers, glue, tacking strips and cellulose dope. At four in the morning they sent me away to get some sleep and promised the Kranich would be airworthy before noon. And so it was.

On Glendale Airport I met Klemperer and his wife who made everything easy for me, though I was beginning to feel guilty again about the swastika on the rudder of the Kranich.

In an attempt to repay all the work that had been done I put on a rather reckless show of aerobatics for which the Kranich was not really designed. As usual I continued until very low down and saw thousands of upturned faces quite close as I passed upside down over the top of the last loop to dive again, pulling out upright just inches from the asphalt of the runway to land. The show took only a few minutes and the public seemed anxious for an encore so I did it all again, trying even harder. I survived. I knew the strength of the wings exactly and was sufficiently light in my touch on the controls to avoid over-stressing the structure or misjudging that final manoeuvre.

Three days of frustration in discouraging weather followed. I had hoped by now to be crossing Texas! But I had a chance to meet more of Hans Wolfram's friends, to visit Klemperer at home and also make a speech at a breakfast club. This event is worth describing. On a sunny morning at about eight o'clock, Wolfram drove me to a big hall where hundreds of people were seated at long tables. It reminded me of one of the big tents at the Munich October Fest. I was taken through the crowd to a high table at the end of the hall. The dignitaries of the breakfast club were waiting and there was a lectern. Music and community singing began, creating a festive atmosphere. Pancakes, ham and eggs, coffee and milk were served to all the tables until the moment came to start the official talks programme. The chairman welcomed the members and introduced the various guests who were to speak. It was a rather strange affair to European eyes.

The first speaker was an elderly American gentleman who had spent seventeen years of his life in Albania and had lost his heart to the fiercely independent people who, since Easter, had been under Italian military occupation. The speaker raged against the fascist Mussolini who had ordered the invasion in April. The old man was well supported by the crowd and I found myself agreeing with all he said. Yet Hitler and Mussolini were supposed to be so friendly! Where did my loyalties lie?

Then my turn came and to much applause I was introduced as 'the gallant master of the beautiful art of soaring'. I was embarrassed but told the audience how I had built my first crude glider at home and tried to fly it. The wing frames of laths had been covered with expensive parchment paper which had turned out to be no good, splitting and tearing at the least opportunity. Still, it had lifted me off the ground a couple of times even though I was not in control of it at all. Then, as a fourteen-year-old in 1920, I had participated in the first gliding competition flying my second home-made biplane glider, the PR 2, now more sensibly covered with ordinary packing paper. It had flown very well too. Dr Klemperer had become my hero then. I went on to give an account of some of my more recent adventures, especially that wonderful flight to Washington and I described my plans to soar across the continent. It was all well received.

The third speaker was the reluctant Dr Klemperer himself. He was obviously much embarrassed by my hero worship but he said a few words in response to my remarks. The session of the breakfast club ended in a happy mood.

The next day I started again on my intended flights, this time being launched from San Bernardino Airport, some 100 km (60 miles) inland from the city. Klemperer had convinced me that the local climate of Los Angeles, with the chilly offshore current promoting fogs, tended to inhibit the formation of thermals during the summer months. April would have been a better time to start, he said, and I expect he was right. I got away in my first thermal from the launch and worked my way along the picturesque mountain ranges towards the gap leading to the great desert of the Imperial Valley, much of it below sea level. Here after about 80 km (50 miles) I was forced down in very difficult terrain not far from Palm Springs. The tiny field I chose to land in was surrounded by fences and hedges but I got down safely and was immediately surrounded by a crowd of dark skinned farming people. I had landed in the Morongo Indian Reservation. Children in blue overalls with lively oriental faces played around my Kranich while I waited for the arrival of my crew with car and trailer.

One of the Indian men sat with me in the dust, our shoulders against the fuselage, discussing soaring. My attention was taken for a while by three young girls who came along to inspect the glider. All three were dressed like ordinary American teenagers, talking English and giggling. When they had gone my new friend took up the theme of preserving the old Indian customs. The Morongo people had once inhabited a much larger area of Southern California but now I was told that youngsters were not using the Morongon language any more, seeming almost ashamed of their roots and trying to be as American as possible. He made no special comment, merely reporting these things as facts.

A very old Indian, his grey hair hanging down in long strands from under a battered straw hat, had been standing nearby during the last few minutes of this conversation. He seemed abstracted, staring with a blank expression at the bare rocks of Mount San Jacinto which rose starkly on the other side of the valley. I thought he had not been following our talk and wondered if he even spoke English. But when I expressed to my companion my regrets about the loss of the language the old man interrupted. 'Oh, we don't care. We don't care. Some day all people will speak one language. It will be English.' He fell silent again and shuffled away.

I had lost so much time with all the false starts and delays that I should not be able to complete the transcontinental journey in the few days that were left of my holiday. I decided to take things easily, to fly when the weather was good and not worry if I did not make much progress. There was, I thought, always next year! How wrong that turned out to be!

The next day, launched by car tow from Palm Springs Airport baking in the sun, I climbed in strong thermals from sea level to more than 10,000 feet altitude. Several times I passed over the very top of Mt San Jacinto to prove to myself that I had fulfilled the altitude requirement of 3,000 metres (9843 feet) climb for the International Gold soaring badge.[1] Taken with the Washington distance flight, that completed the requirements. I landed back at Palm Springs to get the barograph checked and the various papers signed to prove my claim, abandoning for the time being any cross-country distance plans. Two days later we drove across Southern Arizona to Winslow, an aerodrome at 4,878 feet (1,490 metres) above sea level. 'Caution, Rattlesnakes' was written on a sign by the hangar.

---

[1] Riedel was the thirty-ninth person in the world to complete all requirements for the Gold badge. The full requirements were for a height gain of 3,000 metres after release from tow and a distance flight of 300 km.

On 21 June I prepared only for a short flight as a demonstration to the handful of friendly airline employees who had been helpful to me. The sky was completely lacking in clouds so I did not expect good thermals and there was a stiff north-easterly breeze which would be against an eastward distance flight. A few small puffy clouds did appear thirty miles or more to the south. After taking off, conditions proved to be much better than I had expected. I flew at once into a very strong thermal with no cloud to mark it, what is called a 'blue' thermal. I reached an altitude of 10,000 feet (3,050 metres) above sea level in a few minutes of tight circling. There far below was the meteor crater which I had visited yesterday, surrounded by mile after mile of flat plateau country. I could see across the plateau to the edge of the forest and towards the mountains where those clouds were now billowing. I decided after all to set off towards the south-east. I was in shirt sleeves, had no food and my only maps were still just auto road maps picked up at a service station. When I left the thermal I immediately met strong downcurrents. When air goes up rapidly in one place it comes down just as rapidly somewhere else! I pressed through the sink and soon ran into another thermal as good as the first. I climbed swiftly in it and set off gliding again.

After some progress in this way I approached the edge of the forest. Those fat clouds still seemed far away over the peaks. Could I reach them? There was a long, worrying glide over the forest but I saw a timber mill in a clearing which, if the worst happened, would allow me to land safely. As I lost height the ground was rising towards the mountains so, although my altimeter read thousands of feet above sea level, I was fast running out of height. Soon I could pick out individual trees reaching up towards me, as if to snatch me down. I must find lift! I flew a little further on towards the steep slopes and there it was. The Kranich surged upwards, I banked into the turn and the variometer needle swung round against its upper stop. I was climbing at more than 15 feet per second, about 1,000 feet (305 metres) per minute vertically upwards. I watched the altimeter needle smoothly winding upwards like the second hand of a watch. These mountain thermals were strong! From 17,000 feet (5,200 metres) above sea level I headed due east again. The flight from here was full of tension and surprises, taking me from thermal to thermal over miles of absolutely empty country, steep mountains poking up at me, desert and desolate forested areas in between.

Despite the sun it was bitterly cold and I closed the little windows in my cockpit canopy. Delicate fronds of ice appeared where moisture from my breath froze as it touched the transparent plastic. For five hours I remained between 13,000 and 18,000 feet (4,000 and 5,400 metres). As I entered a good thermal it was as if I was literally thrown upwards. I would circle only a few times to regain all the height lost in the preceding downward glide. I thought I might reach the Rio Grande del Norte but there were no roads or trails, no human settlements. I became stiff and cold. The longer I remained at these high altitudes the harder it became to concentrate. I was beginning to wander mentally, not realising that I was short of oxygen. I should have known better but the trouble with anoxia is that judgement is the first thing to be affected. I tested my alertness by talking aloud, telling myself what to do next. I tried to sing but could not control my breathing sufficiently. I did not know my position on the map for it had been a long time since I had seen the bluish colours of the painted desert far away to the north. My mind slipped again and again to matters that had nothing to do with the flight.

About four o'clock in the afternoon I realised that I was quite low near the desert floor having in my dreamy state missed several chances to circle up again. I was in danger of being forced to land in this lonely wilderness. Two alarming thoughts brought me wide awake: rattlesnakes and canyons! I was wearing only very light, low cut sandals, no protection against snakebite or thorns. The dark and forbidding canyons filled me with horror at the thought that after landing I might have to climb down and back up those rocky cliffs which were cut vertically into the surface of the Colorado plateau. I become hopelessly dizzy when looking down precipices. To stand on the top of a skyscraper makes me shake, contradictory though it seems for a flier to suffer in this way. Looking down from a tall building or cliff is quite different from being thousands of feet high in an aircraft. Coming to my senses I carefully used every scrap of lift I could find and managed to work my way up to 17,000 feet (5,200 metres) again. Now I was freezing again and short of oxygen. My fingers and toes were stiff and numb.

Highway 60 was the nearest possible contact with civilisation. In the rear cockpit I had hung a gallon bag of water. This had been intended only for my proposed short passenger flights above the airport. It did not seem anything like enough now if I should be faced with what might be a twenty mile scramble through the desert to reach the road. With darkness approaching I realised I should have to land the Kranich even though the thermals were still strong. But where should I land? The sun now seemed to be sinking far more rapidly than usual. If I were not careful I should be forced to put down in darkness in this awful country and that would be the end of me. Surely now I must be somewhere near habitation?

Far ahead, but within gliding distance, I spotted a shallow valley and a ranch some distance down it. I headed towards it. Of course, when I did not really need it I found a thermal immediately over the buildings. Circling a few hundred feet over the homestead I shouted down to announce my arrival and after a few minutes saw a little group of people rush outside to see what was causing the noise. As I approached to land a group of five horses took fright and galloped right across in front of me, fortunately running faster than the glider so they were clear before I touched down. The place turned out to be the Rancho Montoso, with a fine herd of Hereford cattle, 7,000 feet (2140 metres) above sea level at the extreme end of a wide, lonely plain several miles from the small town of Magdalena, New Mexico and within the western catchment of the Rio Grande. I had crossed the continental watershed, the first person to do so in soaring flight. The distance I had flown from my release from the car tow to my landing was 314 km (195 miles) and I landed at 7.20 pm, mountain time.

I was greeted with great hospitality and thawed out gradually. I sat down to dinner with the rancher, Art Myrland, his wife Gretchen and five cowboys. They had not heard my shouts from above. They said they had been sitting down at dinner when their dogs suddenly started a furious and very excited barking which was what had brought them out of the house. They did not see what the fuss was about until they happened to look up to see me circling round and round above them. I told my story. Art Myrland was English-born but had lived in Chicago before turning to ranching. Later I wished I had told him the name of the only other person I had ever met who came from that city of four million people. I had met Bill Walsh in Colombia when he was on a business trip there and had made friends with him. I had never visited Chicago and had never taken up his invitation to call on him there. It seemed silly to mention his name in that isolated ranch house for the chances of my host having heard of Bill were utterly remote. Yet a few days afterwards when I was back in Washington I received a telegram from the ranch. Bill was there to visit his old friends the Myrlands and heard immediately about the crazy German glider pilot who had literally dropped in on them a few days earlier. 'That sounds like Peter Riedel!' Bill had said. 'I knew him in Colombia!'

My crew arrived with the trailer and we loaded the dismantled Kranich onto it. My vacation had run out and I had calls to make at more aircraft plants. We drove with the glider trailer in stages across the country. I called at the Beech and Cessna factories and at the Stearman factory in Wichita, Kansas, at the end of June. I was treated royally and got the Kranich rigged to give a few of the staff some brief flights. Then it was on to Washington. Stearman was building trainers for the Army and Navy, Beech and Cessna were busy with small transport and sporting aircraft of very slight military importance. In St Louis I saw the new Curtiss CW-20, a transport plane somewhat bigger than the DC-3.

Back at my desk I dutifully made out a long report on my impressions of the Californian and Mid-Western aircraft industry. Everything I saw confirmed what I had already said. I dared not make any political comments in what was purely a technical paper but I tried at least to make it plain that the possibility of war was not being considered seriously on the American side. In June and July 1939 the American aircraft industry was concentrating its attention entirely on peace-time requirements. With Wolfram's additional information about Hitler's state of mind and his fear of aggression, I emphasised that I had seen no military preparations whatever. I hoped this would drive home the point than no pre-emptive strike would be necessary, there was not the smallest hint of anyone in the USA preparing to attack Germany. It was true that Roosevelt had fulminated against the aggressive nations of Europe but such speeches are very far indeed from threatening an attack and in any case the President of the USA had not the power to precipitate a war.

Helen and I were beginning to feel rather desperate. With the threat of conflict always ahead we had previously thought marriage inadvisable. Now, we convinced ourselves, was the time. If war was coming, remembering what Wiedemann had said to Hans Wolfram, we should make the best of the peace while it lasted. We had better be married soon. If war did not come, so much the better. I was German and nominally at least a soldier. Helen was a foreign national and marriage to her would not be allowed without a great argument. I should need special permission from the *Wehrmacht*. Persuading Bötticher would be the first necessary step and I knew it would be the most difficult. Nevertheless I could not let things go on as they were, it would be unfair to both of us. I decided to approach General Bötticher within the next few days. How ironic that we should choose just this time to make our decision! The interview I had planned was postponed.

The Ribbentrop-Molotov pact of 23 August 1939 shattered the complacency of the Western powers. It came as a huge surprise to almost everyone, not least to the communist politicians who had, till this moment, regarded Nazi Germany as the arch enemy of the USSR. How could anyone believe that such an agreement would be made? Some of us who were involved in German aviation were not so surprised for we knew a secret. This 1939 pact was not the first military agreement between Germany and the communists.

In 1927, although not a member, I was closely associated with the Academic Flying Group or *Akaflieg* of the Darmstadt Technical University. It was a well organised group which made large demands on the time and energy of its members, young student aircraft engineers. I did not have time to spare to join since, very hard up, I had to get through college as soon as possible. Most of the *Akaflieg* boys at Darmstadt and other German universities were prepared to take an extra year or even two before graduation so that they could dedicate many days, weeks and months to their *Akaflieg* projects. The Darmstadt group had already made a great reputation, having designed and built some of the most advanced sailplanes and several interesting powered aircraft like the D-14, which was in their workshops in 1927. Work on this exciting venture seemed very slow that year. Mysteriously in mid-summer several leading members of the *Akaflieg* vanished. I caught a few sidelong glances and whispers. 'Lipetsk,' someone said with a wink and a nod. What was going on? It was not long before my friends told me.

After Versailles, Germany was not allowed to build military aircraft or to have an air force, but since 1924 there had been a secret agreement between the emerging *Reichswehr* and the Soviet Union. How much of this was known to the inner circles of the Weimar government outside the War Ministry I do not know. Certainly the elected representatives in the Reichstag did not speak publicly of it, nor did anything ever appear in the press. In exchange for technical help and instruction, the USSR allowed the German military to establish an air base at Lipetsk near Voronesh. Modern military aircraft were secretly shipped there. These were mostly Dutch Fokkers or aircraft of German design, Junkers and Dorniers built in Sweden or Switzerland with British engines. Promising men, some veterans of the previous war, others who had learned to fly on the Wasserkuppe in gliders or were studying for their degrees in aero-nautical engineering, were picked out and enrolled secretly, anticipating a future career in the air service once the restrictions on German military expansion were lifted. The nucleus of a future German *Luftwaffe* was established in this way years before Hitler even looked like coming to power. Two large airfields were established side-by-side at Lipetsk, one for the Red Air Force, one for the German. Advanced joint training exercises by bomber and fighter planes went on, engineers developed new types of bombs and bomb sights. Guns were fitted to the planes, targets set up for practice attacks and new tactics worked out. At the time I heard about all this I was disappointed that no one ever offered a place for me in the select band who, each year, left quietly for their courses at Lipetsk. I suppose I had already made something of a reputation . . . *Ah! That Riedel, he'll never make a soldier!*

But, knowing this old secret, when the 1939 pact was announced it did not seem so strange to me as to other people. I supposed the basis for peaceful co-operation had been laid long before and this was merely its open continuation. The existence of Lipetsk seemed to prove that, despite the propaganda, peaceful relations would continue in the East. When it suited them, the Nazis could always point to the title of their party. They were, in full, the *Nationalsozialistische Deutsche Arbeiterpartei*, the national

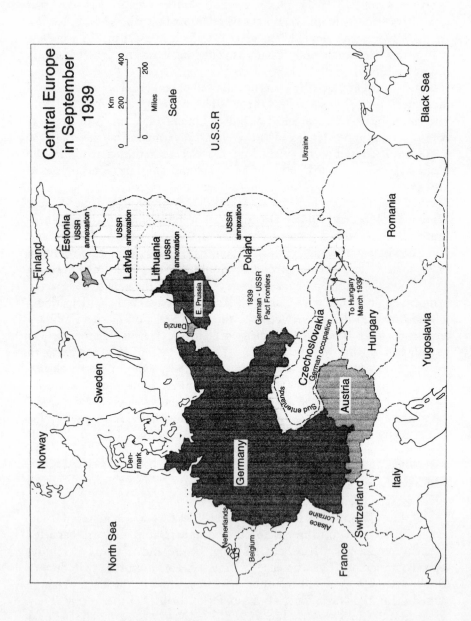

Central Europe in September 1939

Some significant place names
Pre 1939 frontiers shown

socialist German *workers'* party. The apparent *volte face* of August 1939 was in reality not difficult for the propagandists on both sides to deal with. There were elements of communism in the Nazi doctrines. On both sides, there was a certain egalitarianism, a glorification of the common working man. They broke the power of the old aristocracies. Promotion in the armed forces was now supposed to be on merit rather than through family connections, birth or wealth. Nationwide health and welfare schemes for women and children were set up, there were mass youth movements, strict state control of the news media and so on, labour camps and arrests of political dissidents on both sides. There was more in common between the USSR and Nazi Germany than anyone had cared to admit openly. Communist parties throughout the world fell into line at once.

For the whole of that week I still persuaded myself that there would be no war. I misunderstood the situation completely. I told Helen it meant a peaceful solution of the Danzig problem would be reached along lines similar to those of the Munich agreement; there would be some adjustments of the Polish frontier. The USSR would be as compliant as France and Britain had been over Czechoslovakia. The Führer would achieve everything he wanted. All the wrongs inflicted on the German minorities would be corrected.

There was a small specialist photographic shop in Washington where I bought a cine-camera and some film. The proprietor was Jewish. He told me he was worried because he had relatives in Poland. I assured him there was no problem. In all good conscience I said there was nothing to worry about, mails were still getting through. The American press was getting worked up about nothing and there would be no fighting. He seemed relieved, saying that anyone working in the German Embassy should know the truth. I was more ignorant than he. The Embassy staff were kept in ignorance so that we couldn't give anything away. On 29 August the General warned me confidentially that we should soon have to take in quite a large number of additional personnel. He obviously had special information which he had kept to himself. In a sudden sweat I could think of only one reason for this development. War was imminent

The first morning of September came with newspaper headlines shrieking GERMAN TROOPS INVADE POLAND. The British ultimatum followed. War between Britain, allied with France, against Germany was declared on 3 September. The atmosphere in the Embassy was dreadful. I saw nothing but gloom on people's faces, although everyone concealed their feelings in public and dared not speak in private. The General hid himself away behind mountains of paper and was altogether unapproachable. I never knew whether, at some deep level, he felt the same way as I did. The German people had wished to see Germany strong and prosperous again and on an equal footing with the other European countries. 'Work and Bread' had been the main slogan of the Nazis before 1933 and they had fulfilled this demand. For this reason they had widespread support among the ordinary people who want nothing more than to live and work peacefully. We had not voted for Hitler to lead us into war. But our fault had been to yield unrestricted power to one man and his clique. We had failed to make the Weimar Republic work, failed to understand that dictatorship leads invariably to oppression and war.

Soon the Embassy was swamped by a mass of propaganda including reports and eyewitness stories of atrocities allegedly committed against Germans. I no longer knew what to believe. Nationalistic and racial hatreds were fanned, fanaticism became commonplace and, despite myself, I was not unaffected. I had to accept the fact of war and that I had committed myself to the German side. When had I made this decision? When I was born German? Hardly my decision, that! I had even left the country when the opportunity arose in 1936. Why, now, did I feel myself to be so much a patriotic, duty-bound German? At which moment had I decided to return? When I informed Bötticher I would take the job he offered after all? When Udet's official letter arrived in Colombia? When I was in Berlin wandering, muddled and mystified through the bureaucratic maze?

I could not say when the decisive moment had been but here I was and it was too late to draw back. Duty demanded I should stay at my post, obedience and tradition required me to serve. Common sense pulled me the other way. Somewhere my country had taken a wrong road and I did not wish to follow it but to leave now would be downright treachery. I began to suffer frightening changes of mood, from exaltation one minute to the depths of black depression the next. I suppose my character had always been like this to some extent, especially since my mother died. Often there were good reasons for feeling the way I did, the joy of accomplishing a good soaring flight or doing a difficult task well, the sorrow of a friend's death or a disappointment in love. There were reasons enough now, to feel torn in two directions and to swing from one emotion to another.

As before, the tensions eased in our small world and we settled down again. Hard work and the comfort of routine enabled me to quieten myself. Demands on us increased and new staff were taken on. I found myself with three new assistants: a couple of young German women who had found themselves in the USA at the start of the war and responded to the Embassy's call for staff; a young male engineer who had come from Bavaria on an academic exchange and decided to work for us now. I set them to expanding my statistical researches, developing the system of news gathering. Still the never-ending stream of published information continued. Everything we needed to know and more than we could really handle was presented to us at the cost of a few magazine subscriptions or, sometimes, for nothing since government leaflets, pamphlets, reports of commissions of enquiry and congressional records, were all handed out freely.

Within three weeks the Polish campaign was over. Six months followed without any serious land battles although there was warfare at sea. The British had an aircraft carrier, HMS *Courageous*, sunk by a U-boat within a fortnight and in December came the naval battle of the River Plate which ended with the German battleship, *Graf Spee*, being scuttled in the estuary off Montevideo. These events made big headlines in the USA but otherwise little seemed to be happening. Henry Ford called it a 'phony war'. Both sides avoided heavy engagements and the British RAF did little other than dropping clouds of propaganda leaflets over the Rhine and Ruhr industrial cities. One could still hope for a sudden armistice and Hitler himself seems to have expected this.

Helen and I began to breathe and make plans again.

7

All the News that's Fit to File

In the USA two problems took the limelight at this time. The first had to be decided in Congress but there was strong public opinion to be taken into account. Should the Arms Export laws be relaxed in favour of Britain and France? Applied strictly the law decreed that on the outbreak of a war anywhere exports of arms to the belligerent countries must cease. If Hitler and Ribbentrop had been relying on this they made a gross miscalculation. Anyone who knew America could have forecast what the decision would be. Common language, common heritage and common ideas of freedom and democracy made the USA a natural ally of Britain. At the end of October 1939 the law was changed and exports of armaments to Britain and France continued with only a month's interruption. But to begin with, as we had foreseen, there was the merest trickle of supplies.

The other major issue was also of immediate interest to us, the expansion of the aircraft industry. Leading businessmen hesitated. They distrusted Roosevelt's 'New Deal', feared increased taxes and believed they would be ruined should peace suddenly be declared after they had invested millions in new projects. Wall Street bankers made long faces. Nobody had a heart, let alone any money for this distant European war. Some of the financial commentators believed the very structure of capitalism itself was threatened. Investors lost confidence in the future and there was even a hint of a new economic depression.

A compromise was worked out before long. Guarantees were given about taxation and Britain and France came through with capital to finance the erection of some of the new workshops. It was only then, in Autumn 1939, that the expansion really began.

The Winter War, which began when the USSR attacked Finland at the end of November, excited American public opinion much more than the apparent stalemate between Germany, France and Britain. The USSR had never been popular and to many businessmen that was where America's real enemy lay. A wave of sympathy for Finland, such a small country struggling against the great Russian bear, swept the USA. There was a call for massive material aid and it was only then realised by the ordinary American people that the USA was quite unable to provide anything of the kind. All that could be sent were a few dozen Brewster Buffalo pursuit planes unwanted by the US Navy. They were unwanted because they were totally out-of-date, too slow and under-armed, but there was nothing else available. The newspapers were sharp in their criticisms and public opinion was stirred up. How could the mighty USA, they cried, have so neglected its air forces that in this emergency it could find no modern warplanes for a little country that needed them so desperately?

Leading men in the industry and in Congress struggled to placate their attackers with ambiguous statements and wildly exaggerated predictions. One asserted that production had reached 10,000 aircraft per year. This was nonsense, as I knew perfectly well. I suppose the fellow was not deliberately lying but he must have included in his figures all the little Piper Cubs, Aeroncas and perhaps even amateur home-built light aeroplanes that had no military value whatever. The significant figure was less than a third of this published claim.

The same need to calm public fears prompted a transparent little stunt by the Boeing Company. General Bötticher called me to his office one morning to show me a newspaper story from Seattle which stated that two Flying Fortress B-17B bombers were rolling out of the factory every day. He became irritated when I laughed.

'General,' I said, 'just now I don't doubt they are rolling two out every day. But it will only go on for two weeks. The entire order they have received for the B-17B is 26 aircraft. When this is filled, production will stop again. In three weeks there won't be any B-17s rolling out at all.'

'Are you quite sure of this?' he demanded.

I assured him I was. We knew that more orders had been placed quite recently, a small one for thirteen of the B-17C and larger numbers of the B-17 D and E versions. Experience showed that it took around eighteen months from the day an order was placed with the firm before the first plane could be completed. To build big aeroplanes requires long preparation by the parts and sub-assembly divisions of the factory. It would be months before any more B-17 deliveries could take place. I tried again to explain to the General the system whereby I had arrived at my conclusions but he balked at this and assured me, as usual, that he had perfect faith in my judgement. The only result of this Seattle story was that I could add to my records the fact that the US Army Air Corps now had a total of thirty-nine Flying Fortresses, thirteen of the A and 26 of the B version. Not a single one had gone to Europe.[1]

We in the embassy were now under military discipline. More staff joined until General Bötticher found himself at the head of a small army of ten

[1] A few Flying Fortresses entered service with the RAF in Spring 1941.

including himself, six men and four women. Our first task every day was to scan all the newspapers and cut out anything that might be of value to someone in our staff. I was assigned to the *New York Herald Tribune*. We soon developed the ability to pick out from the general background of agency reports and shared stories the significant little items that, on analysis, could tell us something of military importance. One of our new men who had been an officer on the ship *Columbus*, which had been scuttled off the coast of Florida, was set to work gathering information on Canada and on British possessions in Latin America. The Canadian aircraft industry was expanding now in close co-operation with the Americans and a big flight training programme for pilots and aircrew recruited from all parts of the British Empire was beginning, using mostly American aircraft and equipment.

General von Bötticher remained in overall charge, but my work on the aviation side and his on the army became more clearly separate because there was too much for one person to comprehend. His reports went directly to the German War Department and mine now were simply forwarded unchanged to the Air Ministry in Berlin. The naval people tended to keep to their own little group. We had almost nothing to do with the Foreign Office or the Ambassador. This led to a good deal of interdepartmental jealousy and friction. Dr Tannenberg, a Foreign Office diplomat, had general responsibility for economic affairs but my General appointed his own economic adviser. The two economists were in constant rivalry, manoeuvring jealously and secretively to outwit one another while maintaining an outward semblance of polite co-operation. Their reports were not co-ordinated and, treated as highly confidential, went to entirely different departments in Berlin. I was amused in a way by all this, but when I stopped to think about it I knew it was a serious failure of our system. What confusions were caused I could not say. The feelings of distrust and dislike became mutual and the fault was not all on the side of the FO personnel.

The General and I were supposed to attend a regular conference, which was presided over by His Excellency Thomsen the Ambassador, in the main Embassy building which adjoined our offices. We were treated by some of the diplomatic staff as unwanted guests in their home. We all sat round a big table in the Ambassador's room and listened to his comments on the latest news. Sometimes he quoted telegrams from Ribbentrop telling us that he wanted some new situation report or action by us in our contacts with American officials or business people. After this the 'big shots' in the conference were allowed to make their remarks. If some question about aviation came up the General might ask for my opinion but mostly the few younger men present, assistants and secretaries, were expected to listen to the great men and speak only when spoken to. My own chief would have his say and then sometimes the Naval Attaché, Vice-Admiral Witthoeft-Emden.

Tannenberg would usually have some remarks about the war economy. A smooth, ambitious man, he spoke such exquisite and studied German that one was forced to wonder if he had any attention left for the actual content of his speeches. Yet he worked hard and seemed to know what he was talking about. Sometimes Herbert von Strempl, an irreverent and intransigent playboy whose department was press and propaganda, would have something to offer. The Embassy Secretary, Dr Resenberg, was a lazy, slow-thinking former classmate of Heinrich Himmler and as a rule remained smugly silent. He had enough weight, through the power of his friend at home, to escape criticism for his lethargy.

Some of the best contributions to the discussions were made by Dr Sell, the Washington representative of the German News Service. This was especially true when the question was one of judging the reaction of the American public to some action by Hitler. Sell appeared to me to be an excellent man. As press correspondent he made many contacts with ordinary Americans. He listened to their ideas about events and did not hesitate to speak the truth in our meetings, even if it meant passing on criticisms of the government at home. In contrast, the regular diplomats moved only among the upper echelons of American society. I knew from my own experience that being invited to their social events usually meant meeting other diplomats or high officials of the American government and usually in a formal and stiff manner. I had been at such affairs with Bötticher where I had met Generals Arnold and Marshal for example and various other famous Americans. I was invariably only there as a sort of underling or makeweight, ready to advise the General if some question of aeronautics cropped up. Very rarely was an average American to be found in this stratum. How, then, could our diplomats report about the opinion of Americans? Often enough the man in the street had a different point of view from that of the 'bigwigs'. This was clearly shown in 1940 when Roosevelt was re-elected to the Presidency when most of the press was against him.

I became gradually aware that it was difficult if not impossible to report unpleasant truths. The younger soldiers in the attaché group lived in permanent fear of displeasing their superiors and these superiors had a corresponding dread of their own high chiefs in Berlin. The same was true on the Foreign Office side. Unfavourable news was simply not mentioned, played down, under-emphasised or passed over lightly while any good news was inflated out of proportion. The fault of the German diplomatic corps at this time was that they refrained from reporting harsh truths for fear of losing their positions. To contradict or disturb the powers at home led to disgrace, being summoned back to Germany, giving up the very comfortable life and social round of a diplomat in Washington for the harsher style of a country at war.

Soon after the start of the war the mutual hostility between the diplomats and the military men caused the General to cease attending the big Embassy conferences unless he was ordered to do so. Instead we assembled each morning in his room carrying the press cuttings we had clipped out and reported to Bötticher and the others what we had found. Any clipping of interest to a colleague was handed over. It proved a good system because, in spite of the overlapping of the main stories, each paper would carry some additional information not found in the others, especially when it came to the economic section.

A typical incident illustrative of the lack of co-operation between us and the Embassy arose one day in spring 1940. A young engineer working under Tannenberg in the economic unit of the Embassy almost crept into my room and after closing the door put a bundle of press clippings on my desk.

'Take these, Herr Riedel,' he said guiltily. 'I put them on one side for you because I thought they might be useful. We read a number of economic magazines and papers which your department doesn't seem to have.' I was very pleased and thanked him for his help.

'Don't make a point of it,' he said. 'It's our duty to help one another. But not all those over there are of the same opinion.' He nodded through the wall towards the main Embassy. 'I went to Tannenberg and showed him these clippings, suggesting we should send them over to you regularly. He was furious! He forbade me to give any material at all to General von Bötticher's office. You know, Tannenberg and Bötticher hate one-another, but there's a war on.' I was depressed for I knew there were others with a similar attitude on our side.

In October 1939 all the German consuls stationed at various cities throughout the USA were called to Washington to be briefed about their new duties during the war. We met in the Embassy building in a great hall which reminded me of the dingy backstage area of an unused provincial theatre. There was a large table around which we all sat. At the General's request in due course I was given the chance to tell them my own needs.

'Gentlemen, I will give each of you the names and addresses of the aircraft factories in your district and I ask you please to subscribe to one or two local newspapers in every town where there is an aircraft factory. Let these papers be read regularly and clip out every article or advertisement, however small, where the name of the factory is mentioned.

Send the clippings to me every two or three weeks. We will do the rest of the work here.'

They did as I asked and floods of news clippings from all over the country began to arrive on our desks. My assistants and I had our hands full with the business of analysis. We were easily able to discover, for each factory, the number of workers, the area of shop floor, the type of aircraft being built and information about its technical weaknesses and the exact dates of test flights. When advertisements for more workers appeared in the local papers we knew that a certain plant was expanding. For example, reporters of the *Wichita Star* or the *Kansas City Observer* regularly visited the factories of Beech, Cessna and Boeing-Stearman in their home towns. With pride they wrote long articles giving their impressions. They never forgot to mention plans for expansion which, they said, were going to make Wichita, or whichever town it was, an important aviation centre in the USA. These assiduous patriotic authors were my best agents! Often in their pride at local achievements they revealed military secrets which in any European country would have resulted in their arrest. They did not realise that they were telling everything immediately to me in the German Embassy.

The Aeronautical Chamber of Commerce in Southern California became another valuable source. They began publication, in mid-1939, of a little typewritten monthly news sheet entitled *Aviation Progress in Los Angeles*, which was always gladly received in my office. Month by month it told us the number of workers in the Douglas, Lockheed, North American, Vultee, Consolidated, Northrop and Ryan plants. Every expansion was reported and backed by a full description of work going on. The traditional love of Americans for publicity was of great help. I blessed the advertising managers of the various companies. On the day of Pearl Harbor this news sheet was still going strong.

Among my best informants was the aviation editor of the *Wall Street Journal*. He evidently made regular trips to all the important plants and often mentioned details which did not appear anywhere else. I did not need to go to the plants myself, or prowl around them secretly with a telephoto lens on my camera. He did it all for me and far better than any spy could do.

We also glanced through all the well-known American aviation magazines such as *Aero Digest, Aviation, Western Flying, Popular Aviation* and so on. They did not add much to our more exact and particular data but they contained interesting articles, drawings and photographs which commented on and illustrated the expansion of the industry. I recall one particular example. An advertisement for the Glenn L. Martin Corporation carried in *Aviation Digest* during the winter of 1939-40 showed in pictures how the production space of this works was doubled within one hundred days. The exact dates of starting and completing the new workshops was given. Its significance was not lost on us.

Besides all these sources there was a ceaseless flow of information from Capitol Hill, via the government printing presses. The public was apathetic but we were interested. There were the proceedings of the two Congressional Committees for Military and Naval Affairs, issued as booklets sometimes with several hundred pages, quoting every word of the discussions between Congress on the one hand and senior officers and experts of the armed services on the other. General Arnold, chief of the Army Air Corps, Admiral Towers, commander of the Naval Air Force, and many more officers were called to answer questions. They described the types of planes required and gave exact reasons for their opinions. Delays in delivery were criticised and explained. Detailed lists concerning present and future strengths of the Army Air Corps and the Naval Air Forces were made public. The military men's replies were rarely deleted from the transcripts and then only on special request. When they made such a stipulation it was usually easy to work out what it was they hoped to conceal. With what we already knew we filled in most of the gaps.

General Bötticher always wanted to have a clear picture of the strength and disposition of the American aerial forces. From the Congressional hearings, together with the lists published in the *American Aviation Yearbook*, my assistants were able to figure out at any time the exact number of aircraft which the US Military forces had at their disposal. We used the *Army and Navy Journal*, the *Army and Navy Registers* and the postal register of US Military units overseas. Even the *Air Corps Newsletter* was sent to us regularly by mail from the War department. It was a lightweight journal intended for serving men and was an excellent source for discovering where various units were, what they were doing there and where they were to be posted.

Another source I learned to value highly was the *Arms and Export Statistics* of the US Department of Commerce. All aircraft exported were listed here with the country to which they went. The relevance of these figures to our immediate problem was obvious and we received several copies of the survey report every month. We were even able to discover which ports were used by the ships taking the aircraft to their various destinations. For example, the A&E Statistics showed that each month a certain number of planes, at a cost of so many dollars, had been shipped from Baltimore to France. It was very simple for us to show that these were Martin Maryland bombers. We knew that 200 had been ordered, now we could say, month by month, how many had actually been shipped. It was a little harder to analyse the figures for a port like Los Angeles where several different types of aircraft were involved in any one month's shipments but with a little elementary algebra and detailed understanding of all the other material at our disposal we could say exactly, for instance, that 9 Lockheed Hudson bombers and 8 Harvard trainers had left for Britain.

The idea of publishing all this material was that the American taxpayer could see where all the money was going and how the regulations were being administered. It was a good democratic principle but the drawbacks were obvious. America's unpreparedness for war became all too obvious to those who planned aggression.

As my assistants handled most of the routine reading and collating I was able to devote most of my time to improving the system. I was hoping to reach a point where, at any time, I could respond with authority to any question about American aircraft production and distribution all over the world. I determined never to base a report on a single newspaper story which might be inaccurate or exaggerated but to build up a self-consistent and factual mass of data.

I set up a system of filing cabinets, boxes and folders under nine main headings:

1. Aircraft Industry, general
2. Aircraft types
3. Aircraft Orders (Army, Navy, the European Allies, Neutral countries, US Airlines)
4. Production facilities (space, workforce, man hours per week, future plans etc)
5. Value of production $US per month, quarter, year etc
6. Graphical picture of development since 1 July 1938
7. All countries of the world with list of all American aircraft delivered
8. All US Airlines with list of aircraft
9. Flying units of US Army, US Navy and their aircraft

File 1 was mostly a collection of news articles. For the industry as a whole the main source was the *Wall Street Journal*. There followed a number of separate sections relating to each factory. This included our own summary listing the names of the men in charge, business partnerships and cross-ownerships together with all the little news clippings from the small newspapers with facts about visits of foreign buyers, accidents with experimental aircraft, bottlenecks which slowed production and so on.

In File 2 were detailed technical descriptions of all American aircraft types and sub types with pictures and drawings. Each time a new aircraft showed itself in public all its technical details were given to the press. Often I received information from the papers about types that were still in the experimental stages. For example, a good deal was written about the initial difficulties with the Martin 179 of which 1,100 were ordered for the Army in September 1939 and which eventually became the B-26 Marauder. It was no secret that production of this type was delayed by five months because of technical difficulties. It was all in the papers. Another example was the Curtiss Model 84, a dive-bomber for the Navy which was ordered in quantity before the prototype had even flown in 1940. A new factory was built at Columbus, Ohio but production of the SB2 C Helldiver could not begin because problems were found with the longitudinal stability, requiring many modifications.[2] Sensational news stories were published about it all.

Under heading 3 we entered all the material about sales. The factories hastened to publish news of orders received from Britain, France or other foreign powers while the US Military continued to give out official statements about their own purchases. Another significant item was the regular publication of the factory backlogs of unfilled orders. This was useful because I could gauge the pressure driving the expansion programme of each plant. The longer the list of outstanding orders, the more likely an extension of factory space would result and this would before long be correlated with something in File 4 where difficulties such as the lack of specialist tool-makers, shortages of certain machines, changes of production methods for increased output by semi-skilled and unskilled labour, all freely discussed, were filed under the same heading.

Under 5 were included all the financial details. Even when only the costs in $US of an order were mentioned in a report it was not difficult to work out what this meant in terms of, say, twin-engined Douglas bombers at the price I already knew. If a plant was building only one type of aircraft my estimates were very close to the truth. I soon learned to make allowances for hidden items such as spare parts. The Lockheed Company, for instance, published for 1938 and 1939 not only the total output in dollars and cents but also the number and type of each plane. From these figures I was able to show that extra production such as spares amounted to about 15 per cent of the total output. I made due allowance in all my costings after this.

Under 6 we filed the graphs and charts which I drew and came to regard as my most important summary of results. I used ordinary squared graph paper, setting a scale of months along the base of each chart and three vertical scales showing factory space in square feet, number of workers and

---

[2] The prototype SB2C-1 flew in December 1940. After several accidents with test aircraft and numerous modifications the first few Helldivers entered service in December 1942 but were judged unfit for combat. A further year passed before any saw action. The Helldiver was never satisfactory despite quite large quantity production. Most were withdrawn soon to be used as trainers and target tugs, etc (Peter M. Bowers, *Curtiss Aircraft 1907-1947*, Putnam, 1979).

value of output in dollars. They showed at a glance how each factory stood at any time but, more importantly, it was possible to predict what production would be a month, six months and even a year ahead. One of the interesting and important things I was able to plot on these charts was a comparison between the expectations of the various companies and the realities that emerged over time. A publicity manager would announce to his local press reporter that within two months the plant would be increased in size from so many thousand square feet to, say, twice that figure. The number of workers employed, he might add, would go up from 4,100 to 10,000 as soon as the building was ready and output of aircraft would then be more than doubled. I would mark a faint line on my graph for this factory showing the prediction for two months. Later there would be another report or some hard facts from our other sources would appear. Almost invariably the building would not be completed on time, the workforce would not reach the predicted figure so soon, output was not what had been expected. But the publicity man, bearded again by the energetic reporter, would assert: 'The difficulties will be overcome. By the end of this month we expect . . . and in three months from now there will be . . .' and so on and so on. I would mark a hard line on the chart using the realised figures and could see, over a period, how the rate of expansion achieved compared with the predictions. I was even able to allot to each company publicity department an exaggeration factor which proved remarkably consistent over a period for each enterprise. My own realistic predictions were still impressive enough. All was passed regularly to Berlin.

In File 7 was an alphabetical register showing what aircraft each country had received from the USA during the last few years. For instance, when Norway, Denmark, Belgium and Holland were invaded I could promptly report the precise numbers of American aircraft which had been delivered to each. Later the Japanese Air Attachés were given access to my File 7, which listed American deliveries to the Dutch East Indies, Australia, China, the Philippines and the Malayan peninsula.

Under items 8 and 9 we assembled information about production of aircraft not destined for export and could subtract these from the totals going directly to the war. Any discrepancies which appeared in our estimates could then be explained and the true situation clarified.

All this information was assembled perfectly legally but as the months went by I recognised some signs of tightening security. Some of the official figures began to give results not correlating properly with the rest of our information. I suspected that some attempt was being made to impose censorship or even to promote disinformation, deliberately putting out falsehoods. I was able to find ways round this without much trouble. We

81

had so many different sources of news and so many ways of cross-checking now that it was almost impossible for us to be misled.

Each month I reported the number of military aircraft produced, subdivided as to types, and added an estimate of distribution to the various customers. Every three months I sent telegrams concerning the production capacity of the American aircraft industry as a whole with a summary concerning each individual factory. Every six months I sent a telegram about the development of total American military air power. In between times I was able to answer immediately most of the routine questions from headquarters. I did not know what effects my reports were having in Berlin but the trend was perfectly obvious to me and I worried.

As new information came in I was able to re-check and show that generally my predictions were proving right within 10 per cent. We had said that if war broke out in 1939 America would not be able to send much in the way of military aircraft for two years. I warned Berlin at every stage of the growth of the American industry and began almost counting the days until American air power could begin to make itself felt either in the form of aircraft delivered to the allies or, if America should enter the war, as active combat units of the US Army and Navy. Did Berlin realise what this meant? No reaction came to me from that quarter.

8

The Sleeper Wakes to Nightmare

The Winter War in Finland had been underway for many weeks when General von Bötticher summoned me one day to his office.

'Herr Riedel, I want you to meet some officers from the Soviet Embassy who are here.' This would be interesting, I thought, hurrying through to his room. There they were, two men in military dress, representatives of the Red Army which at that time was regarded by most of the American public as a monster devouring a gallant but helpless prey in Finland. The General introduced me via a third man, an interpreter in civilian clothes. I was told that the two newcomers did not speak German and could not yet speak English well. Major Ovchinnikov, I learned at once, was a soaring ace who held the Soviet National record for altitude in two-seaters. He was a short, jovial man and grinned cheerfully at me as we shook hands. I grinned back, for we knew we had something in common, the feel of a sailplane climbing in a thermal! The other officer, taller, haggard and melancholy, was Major Beresin, looking like a figure out of Dostoevsky. He wore horn rimmed glasses and was, I was told, a tank officer. I wondered how he could manage in a tank, shaken up and down by the violent motions over rough ground and his glasses falling off.

The ice having been broken it was up to us now to repay this courtesy call and out of curiosity, as well as diplomatic etiquette, I made my first visit to the Russian Embassy some few days later. I took with me some material which I thought Ovchinnikov would find useful in starting his information gathering. There were two lists: one containing all the modern American aircraft types and a second one with the names and locations of all the important aircraft factories. There was nothing secret here. I had made the lists from published sources and took them as a gesture of friendship.

Both Ovchinnikov and Beresin received me and I discovered they did after all have some knowledge of English and so we were able to converse in halting fashion. Ovchinnikov turned out to be, as I had thought, a lively fellow who enjoyed telling jokes and we got on quite well together. We avoided politics. I came to know Ovchinnikov better as time went by and his English improved although he never became very fluent. I continued to meet him fairly often although he and Beresin hardly came near our Embassy again after their first visit. Our staff seemed distinctly cool towards the Russians but Bötticher did not discourage me from keeping in touch. I was sure my duty lay in establishing a good relationship. One day I took my precious file of graphs to show Ovchinnikov but I soon realised that he was not taking in what I was showing him. After a while he looked at me with an enquiring expression.

'Tell me, where are your men in place?'

'What?' I was slow in the uptake. He smiled slyly, repeating the question, making it clearer by some pantomime gestures, peering, looking through binoculars, copying. I realised he wanted me to tell him where I had agents, spies, working for me in the American factories. He had totally failed to understand how I had gathered my information.

'I have men in Grumman. Where are your men?'

'I have no men. I find out everything in this way!' I pointed again to my statistics. Clearly he did not believe me.

At last in January 1940 after many hesitations I approached General von Bötticher about marrying Helen. He flatly refused to support my application and without his approval there was no hope. To press my case would only anger him. It was in Bötticher's power to send me home at any time, probably via Japan and the USSR. I was deeply depressed, borne up only by Helen's cheerful support.

I was desperately anxious to get away sometimes into the clean air. Since coming back from my holiday in the west my sailplane, the Kranich, which I had hardly touched since bringing it back from the west, had been stored at Bolling Army air base near Washington. As the winter drew to an end I checked the sailplane over to make sure it was still airworthy. I showed it to Ovchinnikov one day and promised him some flying in it when the weather improved. When he realised I was allowed to keep my Kranich at Bolling he told me he was hoping to get an aeroplane of his own from Moscow and wondered if it would be possible to keep it at Bolling too. A lunch was given about this time by the American War Department for a group of military attachés, carefully chosen from the Axis side and nominally neutral countries to avoid conflict. Ovchinnikov asked me to make the enquiry and Colonel Crane, who was the officer responsible for organising the occasion, said 'No objection whatever!' without hesitation. Ovchinnikov looked very down in the dumps at first because he had taken the Colonel's first word for a downright refusal. He was delighted when I explained, but his aircraft never arrived.

On the first weekend that the weather looked good enough after the winter, with Helen to help me, I towed the Kranich by road to Hybla Valley airport for some flying. A man who had been sitting in a car outside the hangar saw us preparing to get the huge wings off the trailer. Clearly we needed help. He jumped out and came over. To my amazement I recognised him. It was Georges Abrial, a great French gliding pioneer. I had met him nineteen years before in 1921 when I was a teenager at the second gliding competition on the Wasserkuppe! We forgot entirely that we were supposed now to be enemies and shook hands delightedly. Georges was the oldest glider pilot in France! Then Ovchinnikov, whom I had invited, arrived in his red car and the four of us, a German, a Russian, a Frenchman and Helen, an American, rigged the sailplane. I strapped myself into the front seat, Georges ran with the wing tip as Ovchinnikov drove my tow car with Helen by his side to tell him when I released the steel cable. It was a good day and after a quick soaring flight to 7,000 feet I came down to take each of the others up for a flight. Georges told me he was living in Baltimore and I assumed he had been sent there by the French Air Ministry to oversee the deliveries of the Martin Maryland bombers which I knew about. Neither of us mentioned it on that Saturday. Some American friends who turned up were at first astonished that we four should be working together in such a friendly fashion but they were interested in soaring too and that seemed much more important to us all. I wonder if we should have been so relaxed and friendly if I had met Abrial a few days later?

On 1 April 1940 General von Bötticher celebrated his thirtieth anniversary as a soldier. His small staff assembled that morning to offer him congratulations. To my astonishment when the little ceremony was over he announced another. He congratulated me on my promotion to Second Lieutenant!

'This,' he said, 'is the first time in the history of the German Army that a soldier has been promoted from *Gefreiter* in the reserves directly to the rank of Second Lieutenant.' Perhaps he exaggerated a little in this but I thanked him heartily for, surprised as I was, I knew he was responsible for my sudden rise. It gave me several immediate advantages. Officially I became Assistant Air Attaché whereas previously I had been classified only as a Technical Assistant. Now that I had some rank, my name appeared on the Diplomatic List which entitled me to honorary membership of the Army and Navy Club and the Army-Navy Country Club. I was given diplomatic licence plates for my car, which guaranteed some immunity if I should be caught infringing the speed limits or commit some other small traffic offence. My salary jumped considerably, which would make it easier for Helen and me to marry, if only we could overcome all the objections. Was it time to try again?

Sad news came on 9 April, though it was soon overwhelmed in my mind by bigger developments. We heard that Patricia Donovan, the happy girl I had known briefly, had been killed in an auto accident, a shocking affair. On an icy road near Fredericksburg, Virginia, she had skidded and lost control, the open car overturned and she received severe head injuries. It was a road with little traffic, no one saw the smash and she had lain unconscious for a long time in the bitter cold when quick medical attention might have saved her. She died in hospital.[1] Inadequate though it was, I sent a note of regret to her father. I was reminded bitterly of my younger sister Beate's death in 1932 when she was being driven by an irresponsible glider pilot friend, Günter Groenhoff. He had lost control of the open car on a bend, run off the road without rolling over but Beate was struck by the branch of a tree and killed. Günter was unhurt but was never the same again and died himself in a sailplane accident soon afterwards.

I had barely adjusted to my new status when the phoney war came abruptly to an end. I was called to the General's office early and he asked me what I knew about American aircraft deliveries to Denmark, Norway and Sweden. Could I make an immediate report? I did do so within five minutes by extracting the figures from File 7. Norway, since February had received some of the 24 Curtiss P-36 fighters that had been ordered. I knew the exact number delivered and also that the P-36 was much slower than the Junkers 88 bomber and barely capable of equalling the speed of the Heinkel 111. So much for the American so called 'pursuit' planes at this time. They might pursue but they couldn't catch a modern bomber. Against a fighter like the Messerschmitt 109 it would be suicide to fly a P-36 with a 90 mph disadvantage in speed. Sweden had ordered some Seversky fighters from the Republic Aircraft Company but most of them had not arrived yet. Denmark had nothing at all from the US. By the time I was answering the General's questions Denmark had already been completely overrun in any case. The invasion of Denmark and Norway came as a shock. To us in the Embassy, Norway had meant pre-war vacation trips, a beautiful landscape and a friendly population. Now we must consider them enemies.

The *Luftwaffe* deployed 500 combat aircraft, most of them bombers, and 571 troop transport planes. The campaign in Norway was over within two months, ending with complete occupation of the country, but before this the war had moved on with speed beyond anyone's imagining. On 10 May the German Army, supported by the air force, advanced into Belgium and Holland, outflanking the French defensive Maginot Line. For the first time, gliders had been used to carry troops into battle. On the first morning of the offensive I sent a telegram about deliveries of aircraft to Holland and

---

[1] See *The Last Hero*, op cit.

Belgium. I had reported before about deliveries to France of the few Martin Marylands and about 120 Curtiss P-36 pursuits similar to those sent to Norway.

In the office we were now greatly overloaded with work. I was in a high state of anxiety, fearing that Europe was in for another drawn-out period of trench warfare with huge casualties. I wanted peace to come again soon and the only hope, it seemed, was for a very quick German victory. I was very far from confident of this, lay sleepless night after night, scanned the newspapers with desperate anxiety and worked myself into a mental frenzy. I believed Hitler's own words at the start of the offensive: 'This campaign will determine our fate for the next thousand years.' I was soon in an almost permanent state of fever, desperately needing rest and on the point of breakdown. Yet I could not bring myself to leave my post while others were dying in battle.

By the end of May it was clear that France would be defeated. Shortly before the capitulation the French prime minister, Reynaud, made a desperate appeal to Roosevelt. 'The *Luftwaffe* entirely dominates the air. Unless you can send us 1,000 first-class combat aircraft immediately, we are lost!' The French had received a positive answer and the aircraft carrier *Bearn* was said to be its way across the Atlantic to pick up the first load. Bötticher required me to report on whether such a contribution could be made.

'They cannot possibly send 1,000 first line planes,' I told him, almost stammering, 'because they simply do not have them. General Arnold himself stated in the Congressional hearing that the US Army Air Corps itself had no more than six first line fighters, six Curtiss P-40s! Six, General! Not sixty or six hundred. Six! Six! And the Naval Air Force has only obsolete equipment.'

'Very well, my dear Riedel, very well, calm down. Draft a telegram as quickly as you can.'

I did so and what I said was later proved correct. America could not help. The American war planes were obsolete and could not hope to stand up against Messerschmitts, Dorniers, Junkers and Heinkels. During these last few weeks American public opinion had been stirred up again. This time, no one came forward to make soothing statements. Dorothy Thompson, an intelligent and fearless newspaper correspondent who visited many different aircraft factories wrote furiously that she had tried to get exact information about the present rate of American warplane production but there existed no office and no person who could or would answer correctly. When I read this in the *Washington Post* I thought I could send her a postcard with only three words on it: 'Come to me!' I didn't post it but I knew the answers to all her questions.

France surrendered but the British managed to get most of their troops off from Dunkirk. The armistice with France was signed in mid-June. The campaign was finished and I was just about finished too, on the verge of collapse. On the day of the capitulation I was forced by doctor's orders to stop work. I was behaving erratically and was very miserable.

The doctor had wanted me in hospital but I decided I would try to cure myself by a period of total relaxation in a beautiful mountain resort in West Virginia. I took my leave and drove to the Greenbriar Hotel at White Sulphur Springs. It began to seem likely in that summer of 1940 that my wish for an end to the fighting would be granted. Most of my colleagues expected either an armistice with Britain or an invasion followed by surrender.

I decided to write to the General and ask him again to support my marriage. Within four days I had his answer, negative again. My illness returned with renewed force. Had Bötticher been within reach I might have assaulted him but I gradually calmed myself. As I cooled I began to think along another line. It had been in the back of my mind ever since September. Should I leave the Embassy?

For years I had felt more at home in the USA and I had not lived continuously in Germany since I took up my airline job in Colombia back in 1936. I was altogether divided in my mind. Everything pointed to a complete German victory in the very near future, the war was virtually over. I had done a good job during the critical months and to remove myself at the time of triumph ought not to be construed as treason. This might be the time to go. It occurred to me that my illness might provide me with an excuse.

Or would it? What would Ernst Udet and Hanna Reitsch and all my other German friends think of me if I deserted before the war had truly ended? I admired Ernst who had recommended me to Bötticher in the first place. He was as international in his outlook as I but had stayed on to do his duty and was still in his Berlin office. I should let him down if I gave up now. Hanna had never seemed sexually attractive to me, too small for one thing, but I considered her to be a great friend. We had been through many adventures together since we met in 1933 at the Rhön gliding competition, which I had won while she got the wooden spoon. No, not a wooden spoon. It had been a set of kitchen scales and a meat mincer, a crude sort of message from the male sponsors that a woman should stay in the kitchen! She had been rightly furious. But Hanna had not let this humiliation divert her from her dedication to flying . . . and to her beloved Germany . . . and to Hitler. She had gone on to become a quite outstanding pilot capable of equalling or surpassing the best men. I knew how fervently she would react if I should, in her eyes, betray my country. We had both been on that extraordinary gliding expedition to Brazil in 1934. There would be many others once the war ended and I should find it hard to bear if she came to despise me.

After all, the war was almost over and I could wait a few more weeks. Real peace did not look so far off and then I might resign with a clear conscience, having done my job well for the vitally important period. I would no longer be so strictly bound by tradition and duty.

I now wanted nothing else but to settle down in America with Helen and to become an American citizen. Once I had faced the issue I thought I could take the first steps without committing myself. I decided to return to Washington at once to see a lawyer and find out what my status would be in the USA.

Confronting this legal man, Howard Le Roy, was a little awkward at first. He seemed suspicious and hostile but when I had explained my situation he became more friendly. Nonetheless he said that things would not be easy. I had entered the USA as a diplomat. I must surrender my diplomatic status and obtain a regular German citizen's passport, seek the appropriate visas and only then could I make application to the US Dept of Immigration. Nothing would follow automatically. I should be considered along with others and there would be no guarantees.

I knew if Bötticher came to hear even of this preliminary enquiry, he would require an explanation and I should be on my way back in disgrace immediately with no hope of returning. Once I went back, or was sent back, to Germany, suspicion would remain on me there so that I would probably never escape again. Le Roy pointed out that it would probably require an Act of Congress to change the laws. He would make further enquiries and would let me know if there was anything else that might be done but I knew there was no chance.

Thoroughly depressed now I submitted to my doctor's advice and went into hospital. Under treatment I began slowly to improve. I had lost all interest in the war and expected to hear that it was over but about the middle of July, as I began slowly to take an interest in the world again, I wondered why no invasion had taken place. In June it had seemed likely that German victory would soon be complete. Now, despite Britain's weakness after Dunkirk, there had been no triumph and no armistice. Churchill had replaced Chamberlain and Britain showed no signs of collapse.

Some slight classical learning had been forced into me at the grim school I had attended in Aschersleben. Now, unwanted it came to mind. After their disastrous defeat at Cannae, Roman citizens had been warned by the words *Hannibal ante portas* (Hannibal is at the gates)! They had expected the armies of Carthage to invade the city and lay it waste at any time.

Defeat and despair were all around, they were done for! But Hannibal never launched his final assault, the reason being forever a mystery. Perhaps inspired by my nervous condition I made the equation, Hannibal and Hitler, Rome and Britain. In Rome Cato the orator had repeated, time and time again, *Delenda est Carthago* (Carthage must be destroyed). In the end Carthage had been totally devastated by Rome despite the earlier catastrophic defeats. They ran ploughs over the once mighty city when it was all over. Was Churchill another Cato? Was Germany to be ploughed into the earth as Carthage had been? If so, what did the future hold for Helen and me?

I could not leave the Embassy as long as the European war continued. Only if peace came we might then be able to sort things out. I explained all this to Helen. I also warned her that if the time came when Germany and the USA should break off diplomatic relations or declare war, I and all the other diplomats would have to return to Germany. She was in favour of getting married immediately and hang the consequences. The General would not be able to prevent us if we were quick about it and then we should see how things worked out.

After the doctors had finished with me they insisted I should take a real holiday and I spent six weeks exploring the west, staying mostly in New Mexico at Taos. There I met and made friends with the Indians who lived in their big, two-storey adobe houses. On one occasion I was invited to ride with one of them into the mountains. The Taos had been supposedly converted to Catholicism by the Spanish missions centuries ago but I found they still had their medicine men and their ancient religious rituals and beliefs. I was permitted to see some of these ceremonies and was taken to holy places but sworn to secrecy and not allowed to take photographs. Even my presence was disapproved of by the tribal elders but some of the younger men showed great trust. Removed for a time from the stresses of my work I found it possible to regain my sense of balance and perspective. After all, against the landscape of the mountains and desert the troubles of humanity did not seem so vast. Early in September I was fully recovered in health and went back to Washington to start work again. But I resolved not to accept the General's rejection of my marriage without a fight. I wanted his official approval if it could be given. Ernst Udet had made my appointment possible. Perhaps now he would understand and would be able to pull some strings in Berlin. I wrote to him and to Hanna.

The USA was again preoccupied with internal politics. Franklin D Roosevelt decided to stand for a third term of office as President. No paragraph of the Constitution prevented this but George Washington had established a sort of tradition by refusing a third term. To ignore this was considered scandalous by many but Roosevelt and his supporters saw things differently. Roosevelt wished to push on with the 'New Deal' and called on the electorate not to change horses in mid stream. They re-elected him but in September 1940, before the vote, he declared a State of Emergency for the nation. Roosevelt suggested in his speeches that since the huge French possessions in Africa were now effectively under German control there was a possibility that, with the relative narrowness of the Atlantic Ocean between South America and the west coast of Africa, German and Italian forces, possibly in alliance with Franco Spain, would be able to establish a foothold in Brazil and even in Central America. The USA then would be within range of German long-range bombers. (The US Navy had always been uneasy about the growing influence of Germans in Latin America. Even our little airline, SCADTA in Colombia, financed originally by German capital and staffed mostly by Germans, had been seen as a potential threat to the Panama Canal!) The state of the armed forces in the US, as now everyone recognised, was such that emergency measures to re-arm must be taken urgently. This decision stirred the American people profoundly. Many had been greatly worried by the fall of France but it needed Roosevelt's warnings to make them understand the need for positive action.

Charles Lindbergh, the popular hero of the transatlantic solo flight to Paris in 1927 and regarded as a leading expert on aviation, ridiculed these notions knowing well that the danger of an air attack on the USA from Germany was quite remote. But the political balance was already against him. Roosevelt had a broader vision and his view prevailed. The automobile industry would be converted to the production of armoured vehicles and aircraft. The Federal Government would finance the operation, which would be co-ordinated by a national armament supremo. Among all the rest, a programme to build five hundred heavy four-engined bombers every month was to be launched. In other words the President was proposing that six thousand bombers of the Boeing B-17 and Consolidated B-24 types would be turned out each year. 'The present trickle of deliveries will increase to a stream and later to an all-drowning flood which will overcome the common enemy.' My professional interests and duties were to report immediately about the effect of these decisions on aircraft production.

Six thousand four-engined heavy bombers per year seemed unbelievable at first but, with my assistants, I set out to make an assessment of the possibility. Five hundred of these aircraft per month would require 2,000 engines and in addition one or two motors in reserve for each plane, with spares and all the servicing equipment necessary to keep the bombers serviceable. There would have to be 54,000 accurately machined cylinders and cylinder heads every month, each with a crankshaft, valves, valve springs, pistons, piston rings, connecting rods, gudgeon pins, sparking plugs and so on and so on and so on. Planning on such a scale had never been attempted before.

I did not doubt that American industry would be capable of this kind of output given sufficient time. The question was how long it would take for this to be achieved. Our information was that Boeings were now turning out about ten of the B-17 Flying Fortress per month. The Consolidated Aircraft Corporation in San Diego, where hardly anything had been going on when I visited them in 1939, had recently delivered seven experimental models of their B-24, later to be called the Liberator. These were now undergoing service trials. (The prototype had flown in December.) To boost these numbers to 500 per month would require some radical measures.

The reaction to Roosevelt's announcements by the general public was favourable and I felt sure that American industrialists would be willing to make the efforts demanded of them but in our morning conferences another illustration of America's lack of preparation for war appeared. In the US Army manoeuvres in summer 1940 there were no armoured cars. Normal automobiles simulated these vehicles by being fitted with wooden superstructures to give the American GI some idea of what an enemy might look like. I could hardly quibble when my Army colleagues chuckled. Imagine an American army with wooden imitation tanks coming up against a modern German panzer division. Ludicrous! But now it was declared that the USA would have huge armoured divisions within two years.

I looked at all my records again and did my best to estimate what would happen. I decided that it would take about six months for the necessary conversions and expansions of the many existing aircraft and auto factories to be completed and then another eighteen months before the figure of five hundred bombers per month would be achieved. In other words, I predicted that by Autumn 1942 the Presidential targets would actually be reached. It will all be over long before then, the Army men said.

My task was to follow the development of the programme. The national armaments chief appointed by Roosevelt was Donald Nelson, President of General Motors. He took this extraordinary government post at a salary of $1.00 per year because he would keep his existing executive salary. It was a clever move by Roosevelt for he knew he had a man with great ability, an expert industrialist used to managing people, organising and co-ordinating a huge conglomeration of factories. Henry Ford, despite his general opposition to Roosevelt's policies and his commercial rivalry with Nelson, wished to demonstrate that when called upon in an emergency he and his companies would respond better than anyone, needing no direction from a government-appointed overlord. He asked the War Department to send one example of a selected four-engined bomber to Detroit and at the same time bought a large piece of flat land at Willow Run on the outskirts of the city. As soon as the bomber, a B-24, arrived he and his team of production specialists swarmed around it and proceeded to analyse it for mass production. The Liberator was divided into sub units which could be put together on moving production lines like Ford cars, all the lines coming together at the end for final assembly. Within days the ground at Willow Run was broken and the new factory begun: one building half a mile long and quarter of a mile wide, a hundred and fifty feet high. Ford was prepared to spend thirty million dollars of his own money to prove his point.

All was duly described in the press.

Winter was approaching and frost would prevent concrete being poured. The whole project would be delayed by months but Ford was not going to allow this. The building site was first covered by a vast temporary structure of wood and cardboard within which the temperature could be maintained and floodlights installed to allow work in shifts round the clock irrespective of the temperature outside. The additional cost, an extra million or so, was unimportant compared with the time saved. Traffic problems arose in getting the thousands of workers to the building site. Ford bought up the old First Avenue Elevated Railroad, which was being demolished, and had it rebuilt to take people from the city to Willow Run. As the workforce grew so rapidly accommodation in Detroit, which had many more industries than Fords, was a severe problem but beds and rooms were hired out on an eight hour basis, three persons taking it in turns to sleep.

I read about it. It was all in the papers!

Under more direct government control the other manufacturers began to convert and expand their plants. Existing aircraft companies were merged for production purposes with automobile firms like Chrysler, Chevrolet, Fisher and many others. Parts made in the former automobile factories would be brought together at huge new assembly works at places in the middle west, Omaha, Dallas, Fort Worth, Tulsa, Nashville and other places where there had been very little aircraft industry before.

Many of the new factory buildings were of revolutionary design without windows but with air conditioning. Temperature and humidity could be controlled despite the variations of weather outside, the workers could be kept comfortable. Metal parts which otherwise would expand and contract in varying temperatures could be more accurately made and would fit correctly when mated with other parts. Lighting was indirect and agreeable. Blackout, though unnecessary in the USA, would be no problem if there ever were air raids. Work could continue day and night without interruption.

We in the Embassy learned of all these things as before. We read of a car factory where expensive machine tools not needed for aircraft production were simply taken out of the works and, covered with grease and oil paper, allowed to stand outside in all weathers while the conversion proceeded. Even allowing for the exaggerations, which we knew were likely to appear in many of the stories, the progress during that winter made very solemn reading for us.

Meanwhile the Italian army was driven back in North Africa and there was the Italian involvement in Greece which required German intervention to save Mussolini. This involved yet another attack on a neutral country as German troops moved into Yugoslavia. The General and I pondered about Hitler's policy at this time, wondering why he did not, as even Roosevelt had expected, occupy French North Africa. Could it be there were not enough German soldiers available? If not, why not? Was he assembling the divisions on the Channel coast for the attack on Britain? Might we, after all, have peace soon? The English Cato rumbled on, *Delenda est Carthago!*

The American devotion to publicity continued, revealing to us all we wanted to know. When Rommel's offensive in the desert was being prepared in 1941 the High Command knew in advance how many American aircraft had been delivered to Egypt. We learned early in 1941 of the despatch of the first PBY Catalina flying boats for Britain from the Consolidated factory in San Diego. I had seen a few of the type there myself at the time of my visit.[2] The PBY could remain airborne on patrol for seventeen hours at a time and had a range of 6,400 km (4,000 miles). It would be used over the ocean. The take off and stage by stage flight to Canada of each PBY was fully described in the press and duly reported by us to Berlin. Whether the German Navy took notice I do not know. Catalina patrols played a critical role in the location, shadowing and eventual sinking by the British Navy in May 1941 of the Bismarck. I was so intensely involved in all these developments that I was in danger of making myself ill again.

[2] The first Catalina for assessment was delivered to Britain in July 1939 and on the outbreak of war 50 were ordered for the RAF Coastal Command. Deliveries began early in 1941 (O. G. Thetford, Putnam).

9

Invasion of the USSR

On 24 January 1941 the porter of the Embassy telephoned me from the reception desk.

'Captain von Werra has arrived and wants to present himself to General von Bötticher. Will you look after Herr von Werra until the general arrives?'

I was delighted. I was eager to meet this young German officer who we all knew had succeeded in escaping from imprisonment in Canada. Two days previously the newspapers had reported Werra's arrival on United States soil after he had crossed the St Lawrence river in a boat. He was a pilot who, during the French campaign, had won his Knight's Cross, which at the time was a rare award. He was already something of a star because he had been featured in the *Luftwaffe* magazine with his pet lion cub, which he played with before taking off into action. My first impression on shaking his hand was of a lively young man of great vitality. His face was radiant, full of energy and it was not hard to understand that he would never be content to stay in a prison camp.

He had to tell and re-tell his story. He gave me an outline on that first morning and then I heard more details over lunch with the General and the rest of our staff. Subsequently General Arnold and some of his officers were greatly entertained by Werra's version of his adventures, given in his elementary English.

He had, he said, been shot down in his Messerschmitt 109 by three Spitfires when returning with little fuel left after escorting Heinkel bombers attacking targets near London. He made a crash-landing near Canterbury and was arrested by the British Home Guard. After inter-rogation in London he had been sent to a rather sloppily run prison camp in the Midlands and made his first escape attempt from there, running away from an escorted party out for exercise. He was caught after a week when, exhausted and very hungry, he was found asleep in a barn. He was then imprisoned under harder conditions in Scotland where he escaped with thirty others through a tunnel. Most of the men had prepared civilian disguises but were soon caught.

Werra kept his flying suit on and, after getting as far away as possible from the camp, presented himself at a railway station pretending to be a Dutch airman of the Free Royal Dutch Airforce. He claimed his aircraft had been forced down nearby and he wanted help from the RAF. This worked just as he hoped for he was taken to an air base and welcomed, given a meal, shown round the hangars and even allowed to sit in the cockpit of a Hurricane fighter which he hoped to use to escape in. While he sat there working out how to start the engine his ruse was spotted and he was again arrested. He was then shipped off to Canada. After disembarkation he escaped by jumping out of the train taking him and other prisoners from Halifax via Montreal to the prison camp which he never reached. Pretending to be a Dutch sailor, wearing improvised clothing he hitch-hiked with several innocent drivers, even including a policeman, and reached Ottawa. From there he was given another lift to the St Lawrence River which he hoped to find frozen so that he could walk across. It was not completely covered with ice so he stole a boat and, with a considerable struggle, was able to drag it to the edge of the ice, launch it into the fast current, jump in and row across to leap at considerable risk onto the American ice. From there he had scrambled to solid ground, reported to the police and soon arrived in New York.

Werra did not want to stay in the USA and dreaded the prospect of internment. He demanded, in rather peremptory fashion, quick action by the Embassy to get him back to Germany. The ambassador, Herr Thomsen, heard his pleas with diplomatic calm but did not immediately start rushing round to help the young fellow. Thomsen gave the impression of resenting anyone who threatened to disturb the Embassy's Olympian atmosphere. Werra behaved rather like a big child, naïvely wanting everything to be done for him at once. Werra and Bötticher were of such different character that they could not get on with one another and quarrelled almost immediately. The General ordered him to remain in Washington. Werra refused and went to New York where he had friends. Six weeks passed with nothing happening. He stormed back to Washington demanding to see Bötticher again and telling him he must fix his return to Germany. The General was furious and made his dislike of the youngster very clear.

I was sympathetic towards the young pilot. At this time anyone who resented Bötticher and the other pompous stuffed shirts and bureaucrats was a friend of mine! I felt that I understood this simple fellow, a man of action and few complicated thoughts. Unknown to the General or to Ambassador Thomsen, Werra now sought my advice on escaping and we met privately, away from the Embassy. I knew his best chance lay through Latin America.

With the Kranich at Wilmington. The national markings on the rudder were a source of embarrassment.

The Sperber Senior flown by Peter Riedel at Elmira in 1937.
(National Soaring Museum Archives)

Peter Riedel in 1936.

Peter Riedel's photograph of Manhattan taken from the Sperber sailplane in 1937.
Part of the wing is visible on the right.

General F. von Bötticher *(centre)* with Peter Riedel and
Karl O. Lange *(left)* at the 1937 eighth National Soaring
Contest at Elmira, New York.

Peter Riedel; uneasy in uniform.

Peter Riedel aged three with his father, Felix.

Peter Riedel with Hanna Reitsch during the 1934 expedition to Argentina.

The Kranich in flight.

With the Kranich at Medelin in Colombia, February 1938.

Helen.

Helen and Peter preparing the Kranich trailer for the Trans Continental Soaring Expedition in 1939.

Peter at Glendale Grand Central Air Terminal with the Kranich. Note the wheel dolly, jettisoned after take-off.

'How much money do you have?' I asked. He had very little but after reflection agreed that his New York friends would probably help.

'Go back to New York and see if they can let you have $2,000. You will need it if you are to get through South America without papers. If you lack both passport and money you will land up in jail.' He nodded, gloomy at such a prospect.

'Let your friends book a ticket in a false name for you with American Airlines to El Paso, Texas. Your picture has been in the papers. Take a book along and read it or sleep on the plane and don't draw attention to yourself. Your German accent is strong and if you get into conversation with anyone they are quite likely to guess who you are. Don't flirt with the airline hostesses. If you get pally with one of them you'll probably give the game away.' He laughed and admitted I was right and he would be a good boy.

'In El Paso take a hotel room where you can leave your suitcase. Pay for the room in advance and then just walk out as if you were going for a stroll. Leave your case behind, with your hat and coat too. Put your hands in your pockets and wander across the international bridge over the Rio Grande. You will then be in Mexico. There are no passport controls for people leaving the USA on that bridge, I did the same thing myself once. There is a lot of pedestrian tourist traffic, people who just want to spend a few hours in Mexico. You can pretend you are one of them. It is only if you want to come back again that anyone will ask for your passport and you won't be coming back. In Mexico you will be on your own.'

Werra left soon afterwards for New York and three days later the General told me that he had disappeared. Bötticher was angry but powerless. Later I heard indirectly that Werra had followed my advice. He had travelled from the border to Mexico City by rail. He had taken a first class compartment to be alone and was glad of this when a Mexican official suddenly appeared and asked for his passport. Werra opened his pocket book and extracted a $100 note. The Mexican was much astonished, perhaps because of the size of the bribe. Werra told him openly who he was and the man, suddenly very friendly, assured him he would not be disturbed on the train again. On reaching Mexico City late in the afternoon Werra went to the German legation which he found already closed but a young attaché was there. This man helped him secretly by providing him with a diplomatic passport in a false name which enabled him to travel freely by Pan American to South America and then on an Italian flight to Europe and home.

Only a few months later Werra was killed when his Messerschmitt crashed into the English Channel. He was not shot down but his squadron comrades heard him say on the radio that something was wrong with the aircraft. He dived into the sea and was never found.[1]

At last I had encouraging replies from Udet and other friends in Germany about my marriage. Pressure was being applied on my behalf. Helen and I began to hope again.

My friendship with the Russian Ovchinnikov continued but when I still could not tell him about my supposed secret agents he cooled towards me noticeably. We continued to meet from time to time and once I escorted him, Barayev and their wives to the Army Navy Club. I was surprised to discover that they were not already members, as all the other military attachés became so almost automatically on arrival in Washington. The Red Army, it seemed, was not welcome.

Diplomatic banquets and parties at the Soviet Embassy were always very lavish, though after the Winter War almost the only diplomats who accepted invitations to them were the Germans and Japanese. On one occasion late in 1940, Ovchinnikov and I found ourselves sitting together at table. The Soviet Ambassador during his welcoming address pointed us out, saying our friendship, stimulated by a common interest in motorless flight, should be symbolic of the continuing good relationship of our respective countries, united by mutual interests. I even believed what the man said. On another occasion when I was talking to Ovchinnikov and Beresin, another attaché, in their office, we were rudely interrupted by a new man, Sarayev, who, after a barely polite greeting to me, started questioning the other two about our conversation. Ovchinnikov and Beresin were clearly terrified and shrank like naughty schoolboys. Despite this and some other slightly sinister signs I continued with my friendly approaches.

'Herr Riedel, come to my office!' It was the General, tension was in his voice. Something wrong! No, 'please can you spare a few minutes, I'd like a word'. What had I done to anger him?

'There, read that!' Red faced, he shoved a telegram at me, leaned back in his chair and drummed his fingers on his desk.

HIGH COMMAND OF THE LUFTWAFFE TO ATTACHÉ DEPT WASHINGTON: RELIABLE V-MANN[2] REPORTS MONTHLY PRODUCTION AT REPUBLIC AIRCRAFT CORPORATION HAS REACHED FIFTY OF TYPE P-43.[3] TOTAL NUMBER OF WORKERS FIVE THOUSAND. YOUR FIGURES

---

[1] Werra's story, of which there is a good deal of controversy about the details, was told in the book *The One That Got Away*. There was also a film with the same title.

[2] V-mann stood for *vertrauensmann* or trusted confidential agent.

[3] The P-43 was a forerunner of the much more powerful P-47 Thunderbolt.

STATE TWENTY FIVE P-43 MONTHLY AND THREE THOU-
SAND WORKERS. COMPARE YOUR TELEGRAM NO. 1052 OF
APRIL 14TH 1941 IMMEDIATE EXPLANATION EXPECTED.
HÜHNERBERG

A V-mann was an agent of the *Abwehr*. I was angry and resentful that
Bötticher, even now, had so little belief in my work that he questioned me
in this manner. If the General had taken the time and trouble to understand
my methods he would have known at once that such a telegram was not to
be taken seriously. Probably, I told him, the stupid *Abwehr* had found some
lowly worker in the Republic factory who was being paid to give them
information. What could such a man have known about the Company or its
production figures? It was not necessary to engage in espionage when
everything could be discovered in the ways I had developed. I knew and the
General should have known that I was right. We had quite a row but in the
end Bötticher allowed, grudgingly, that I had never been proved wrong on
anything of this sort. He agreed he would stand behind my figures. I was
somewhat placated. It occurred to me that the old man himself was really
very nervous, afraid of making some elementary blunder and being recalled
forthwith to face very unpleasant music in Berlin. He had balked several
times when I tried to show him my charts, graphs and figures. I think he
was afraid of being made to look a fool if he could not follow them.

Soon after this Edgar Hoover, the famous FBI Chief, announced that his
agency had discovered another important spy ring. I recalled the newspaper stories that had greeted me when I arrived in the USA in 1938 and
my heart sank. Had the *Abwehr* made another stupid blunder to bring
Germany into disgrace, making it all the more likely that America would
help the Allies? Yet when the story broke in the papers I could not help
feeling a sort of glee. *Schadenfreude* is the good German word for this
feeling of malicious pleasure at another's misfortune.

It turned out that some young naturalised American of German birth
had visited his homeland on holiday and while there had been approached
by the *Abwehr*, who had noticed, perhaps from his visa application, that he
worked in the Republic Corporation aircraft factory. They offered him
money and applied pressure and threats. He yielded, was given some
sketchy training and taught to use a special radio which fitted into a suitcase
before going back to the USA. On his return he reported all this at once.
The FBI asked him to continue for a while as a double agent, supplying
misinformation to the *Abwehr* and reporting on his contacts, enabling the
FBI to penetrate the espionage organisation. It worked as hoped and now
the whole nonsense had been exposed. In the movie news theatres, films
taken secretly were shown of the young double agent handing over
documents and receiving payments which, the commentaries said, went

straight into the FBI coffers. What pleased me, while feeling sick with the stupidity of it all, was that Hoover assured everyone that the information sent to Berlin by this agent was deliberately falsified or else it had been taken from the well-known aviation magazines which I also used. So this was the RELIABLE V-MANN whose reports had been taken seriously by the High Command of the *Luftwaffe*. I made sure Bötticher saw the point and he assured me yet again, with that charming smile which I never quite trusted, that he had every confidence in me and knew that I worked hard and conscientiously and so on and so on.[4]

A result of this affair, which did not help me, was that on 16 June Sumner Welles, the US Under-Secretary of State, ordered the immediate closure of all the German Consulates throughout the USA. *Agencies of the German Reich in this country including the German Consular establishments, have been engaged in activities outside their legitimate duties,* said the official note. Our government retaliated as usual with closures of American consular offices and of the American Express Company agencies throughout occupied Europe. Soon afterwards similar measures were applied to the Italians. Our consuls could no longer go through their local newspapers and send me interesting clippings. Now too the Department of Commerce lists of figures of exports to Britain were obviously being doctored. The figures were far too small to be accepted. I had to discard what had been one of my most useful references. It looked as if I should have to do some guesswork but I had accumulated three years' experience and believed I should be able to fill in the deficiencies.

As these doors closed, new sources developed. A real goldmine was opened for us in Spring 1941. The *American Aviation Daily* began publication. It was a cyclostyled news bulletin intended especially for the aviation industry, edited in Washington and issued every day. It contained all the material that we ourselves had been gathering from so many scattered sources. Perhaps they used similar methods to our own! My desire for thorough cross-checking caused me to continue using the older methods we had found when I could, but after the *Daily* began to appear I believe we could have relied on it alone.

The War Production Board chaired by Donald Nelson also began to publish monthly figures of total military aircraft production in the USA. The public relations experts had recognised that such figures would make encouraging reading to friends and might have deterrent effects on possible enemies. I was in a good position to interpret them. Everything Roosevelt had predicted was happening. I hoped that Berlin understood.

[4] Years later a Hollywood film, *The House on 94th Street*, with the usual overlay of Hollywood romance, was based on the actual facts of this case.

On Friday 19 June 1941 I picked up the latest edition of the *New York Times* on my way back to the office after lunch. The headline shrieked: GROWING TENSION BETWEEN GERMANY AND SOVIET UNION. It was not the first time such things had been in the news but we had always been reassured by telegrams from home. Such false reports of dissension were merely the enemy's propaganda and must not be taken seriously. So Berlin said again this time. Relations were excellent, Russia had only recently delivered quantities of grain to Germany, more than their trade agreements had bound them to send. All was well, we were not to worry. As I skimmed the paper the Embassy porter rang me.

'Two gentlemen from the Soviet Union are here to see you.' I was astonished. Since that first courtesy visit to Bötticher, no Russian officers had set foot in our building and suddenly two of them wanted me! I dashed downstairs and there were Ovchinnikov and his friend Beresin. I took them back to my room and they sat uncomfortably, struggling as usual with the English language.

'We . . . back to Moscow, soon. Very glad, Moscow better for us than Washington. Sorry. Goodbye!'

'But why?' I asked.

'Don't know.'

'When do you leave?'

'Tomorrow. Wifes gone. Train to west coast, Russian ship, Vladivostock. Wifes, kind regards. Miss Helen too.'

I pointed to the news headlines.

'Is this serious?'

'Don't know! Don't know!'

'Bad mistake!'

'Yes, bad, bad. Big mistake. Home, good!' They tried to look sorrowful but their pleasure at the prospect of returning to their own homes was unmistakable. We shook hands and they left quickly.

Later that day I met Tom, a young officer I knew in Department G-2 of the War Department.

'Have you heard, Ovchinnikov and Beresin are going back to Moscow?' I said. 'Do you know anything about it?'

'Yes. They travelled too much!' He winked. After a blank moment I understood. Military attachés are not allowed to have 'men' in various establishments and are not supposed to travel round to keep mysterious assignments with them. They had been detected in their totally unnecessary activities. All they needed to know was in the newspapers! First the *Abwehr*, now the Russians!

And two days later on 22 June the headlines blazed again: GERMAN TROOPS INVADE SOVIET UNION. It was shattering. All my hopes of peace were destroyed and I felt this was the end for Germany. Had Hitler never heard of Napoleon? Better than anyone I knew that the huge quantities of war materials promised by Roosevelt would indeed soon arrive and now Hitler had committed Germany to fight on two fronts, or three with North Africa. Some arrogant army fellow in the Embassy went around saying that the German Army would cut through Russia like a knife through butter. I hoped he was right because it seemed the only possible way out for us. The only hope for my country was a quick victory, another *blitzkrieg*, and peace.

Ovchinnikov and Beresin had left Washington but the astonishing events caught them on the west coast. I opened my paper next day and there they were in a photograph, standing under the wing of a B-24 with some executives of the Consolidated Aircraft Company at San Diego. The caption said 'Russian Attachés inspecting Californian Warplane Factories'. Had I not been so wretched I should have laughed. Suddenly co-operation with the USSR was in fashion. The two names were restored to the diplomatic lists from which they had been removed. Their sins had been forgiven!

For Helen and me now things came to a crisis. We had thought of waiting for peace before marrying but now there seemed less hope of that than ever. All very well to wish for a lightning war. Even if the German army should beat the Russians it would take time, perhaps years, for a final settlement to be reached. Helen and I decided that we would not wait any longer and must face whatever came together, good or ill. Six days after the German invasion of the USSR we finalised our arrangements. We would marry. Such disobedience might result in my being recalled to Berlin. If so, Helen promised she would come with me as my wife. She resigned from her job, we applied for and got a licence. I said nothing to anyone in the Embassy. Although Helen had been brought up a Catholic she cared little about religion and on 28 June 1940 we went through a secular ceremony in the garden of some of her friends in Alexandria, Virginia.

There could be no honeymoon because Bötticher had not been told. I went in to work as usual next day, a Monday. Unexpectedly, the General called me in. Now he gave permission for us to marry! I was dumbfounded for a moment. Unknown to me he had been receiving strong hints from Berlin for some time. Udet and Hanna had been busy pleading for me and a decision had been made at a higher level. Realising that there was some influence at work, Bötticher yielded as gracefully as he could. The wedding, he said, beaming paternally, should be under the Embassy's aegis with all ceremony and he expected the wedding feast to be at his official residence. All I had to do was to name the day!

It was a very awkward few minutes when I told him we had already had our very quiet marriage just the day before, with a simple party afterwards for a few friends! Fortunately for me, after some huffing and puffing, he saw the irony and said, very well, but there must still be a proper reception at his residence. It would be quite unsuitable for our marriage to appear surreptitious in any way. He would handle it as an indication of good German-American relations. Old hypocrite, I thought, he could be trusted to make use of us now his hand had been forced. But at least we should be able to take a honeymoon.

We duly attended the General's lavish reception and, tired by it all and the strain of the past weeks, Helen and I departed on our holiday together with the Embassy's formal approval and best wishes. We first drove to Terre Haute. We expected to stay there with her parents for a few days and then I wanted Helen to come with me to explore the real West, which I had seen and enjoyed but where she had never been. I met the family and we had a quiet and pleasant interlude.

10

Honeymoon with the FBI

Helen's father came into the house looking puzzled and slightly alarmed.

'There's a couple of men in suits along the street there,' he said. 'They've been hanging around for a day or two. I don't know who they are. They don't live round here but they're up to something! They sheared off when they saw me staring at them.' We didn't take much notice and he didn't see them again so we thought no more of it. We stayed a little longer in Terre Haute than we had intended. When Sunday came we got into the car with our luggage, including my movie camera, and headed off westwards on the main highway towards Hannibal. Traffic was quite heavy but we were in a hurry and overtook most of the cars going our way.

After a while I noticed in the rear view mirror that there was a dark blue Ford keeping pace with us. When we overtook someone, the other car also overtook. If I slowed down, the Ford slowed down. Helen and I began to watch, very puzzled and after a while were a bit frightened. It was always the same distance behind, about 200 feet. There was no question about it, we were being followed!

I drove faster and they kept up. I exceeded speed limits, relying on my diplomatic plates and hoping the other car would be stopped by the police. The Ford ignored the limit too and kept up with us, getting even closer, a mere hundred feet and then fifty, then right on our tail. Helen could see two young men in the other car and when they realised they had been spotted they just grinned. What was this all about? If they were gangsters intending to hold us up they would hardly do it here on the open highway with no attempt at concealment or surprise. Why should they pick on Helen and me?

I decided to stop as soon as possible and go to the police to report that there was a car bothering us. I thought it was probably just a stupid prank and these young idiots would be pulled over and warned off. When we reached the outskirts of the next little town we stopped to refuel at a service station and ask where we could find the police. To my amazement the blue Ford pulled in and stopped at the next pump. Now I saw they had a long radio antenna sticking up at one end of their car. Not many cars in those days had two-way radios. Who and what they were suddenly dawned on me but even as I reached my conclusion they gave themselves away even more clumsily.

I paid for our fuel with cash but the other driver, who had his tank filled too, came to the counter and handed over a card. He turned away briefly to the soft drinks stand and I took a quick look as the attendant peered at the card and laboriously copied details from it by hand. There it was, Federal Bureau of Investigation! The driver saw what I was doing and came quickly back to snatch the card away but it was too late.

'So that's what you are!' I said, grinning at him. He was embarrassed and smiled weakly. I hurried back to Helen and grabbed the cine-camera. None of our friends at home would believe we had been followed by the FBI unless I could produce evidence.

'If you don't mind?' I said to the other man in the Ford, and started the camera. He obviously did mind and with a look of astonishment, tried to hide his face. I stopped the camera. The other man arrived hastily.

'Are you going to follow us all the time?' I demanded. He said nothing, apparently not allowed to talk. 'Well, I don't mind if you have been told to trail us. In fact, I'll make it easy for you. We are going straight from here to Hannibal and then through Kansas and after that either to Colorado Springs or Denver. But keep your distance. You have been getting far too close and if I had to stop suddenly or had a blow-out you would have hit us. Keep back at least a hundred yards!' He nodded.

After this they did keep back but they were always in sight. Soon after leaving the town we came to a major crossing with lights. We got through while our FBI men were caught by the red. Rather than taking the chance to lose them we stopped for a while to let them catch up. I waved them down.

'Look, I don't want to make trouble. You can stay close while driving through towns, but when we are on the open road and speeding up, keep a bigger distance, OK?' They nodded. Helen was filming this little roadside conference which they did not realise until too late. After this we worked well together. On one occasion at night I missed a turn off in a small town. Suddenly their car appeared on our off side with lights flashing and the men waving, shouting and pointing, 'This way, this way!' They led us to the right road before taking station again behind. Another time my hat blew out of the open window and they picked it up for me in the road and pulled up alongside us to hand it back.

As we ran into Hannibal this affable pair disappeared but another car tagged on behind us immediately. This time there was no friendly contact. When we checked into our hotel, the Jay Hawk in Topeka Kansas, they parked in the street immediately opposite. In order to show the right spirit I asked the porter to go across to them, saying they were friends of mine. I asked him to tell them we should be leaving promptly at seven in the morning and not to miss us. I watched from the hotel lobby and saw the porter go over and speak to the driver. He evidently received a sharp answer and came back shaking his head.

'They say they don't know you, sir!' Helen and I laughed and I gave him a good tip for his trouble. These new FBI men did their job, following along all the way through Missouri and Kansas, for the most part a dreary drive through endless wheat fields. There were no signs of goodwill but they remained behind far enough and were not a nuisance.

When we arrived at the Colorado state line four men with two cars, each with a big antenna, were waiting by the signboard. Our previous companions turned and went back. Helen and I waved cheerfully as we sailed by but were answered only with sullen looks. We sensed a change of attitude. We had trouble with these two cars all through Colorado. They alternated, one of the cars always latching on less than twenty feet behind even when we were going at 75 mph. This was getting on my nerves a good deal and I lost my temper. After a while I stopped and got out to speak to them to tell them to keep their distance but as I walked back to where they had stopped, their car reversed rapidly away and I had to give up. After getting up to speed again they closed in as before. I told Helen to brace herself and, when we were doing about 60 mph, I suddenly stamped hard on the brakes. I was almost hoping they would hit us and get themselves into trouble, whatever the cost might be to us. Fortunately they swerved and missed us by a fraction but their car almost went out of control on the wrong side of the road.

After this they were more cautious but we felt they were planning some mischief. When we approached Colorado Springs one of the cars overtook us and sped away to reach the town first. We guessed they were arranging something up ahead. All we wanted was to enjoy the town with its splendid backdrop of the Rocky Mountains but these fellows seemed determined to spoil our honeymoon. After more than 500 miles on the road we were hoping for some relaxation but it did not prove very easy.

In the big Antler Hotel my first action was to send a telegram to Bötticher to tell him of our persistent tail. I knew diplomats were not normally subjected to this kind of thing and he would take it up with the American diplomatic people, not for my sake especially but on principle. The room we were given in the hotel seemed very pleasant at first and we began to unpack but I noticed there was a double sliding door connecting us with the next room. It was not fully closed and when I tried to shut it I found it would not move. Anyone next door would be able to hear and see everything in the room. I went downstairs to complain. I first asked the young man at the desk who was in the next room to ours.

'A gentleman, Mr Sorrensen from Denver,' he replied, checking his books.

'Is he a long term resident, or has he just arrived?' I asked.

'He checked in this afternoon sir, about the same time you did.'

'I thought so. Well, Mr Sorrensen is an FBI agent and I don't want him in the next room to mine.' The receptionist was much surprised and withdrew hastily into the office to bring the manager. This man emerged all smiles and false charm. He asked which room was next to the one Helen and I were in. I told him. He looked at the books himself and assured me the young clerk had made a mistake, it wasn't any Mr Sorrensen but a nice elderly couple, Mr and Mrs Jones who had been in that room for four weeks and intended staying longer. I pretended to accept his explanation. I thought that as a German diplomat at a time of international tensions I ought not to create a scene without being quite sure of myself.

When I got back to the room Helen was angry.

'There's someone in there, sitting in the darkness. You can see , there's no light on but I heard him come in. He lit a cigarette and went to the bathroom and now he's sitting in there listening.' Whoever it was heard a few remarks from me that were not flattering and I picked up the internal phone immediately. After my renewed protests the manager agreed to give us another room. The porter arrived and moved our baggage. As we closed the door to follow I waved Helen on and hung back in the corridor, watching the door where I was sure whoever it was had heard all this. Perhaps after all I had been wrong and a nice old gentlemen would emerge after his quiet smoke! In a few minutes the door opened slightly. A young man with a cigarette peered out, looking away from me at first then back. Seeing me he slammed his door and I heard him lock it from the inside.

Back to the manager, who now was not quite so smooth and charming. 'I wonder if you would be so kind as to introduce me to Mr and Mrs Jones? Helen and I would like to meet these nice people!' I said. When he hesitated I mentioned that I had caught sight of Mr Jones going into the room. Perhaps I should stay just outside his room until he came out. All the smooth manner had now gone and the manager admitted, shamefacedly, that he had been compelled to put us in this embarrassing situation. I must not take it too seriously, he would see that we were comfortable and undisturbed in our new quarters. I returned to Helen. In the hotel at least we were not harassed any further but as soon as we drove off towards the Taos Indian pueblo in New Mexico the tail-gating started again and we decided we must devise a scheme.

When we stopped for lunch at a road house we saw an advertisement for take away picnic meals and thought this was a splendid idea, quickly buying ourselves two full boxes. The FBI men, who did not come into the roadhouse, had no chance to see what we had bought. We drove steadily all afternoon, stopping only to fill up quickly with gas and maintaining a high average speed. We eventually left the main highway and entered the pass in the Sangre de Cristo Mountains to reach Taos. As evening came we were surrounded by beautiful scenery. At dusk we pulled to the roadside, opened the car doors and sat outside to eat our packed food. Looking back down the road a short distance we saw, as we had planned, the two cars stopped and the four agents standing there looking in our direction. We enjoyed our meal at leisure, admiring the view in the fast-fading light and made no secret of the fact that we were gnawing chicken bones and peeling oranges. We knew the men had not had a chance to buy anything and must have been debating what they should do. Perhaps they thought of sending one of the cars to get food but they remained, thinking, I suppose, that we should all soon arrive in Taos and they could eat there. They held out as we nibbled, taking our time.

During my convalescence the previous year I had stayed at an overnight cabin tucked away in the hills at the end of a little valley. When full darkness came we set off again at full speed until at about 9 pm and some distance before reaching Taos itself, we turned off. As we went along the by-road we noted that a new grocery store with an illuminated sign had appeared since last year. It was still open, which I had not reckoned with, but we drove on without stopping and the FBI chased us. In the wilderness where the road ended, we reached the cabins. As we checked in and entered our cabin we heard our four unwanted companions grumbling. Only one other cabin was available and it was intended only for a couple of people. All four men had to crowd in there. We heard them asking the receptionist for food but, as I knew very well, there was no catering at this little camp. The open store we had passed required some further action. As soon as we could turn round we went back to our car, got in and without starting the engine rolled off slowly down the hill without lights. Some way off we started the motor and continued. When we arrived at the store the proprietor was obviously just closing up, yawning openly at us. We chatted as, wearily, he locked up his premises and drove off. As we got to our vehicle the FBI cars came tearing down the track, lights blazing, and stopped when they saw us just leaving the closed store. We drove back at once to the cabin with our friends tagging along. The nearest restaurant likely to be open at this time of night was far down the road in Taos. By now they must have been feeling very hungry. Eventually they gave up, all four going there in one of the cars. Had we wished we could have lost them now by driving off into the night and turning off the main road somewhere. They would have a hard time explaining how it could have happened. But we didn't wish to create that sort of trouble so we stayed where we were for the night.

In the Taos pueblo I met some old friends, especially Jim, the Indian who had been my friend and guide on the previous visit. Jim took Helen and me for a two-day trek on horseback into the mountains. The FBI could not follow here. We left them watching our car. We had a very pleasant day, camped overnight and rode back late in the afternoon of the second day. We were astonished to find that almost the entire Taos tribe had turned out to see what happened on our return. The agents had waited and the Indians had little difficulty in finding out they were government men. As far as the Taos were concerned, if the FBI were after us it meant we were sure to be arrested at once. They had come to see it happen. For Indians to be in trouble with the Sheriff was normal but for whites it was something different. A breathless silence fell over the crowd as we rode in. We dismounted and took our gear off the horses, following Jim into his modest house where his wife was praying and close to tears. A few of Jim's friends joined us there and commiserated, not believing us when we assured them we were not in trouble and were not about to be clapped in jail. A medicine man appeared, a haggard fellow with a strangely ecstatic expression. He blessed Helen and me in some strange sort of ceremony which we were told was to make us strong enough to withstand the troubles to come.

The magic must have worked very well. We soon got into our car and drove off, our escorts following at a very respectful distance now! The Taos stood, amazed. What a demonstration of white man's wisdom this was! Helen and I drove on towards the Grand Canyon.

At the Arizona-New Mexico state line two new FBI cars appeared, manned by very young men who at first seemed determined to be a thorough nuisance. One of the new drivers tried the silly and dangerous tail-gating trick but I warned him off in the same way as the others. We reached the Grand Canyon Lodge in the evening and were shown to our rooms. When I returned to the car to get our cases I was furious to find that one of the FBI cars had parked so close to the back of ours that I could not get the trunk open. In a rage I went to the other car and tried to get its door open so that I could push it back, but as soon as I touched it a voice out of the darkness shouted: 'Get away from that car!' A pale young man with a flashlight came running up. I swore at him and demanded he should move his car away. He saw how angry I was and did what I wanted without further argument. I decided we had put up with enough of this nonsense and stormed into the reception hall demanding telegram forms. I sat at a table busily composing a message. I calmed down quickly but thought I would go on with a little charade. I made sure I was in full view of our young followers. Ostentatiously I wrote on one of the forms, addressing it to General von Bötticher.

NEW ARIZONA AGENTS IN CONTRAST TO CORRECT BE-
HAVIOUR OF PREVIOUS GROUP, BEHAVING RECKLESSLY
AND ENDANGERING SAFETY.

I looked at it critically, screwed it up and threw it into the trash basket,
starting on a new form. When I had finished with this I left the table and,
with angry face, marched off to the hotel reception desk as if to arrange for
the telegram to be sent. I knew that as soon as I was out of sight they would
pounce on the trash and read what I had written. I never actually sent the
telegram but hoped it would have its intended effect.

The youngsters thereafter kept at a much more respectful distance but
when we went down for breakfast in the morning we realised one of them
had spent the whole night sitting on a chair on the landing while we were
sleeping. This was becoming altogether ridiculous.

They hung around all the next day as we took walks and were never out
of sight. Helen too decided she had had enough. As we were on our way
to bed after supper one of the fellows dutifully plodded up the stairs a
short time after us, using his flashlight. (There was no electricity in the
place in those days.) Helen had been waiting for this. She had hidden in
the dark behind a corner at the top of the stairs and as he reached the top
she jumped out with a loud 'BOO!' The young man was so startled he
nearly fell down the stairs and dropped his flashlight. Helen retreated
quickly to our room, laughing wildly. I joined her. What was more, after a
short time we heard the men suddenly start roaring with laughter too. It
was a turning point.

The next day again we drove away for more sightseeing at one of the
lesser, but strikingly beautiful, canyons. At one point Helen wanted a cine
film of the two of us looking out from one of the craggy viewpoints. The
agents, as usual, were not far off. She went boldly to one of them, thrust the
camera into his hands and asked him to take our picture. He could hardly
have refused. The best place for him to take it from was a few feet away and
it happened that he had to stand with his back to a considerable vertical
drop. He looked round a little nervously, then before putting his eye to the
viewfinder smiled sheepishly, 'OK. Just don't say BOO!' The film came
out quite well in due course.

Our journey continued from the Canyon across the Painted Desert and
into Navajo country where we began to feel that after all it was a good thing
to have company. The trails were completely without traffic. In that empty
region to have a car break down would have been extremely unpleasant and
even dangerous for there would be no way to get help unless someone else
happened to come along by chance. For mile after mile we saw no humanity
except the FBI men, eating our dust. Only twice during a long day's drive
did we pass Indian settlements, Oraibi and Mishongnovi. It was hard to

believe that we were still in the USA for these places could have been in the deserts of central Asia.

Late in the afternoon we arrived at a place where we could stay overnight, Keams Canyon. This turned out to be a settlement built by the US Government with schools for Indian children and a hospital to serve the entire reservation. There was no hotel but the warden of the school dormitories said we could stay for a night there, since the children were on vacation at this season. Rather to our dismay he treated us and the FBI men as one party and expected us all to sleep in the one dormitory. This was a little too friendly but the boys willingly established themselves in a separate room. Nevertheless at meal time that evening we found ourselves all at the one table. After some hesitation on the part of our companions they began to behave like sensible folk and discussed the extraordinary trip we had made the previous day across the desert. One of the young men knew quite a lot about the history of the region and his explanations were very illuminating. I almost wrote to Edgar Hoover to thank him for sending such an excellent free guide for us.

From Keams Canyon we had to make for home at last. The plan was to drive as far as St Louis where I should fly directly back to Washington to avoid overstaying my leave. Helen would return in the car to Terre Haute for a few more days with her family before rejoining me. I had a reservation from St Louis on Pennsylvania Airlines. We parted with our young friends and a new relay of agents took over, nice fellows again. So it was at each state line, new ones appearing dutifully to trail after us everywhere. The weather was extremely hot. At a roadhouse while Helen and I had our lunch in air-conditioned comfort we sent several tubs of ice cream out to the men in their car. When the girl who served them came back she came to us looking very puzzled.

'They said I should tell you . . . donkey!' She was even more confused when, after a momentary stare, Helen and I laughed loudly. The German word for thanks, 'danke', had sounded like 'donkey' to her. Or maybe that was how the FBI pronounced it.

We approached St Louis. A few miles before entering the city we turned off for the airport. After a little way we realised some thing was wrong. The FBI car had gone. They had not been very close behind us and must have missed our turn and would be in trouble for losing us. It seemed quite strange, as if we had lost something important. I almost turned back to go and look for them! Instead I decided to telephone from the airport to the local FBI Office, which would normally be in the phone book. I could explain what had happened and save them some confusion when Helen and I went our different ways.

When I got to the phone I could not find any FBI number but was able to get one from the directory information operator. I dialled.

'Federal Bureau of Investigation, St Louis Section, Kennedy speaking,' I heard.

'This is Captain Riedel, Air Attaché to the German Embassy in Washington. I am sorry to bother you but your young agents have been following me and my wife during the last eighteen days. They suddenly seem to have lost us. I don't want them to get into trouble, they are nice boys. Will you please let them know I am now at the airport. I shall be flying from here back to Washington tonight with Pennsylvania Airways. The flight leaves at 21.25.' There was a long silence before he replied.

'Just a minute. Hold the line.' The wait was so long I began to think he would never come back. At last he was there again. 'We don't have any record of this.'

'Well perhaps not. But I am sure your men will report in soon to say they have lost us. Please make a note of what I said and let them know.' I repeated the message. He grunted a rough thanks and hung up.

On my flight as far as I could tell no FBI agents turned up and subsequently Helen reported from Terre Haute that she had no companions on her return journey either.

When I got back to Bötticher I learned the explanation for all this. It seems that some branch of the German secret services had been following the American Air Attaché and his wife in Berlin. Every time either of them took a step outside the house, someone followed. This had become a nuisance and an irritation. The Attaché had complained to the German authorities with no effect. Hence the US State Department decided to invoke the usual principle of reciprocity. Our honeymoon gave them just the opportunity they were looking for. Whether they had meant things to develop exactly as they had done we never knew. At any rate, the US War Department assured us that it was none of their doing. Like their counterparts in Berlin they had tried to stop it but without success. Security services make their own laws.

11

Winter of Discontent, Greenbriar Spring

Back to grim reality. In 1939 we had quoted two years before any substantial American material could reach Europe. It was now summer 1941. The war had changed completely. Germany and the USSR were fighting along a front of about 1,500 miles. Britain had a new ally. Until the attack of 22 June my work had been chiefly to determine the share of American aircraft production which was being sent to Britain and Egypt. Now I was required to find out the distribution of American military aircraft to Russia too.

The USA had undertaken the building of a chain of airfields to act as staging points on flights of heavy aircraft to Britain. Workers and all the necessary equipment had been ferried out into the wilderness. Bases now existed in Labrador bringing Iceland, now occupied by American personnel, and England within reach. Planes could fly across in hours almost ready to go into action instead of being dismantled for loading onto ships, then waiting for convoys and requiring re-assembly on the other side. The Alaska Highway too was completed, opening a land route to the USSR through Siberia.

Another line of communication was operating through Takoradi in Africa via Khartoum to Egypt. A Martin Corporation assembly plant was set up in Takoradi for the B-26 Marauder bomber. American engineers were improving key roads in Africa. General von Bötticher realised that feverish preparations to defend Egypt against Rommel's expected offensive were underway. It was very obvious that the British intended to make a determined stand to defend the Suez Canal, loss of which would be a devastating blow and would threaten the British position throughout the Middle East and even India, and cut off oil supplies. From the German viewpoint, capture of Egypt and Palestine would open up a southern route to the rich oilfields of the Caucasus region of the USSR.[1]

---

[1] Paul Leverkühn in 1940-41 had been sent by the *Abwehr* to Tabriz to explore the possibilities of moving troops through this area to capture the Baku oilfield in the USSR.

My boss did his best to impress on the High Command the importance of the American material going in that direction. For my part, I checked my figures and sent through constantly revised and updated estimates of the numbers and types of American warplanes that were now in Egypt and on their way there. As well as the B-26, Curtiss P-40 Tomahawk and Kittyhawk fighters, others were reaching the RAF in quantity. From the American daily press I obtained several reports about the deficiencies of some of these aircraft. The B-26 Marauder bomber was difficult to handle, the P-40 was proving inadequate against the Messerschmitts in combat. The papers carried a story that P-40 fighters were being left in their crates unopened after arrival, the RAF pilots preferring their Spitfires and Hurricanes. P-40s intended for the RAF were instead being diverted to the USSR and so were the Bell P-39 Airacobras. The impression was created that the best American fighters currently in production were not fit for front line service. It mystified me that such information could be openly printed and discussed.

An unusual development was that, following a desperate plea to Roosevelt for fifty more Douglas DC-3 transport aircraft, the President appealed publicly to the American Airline Companies to try to get them. When they attempted to respond, the airlines had great difficulty in finding any planes to spare since home demand was already stretching their facilities. In the rush to get bombers, fighters and attack aircraft into production, little had been done about transport planes. No one in America had realised how important these were to become. This emergency, all exposed to the public view, gave me some important clues since I was able to study my maps and work out where fifty such aircraft might be needed so urgently. It seemed certain that they were for the Takoradi-Khartoum-Cairo route. Everything pointed to a big British campaign in Egypt.

Meanwhile, the converted automobile plants had still not produced any heavy bombers. These were complex aircraft and required much detailed preparation. I knew that they would soon be appearing and that with mass production methods the output would be enormous. Time and again I warned of this in my reports, sometimes couching my draft telegrams in outspoken language. Bötticher insisted I should tone things down.

'The German General Staff tradition has always been to use sober language!' he said. It seemed to me the time for such niceties had passed. The message must have as great an impact as possible. He exerted his right to edit my material so I knew that the full importance of the facts was not being made clear enough.

During the second half of 1941 American production of warplanes exceeded a thousand per month of all types. In Canada the flight training programme was achieving its target figures of 30,000 air crew per year and in the USA a parallel programme was aiming at 50,000 per year. I wondered desperately what resources Germany had to oppose the growing aerial armada. I supposed correspondingly large developments were going on there.

Autumn came and winter. In November, with its dreary grey days, came dreary news indeed for me. The General summoned me on the 18th and I could tell at once he had something unpleasant to say. He was solemn faced.

'I am very sorry, Herr Riedel. I know he was a great friend. I have to tell you, Ernst Udet is dead!' He showed me the telegram which said Ernst had been killed in a flying accident. That was not unlikely for, as Technical Director of the *Luftwaffe* and despite warnings that he should not take such risks, he had often insisted on testing a new aircraft for himself, requiring afterwards that this or that feature should be changed. I was dreadfully upset although I did not doubt that he had died accidentally. I knew he would take every chance to get into the air. He had no formal qualifications other than being a brilliant pilot, relying on instinct and experience rather than scientific understanding. He had made no secret of his loathing for desk work. Now he was gone. I knew I should hear about the accident in detail from my friends before too long.

I became increasingly pessimistic and miserable. For me, the end of the year, reminding me of my mother's death when I was nine years old, was always a time of depression and the news made it all so much worse. Had the time come now for me escape the German service? With Udet gone I need not fear his scorn if I did so. But in the end I told Helen I could not abandon my duty now. With Germany in such a condition it seemed more than ever necessary to remain loyal. We decided again that I must abide by the decision I had made and she would stand with me. But I felt sure now my country was lost.

The predictions emanating from Berlin that the war on the Eastern Front would soon be over with total victory for the *Wehrmacht* were not coming true. We had been assured that the armoured Panzer divisions advancing into the USSR would meet little effective opposition. It was confidently expected by the High Command that the Red Army would break down completely almost at once and General von Bötticher, believing this, thought our troops would be in Leningrad and Moscow within a few days. At first this seemed to be coming true as the tanks penetrated deeply, finding the going easy over the open steppes. Huge numbers of prisoners were taken in the first days. Now the news began to assume a more sombre aspect.

Never mind that Hitler announced that the Red Army was completely destroyed and would never recover. It was soon obvious that this was a monumental lie. Even the ordinary German people must have read between the lines of the propaganda reports. They would hear whispered stories from boys lucky enough to get leave from the front. They would see for themselves the wounded, maimed and frost-bitten who counted themselves lucky still to be alive. A short distance from Moscow the army stopped and the soldiers of the Red Army were still there, resisting and beginning now to make counter-attacks. Yet the German people still apparently believed in their leader, still did as they were told without hesitation. It was all supposed to be over by now, it should not have dragged on into the Russian winter. Goebbels appealed to them to sacrifice their warm winter clothing to send to the front lines. They did so obediently.

I was continuously conscious of the growth of the American effort. To all departments I distributed my detailed lists giving all the different types of aircraft, bombers, fighters, observation, liaison and training planes sub-divided into single, twin and four-engined types and seaplanes. The distribution figures confirmed that half were going directly to the Allies, the rest to a great build up of the American forces themselves. And still the contribution of the automobile plants had not been felt.

Perhaps the only place where Hitler's falsehoods were not recognised was in Japan. Before war broke out I had not met any Japanese. The first contact of any kind was at a diplomatic level late in 1939 when General Oshima, who had been the Military Attaché in Berlin, passed through Washington on his way home. Oshima had a reputation as a supporter of the Axis powers and had been recalled as a tactful gesture intended to demonstrate Japan's desire to remain neutral. Bötticher had previously met him in Berlin and arranged an Embassy luncheon in his honour. Other Japanese diplomats were invited and I met my opposite numbers on this occasion. Some time later I received from Commander Yoshikawa, one of their assistant military attachés, an invitation to a suki-yaki or Japanese dinner.

The occasion was held in a big apartment block. I discovered that this was the establishment of a Japanese chef who worked exclusively for the Japanese Embassy. Other Japanese officers were there and I was introduced to Japanese cuisine and eating with chopsticks, my neighbour at the table, Major Suzuki, guiding me with tact and good humour in all matters of etiquette.

I enjoyed the meal greatly and was fascinated by the methods used in its preparation, Commander Yoshikawa himself cooking some of the dishes in front of us. Afterwards we spent some hours in an adjoining room. Japanese music, which I had never heard before, was played. It seemed very strange to me and I was surprised to find that my hosts also found it unpleasing. It was, they said, old music. At one point Commander Yoshikawa likened the sounds we were hearing to the wailings of a sick cat. These officers responded more favourably to some modern military marches and songs which, they told me, had been written during their war in China and that appealed to the military instincts.

As the evening progressed and the initial tensions lessened the men relaxed with a charming naïvety, revealing a sense of gentle humour. On the following day, responding to their suggestion of a visit to their Embassy, I found the same officers again very formal and reserved to begin with. Our convivial evening just a short time before seemed to have been forgotten but as soon as I took the initiative with a small joke they relaxed at once and became very friendly again. I realised their formality was a kind of barrier they put up when unsure of themselves, but once their visitor behaved naturally they would respond. On other occasions I noticed how easy it was to let formality and stiffness spoil an occasion. German diplomats also tend to rely on the forms and when Japanese and German officials met there would be a round of stiff bowing and expressionless greetings followed by stilted exchanges of words with no contact whatever at more human levels. Afterwards my colleagues would complain that they could not tell what the Japanese were really thinking behind those bland faces. I could readily believe that the Japanese were thinking exactly the same about us.

As time went on I was interested and puzzled by what seemed to be oscillations in official Japanese attitudes to the USA and Germany and I thought I recognised a sort of pattern which I mentioned to Bötticher. There would be some sort of official move demonstrative of goodwill towards the USA and a desire for peace, like the arrival on American soil of the new Ambassador, Admiral Nomura, who made speeches and gave press interviews emphasising his country's love of peace and desire for friendship with the USA. Berlin interpreted these signs as negative for Germany. But a few days afterwards we in the Embassy would receive an official invitation from the Japanese Military Attaché to a formal dinner at which all the speeches and sentiments expressed were on our side. Berlin had to make sense of these different moves as best they could. The same kind of thing happened several times, the most notable being when the 'special peace envoy' Ambassador Kurus, arrived in Washington charged with the duty of establishing a permanent solution to all the conflicts of interest between the USA and Japan that were threatening peace between the two countries. Again it seemed the war party in Tokyo was losing its influence but within a day or two some beautifully engraved invitation cards for a dinner with Admiral Yokoyama arrived on our desks.

After the beginning of the Russo-German conflict Japanese contacts with our military attachés became more frequent and we were encouraged to befriend them and exchange information. When they came to my office they usually brought typewritten lists of questions which, I believe, emanated from Tokyo. Very politely they asked if I could help them with the answers. The subject was always American strengths and formations in the Pacific and South East Asia and the exports of warplanes to the region, about which I had ample information. The Japanese were never able to give me anything worthwhile in exchange for being allowed to see my files and I was not impressed with their general abilities to collect such intelligence for themselves. I excused them on the grounds that they were not very fluent in the English language and, like the Russians, had not realised that most of what they needed to find out was available in published form without any need for spying.

Helen and I were visiting the new Mellon Art Gallery on 7 December 1941 when we met the Italian Air Attaché, Colonel Gaeta. He was in a state of great excitement and almost ran up to us.

'Have you heard? The Japanese have bombed Hawaii!' It sounded too fantastic to be true. The afternoon was peaceful and sunny although chilly with a blue sky. It was not long before we had to accept the news. We could not work out what it might mean for us. It was not clear at first that Germany was to be directly involved. True, there was a pact between Germany and Japan to the effect that they would assist one another if either was attacked but this treaty hardly applied in these circumstances, or so I thought. Japan had not been attacked, Japan was the attacker! The war party in Tokyo had triumphed.

I remembered Helen and I were supposed to be dining that same evening with some Japanese newspaper men who had invited us to join them at a restaurant. It was a strange coincidence and I wondered if they would turn up. There was no reply when I tried to ring their apartment but we decided to go to the restaurant anyway and see if they arrived. If not we could eat there by ourselves. They came very late and were very depressed throughout the evening. I think they knew that their country had launched itself into disaster.

For two days our uncertainty was not resolved. Ambassador Thomsen and General von Bötticher conferred solemnly and concluded that Germany would not enter a war against the USA. Strategically it made no sense. Germany would benefit if the main effort of the USA was directed to the Pacific, away from the fight of Germany against the USSR and Britain. We could still expect some supplies to go from the US to Europe and Russia but the quantities would be smaller. Most of the thousands of aircraft now beginning to emerge from the factories would be directed to the Pacific. It looked good for our side.

Hitler decided otherwise. On the evening of 9 December, a Tuesday, General von Bötticher grimly told me that Hitler had declared war between

Germany and the USA. I should immediately destroy all my papers and records of telegrams. The big incinerator in the basement swallowed tons of paper, including everything I had worked on. I tried to keep back one item only, my graphical statistics which, I thought, might some day be interesting for comparison with American official records when the war ended. I kept the book back and put it in a suitcase with personal belongings. One of my watchful assistants reported this to the General. I had guessed already that this man was reporting secretly on my doings. Bötticher had never liked me much and had kept me on only because my work had been well done and he needed my expertise. I was compelled to hand over the file and it went into the flames. What remained of my respect for Bötticher went with it.

We had expected that within a few hours the Embassy would be closed and we would all be taken into custody prior to a diplomatic exchange of personnel. We would soon be on our way to Germany. This did not happen at once. For about ten days we were allowed to continue living normally within the District of Columbia but I soon noticed that once again Helen and I were being shadowed everywhere we went by the FBI. Agents even moved into the apartment next to ours. Realising that nothing could be helped by making ourselves a nuisance we told them in advance when we were going out and let them catch up in traffic when they looked like losing us. After some initial embarrassment they became friendly and even helped us carry shopping parcels from our car. We were stocking up as far as possible with things we thought we would need to have with us. Relations between us and these young male neighbours relaxed even to the point where they came one evening for a small dinner party when Helen invited some of her women teacher friends and needed a couple of men to make up the numbers. This rather odd celebration was rudely interrupted. The Swiss Embassy, acting as go-between, telephoned to say that all male members of the German diplomatic staff must report tomorrow to the German Embassy building with baggage to be transported to White Sulphur Springs in West Virginia. It was the fashionable resort where I had spent a few days during my illness.

For one night all the men of the former Embassy camped out in the building and next morning a fleet of buses took us to the railway station. Most of the womenfolk joined the group there but Helen stayed behind to see to the final packing up of our household and deal with our furniture. Her position as an American married to a German was going to be difficult.

A special train carried the lot of us to White Sulphur Springs where we were accommodated in the Greenbriar Hotel at the expense of the US Government. After three days Helen joined me there. Had she chosen to leave me at this time she could have done so and I should have been powerless. She chose to stay by me. For her this had never been in doubt.

119

There followed an extraordinary period of luxurious idleness which extended from 19 December until 7 May 1942, almost five months. While the world was going to hell we lived in a kind of fairyland. Soon after Christmas we were joined by the Italian diplomats and not long afterwards the Hungarians and Bulgarians. We renewed old contacts with these various groups and made some new friends among them. It was good to have some new people to talk to rather than being restricted to our own immediate colleagues. The Japanese had not yet arrived.

We had at our disposal all the facilities of a luxury hotel which, until now, had catered for the wealthiest Americans on vacation. We swam in the pool, used the gymnasium, went roller skating in the huge, empty garage, played tennis on the hotel courts, ate like kings and had almost endless cocktail parties and other social gatherings. The staff of the place had nothing else to do but look after us in the same way as they had cared for their wealthy guests before.

The perimeter was guarded and some FBI men actually stayed in the hotel to keep an eye on things from close quarters. We had no contact with press reporters who, to begin with, found us a very interesting but inaccessible group. They had little to write and so made up their own silly tales which we were able to read later in the newspapers. We were amused to discover that the different nationalities were constantly quarrelling with one another and fighting. The truth was we got on extremely well internationally. Internal jealousies and enmities among the German staff did not vanish, however.

One day I noticed a stranger, obviously one of the agents, grinning at me slyly as I passed his table in the dining room. Later one of my Italian friends who, like me, had an American-born wife and so shared many of our problems, took me aside and told me this FBI man would like to meet Helen and me. It was not advisable for us to be seen openly with this man since it could be misinterpreted by my colleagues but we arranged a private session with him. His name, he said, was Morgan. He knew about me phoning the FBI in St Louis. The story had been passed around inside the agency, even reaching Hoover himself, and had created a lot of amusement all the way to the top. We chatted about our honeymoon and he assured us that the agents who had pestered us in Colorado Springs had been severely reprimanded. Spying on us in the hotel had definitely not been part of their instructions. We laughed a good deal about the whole affair but then I received quite a surprise.

'Do you remember what were you doing on the weekend of 7-8 October last year?' he asked me. I had no idea, off hand, where I had been on those dates.

'I will tell you! You left Washington by the 12.42 train for Lynchburg, Virginia. You had lunch in the dining car and stayed there reading. In

Lynchburg you waited a few minutes and then your car arrived, driven by Mrs Riedel with Miss Bötticher as passenger.' It was quite correct. The General's daughter was attending a college in Virginia and Helen had driven there to see her, myself joining them that afternoon. Item by item he went through everything the three of us had done that weekend, every place we had visited, where we stopped to take cine film, where we had crossed the road as he drove past us in his own car. We had been followed the whole time and he was so good at the job that none of us had suspected it for a moment. A different FBI indeed! Why it had been thought necessary to follow us he did not say. Maybe it was just for an exercise. There was nothing in Lynchburg of special interest to an Air Attaché.

Since we could still take newspapers and magazines in the hotel I was able to analyse them as before, though we noticed now that there was more censorship. Nevertheless the various aircraft company reports were still published in the financial pages and from these I was able to see how things were developing. It would have been useful to have my old files to refer to but even without them I was able to make detailed estimates of current and future aircraft production for the whole of 1942. I should, I presumed, be required to make a final report and I began to work on this. I estimated that the total of combat aircraft by the end of 1942 would be about 23,000. Knowing from memory which companies were producing which types I was able to subdivide these totals into single and twin-engined fighters, and twin and four-engined bombers. I reckoned another 12,000 training aircraft would be built. It was obvious too that production in 1943 would be much greater.

As I worked I found members of our former staff constantly hovering round showing much interest in what I was doing. Some of this was mere curiosity but one young man in particular, a member of Dr Tannenberg's staff claiming to be a student of economics, begged me to lend him my statistics so that he could study them. I balked at this, telling him the information was confidential and could be given only to my immediate superior, but I did not cover up my work and he was able to read some of my figures by looking over my shoulder. I was resentful later when he started talking learnedly to little private meetings about American aircraft production. He quoted my statistics as if he had done the work himself. The mutual distrust between the military and diplomatic sides persisted still. I decided the matter was not worth pursuing because in the long run it was best for everyone to know what was happening. The weight of American material was becoming quite enormous and its employment against Germany and Japan would be unrestrained. I had no hope whatever of a German victory now. *Delenda est Carthago!*

12

Return to Germany

Had I not been so skilled at scanning newspapers for small items, I should have missed it. I read one day on the twenty-second page of the *New York Herald Tribune*, a report of a few lines only, emanating from the Polish government in exile in London. It was asserted that tens of thousands of Jewish people had been executed in occupied Poland. The lack of prominence given to the item indicated how little credence was given to it by the American editors to whom it was nothing more than wartime propaganda. I, too, gave it no serious attention. After all, in the First World War, German troops had been accused of eating babies. This seemed to be on about the same level.

In March the Italians, Hungarians and Bulgarians had to pack their cases and they left White Sulphur Springs. Their places were taken by the Japanese and I met my old friends again. A few weeks later we were told this interlude in Virginia was coming to an end. I finished off my report and gave the eighteen pages to Bötticher in both English and German. I found it easier to express myself clearly in the English version and used the most forceful language I dared, for it was clear to me that the High Command in Berlin must be made fully aware of the power that now opposed them. The General, I noted, spent many hours studying the paper I gave him, as if memorising it. He made it available also to the Japanese, our allies, who copied it.

The time came for us to leave. We and the Italians were to sail from New Jersey on the Swedish liner *Drottningholm*. A special train was arranged to take us all to the dock. Helen again had a chance to go her own way but having given her promise she never considered leaving me. Together, but without enthusiasm, we went to the train and soon afterwards were at sea. Even on board the ship the inter-departmental bickering continued and not only on the German side. I was approached by Colonel Gaeta of the Italian military staff who told me that his diplomats were quoting figures of US aircraft production which worried him, since they were so much more detailed than those he had. They had originated, he said, from Dr Tannenberg's section. I knew where they had really come from and with Bötticher's permission allowed Gaeta to take a copy of my report. So at the end of my work in the USA my final report and its implied warnings went to all three capitals: Berlin, Tokyo and Rome. I felt I had done my duty to the best of my abilities. I expected soon to be able to go over the figures with important officers in the Berlin Air Ministry.

We disembarked in Lisbon and thence via Biarritz a special train took us to Frankfurt on Main where we arrived on 25 May 1942. It was Helen's first visit to Europe. She was impressed by the density of the population and the number of villages we had seen from the train. Everywhere we saw uniforms. As we left the platform, in the wide hall of the station crowds of people lined the way to see us as if we were victorious troops. Gigantic banners and placards hung everywhere with slogans and welcoming messages for us. A space was cleared for us to pass through. Rooms had been prepared for us in the Frankfurter Hof hotel.

Minutes after arriving, on the stairs of the hotel I met an old friend from my time in Darmstadt when we had been flying sailplanes there and studying for our engineering degrees. Almost at once he began talking about flying.

'Did you know that Heini Dittmar has reached the speed of sound in Lippisch's new rocket plane?' he asked. Heini was the best German glider pilot before the war, we had both been to Brazil on Georgii's expedition in 1934 with Hanna. Heini had become the first World Champion at the big international soaring contest in 1937. I knew Alexander Lippisch very well too. He had been chief designer at the old soaring institute on the Wasserkuppe where he had been experimenting with tailless aircraft ever since 1927.

'You know,' said my friend, 'Heini is like a member of my family, he always stays with us when he is in Frankfurt. He told me about this new plane several weeks ago. He is only sorry his record cannot be officially recognised because it is a secret. Think of it, 1,500 kilometres per hour! That plane climbs to thirty thousand feet in two minutes!'[1]

I listened with awe. I could not help admiring the rocket plane which, I learned, had been built at the Augsburg Messerschmitt plant. With plenty of such aircraft the *Luftwaffe* might be able to beat off the big attacks. At the same time I was astonished that so soon after arriving in Frankfurt I was being told a military secret! What were Heini and his friend thinking of, to spread this story around? I had expected much tighter control, more seriousness and concentration of purpose, more discipline.

---

[1] The Messerschmitt 163 V1 Komet, powered by a Walther RII 203 rocket motor, was flown by Dittmar at a speeds of 1,004.5 kph (623.8 mph) on 2 Oct 1941 after a towed start to 11,810 feet. During this flight he experienced control difficulties when the wing tips locally exceeded their critical Mach number. The speed of sound was not reached.

Soon after arriving Helen and I visited Oscar Ursinus, the editor of *Flugsport*, who had organised the early gliding competitions. He and his wife, three sons and a daughter had known me since I was fourteen years old when I had taken part in the first Rhön competitions with my home-built glider. I recalled Ursinus asking me, when he met me in Gersfeld at the foot of the Wasserkuppe, if I had run away from home to go gliding.

'No,' I had replied truthfully, 'My father paid for my ticket on the train!' Now we found a sad elderly couple who had lost two sons in the war, one as a Heinkel test pilot, the other shot down in Africa. Their married daughter was interned as an alien in Australia. The third son had survived and at present was in a safe position as a staff officer but nothing could hide their sorrow. The *Rhönvater*, or Rhön father as we had called him, had never imagined in 1920 that sport flying would bring so many young men to their deaths in aerial fighting.

I supposed I would now be required at once by the Air Ministry although no one had given me any orders or suggested a date and time when I should report there. I imagined that all travelling was under control and that we should be required to prove the necessity of each journey before being allowed on a train.

'I'd like to take you there, to the Wasserkuppe where we used to have our gliding contests,' I said to Helen, 'but I think we shall not be allowed to make any diversions on our way to Berlin.' I decided to investigate anyway. I took my diplomatic papers to the ticket office in case there was an argument but when I lined up in the queue I realised that other people were just ordering and paying for their tickets as if it were peacetime. They were booking for their vacations, elderly couples, young mothers with children going to visit relatives, business men with cases, single women, soldiers of course, all going about as they chose. Private travel was unrestricted. Not much sign here of the total war we had been led to expect. Although quite disturbed that everyone still was taking things so easily I was glad in another way, for it meant that I could after all take Helen to the Rhön. I ought also to visit my brother who was my only remaining close relative in Germany.

We had two wonderful days on the Wasserkuppe where heavy new militaristic buildings had replaced the old wooden sheds and dormitories I remembered. Now everyone was in smart uniform instead of looking like the scruffy 'Rhön Indians' I had known. I had been one of them. I remembered how we had slept, that first year, in old packing crates and how Alex Lippisch himself, with the carpenter Gottlob Espenlaub, had wintered up on the mountain through howling gales and heavy snowfalls, sleeping in a huge wardrobe laid on its back. At the end of the cold season, half-starved Lippisch had looked like death and earned himself the nickname, *Rhöngeist* or Rhön ghost. He had come a long way since those days. Now the famous Dr Lippisch was designing rocket planes!

We were made welcome on the Wasserkuppe for I was remembered there as a veteran. I was even allowed to fly one of the superior eighteen metre Weihe sailplanes for an hour. It performed better than any I had flown before and gave me an all too brief period of sheer happiness, concentrating on staying up and making sure of a good approach and landing.

It must have been during our brief stay on the Wasserkuppe that the SS Gauleiter Reinhard Heydrich, the 'Protector' of Czechoslovakia and deputy leader of the SS, second only to Himmler, was assassinated by a hand-grenade which was thrown into his car by the Czech resistance near the village of Lidice. We heard the news later. Heydrich was spoken of in whispers as 'Hangman Heydrich'. He had been a terrifying figure. It was said that the authorities would find those responsible for his death and take revenge.[2] I wondered if the feared 'Hangman' could possibly be some relation to the Heydrich family in Halle. The Heydrichs I knew of were Jewish and ran a Music Institute in Heinrichstrasse. I was told by an aunt that when my mother was sixteen and showing signs of musical talent there had been some brief family argument about whether she should go to a Jewish academy. Grandfather, Professor of Theology in Halle, a Lutheran of course, had been quite angered at this prejudice. Mother was not enrolled at the Heydrich Institute. Could this Heydrich, also from Halle, be secretly Jewish and yet have risen so far in the ranks of the SS and become such a vicious anti-semite? I found it hard to believe yet such inversions and perversions were not unknown.[3]

A day on crowded trains took us to my brother's home. The small town in Thuringia where he lived was quiet and peaceful, hardly affected by the war, but Felix, as I might have expected, was not there. He was away serving in the *Luftwaffe*. My sister-in-law welcomed us and met Helen. We soon made the acquaintance of her neighbour who, with his wife and children, had been living in the apartment above hers for the past four years. To the delight of his family Herr Müller, a soldier, had arrived only yesterday on leave from the Eastern Front.

He was keen to tell me and Helen about his experiences which he seemed to have enjoyed. Helen could not follow German yet though she had picked up a few words. Müller smiled as he talked about how easy they were

[2] The village of Lidice was totally destroyed by the SS, all the men were shot and the women taken to concentration camps.

[3] Heydrich, born 1904, was from a musical family in Halle, his father being an opera singer and his mother an actress. He himself was an accomplished violinist and his brother a cellist. He had nevertheless been extremely anti-Jewish since his youth.

finding it now in the warmer conditions to push the Russians further and further back. Only the partisans behind the lines made things sometimes difficult for the German troops. After expanding on this theme for a while he suddenly changed the subject with every appearance of pleasure at revealing to me a wonderful secret.

'Let me tell you, Herr Riedel, out there in the east they are killing the Jews now, thousands and thousands of them!' Did I hear him correctly? Did he mean it? I admit I was frightened as well as horrified. I dared not reveal my real feelings to this man, a stranger who seemed to be a fanatical Jew hater. Was that little newspaper story I had seen in the *Herald Tribune* true, then? Surely it couldn't be. I lowered my voice because I did not want Helen to follow this, though I guessed she would sense my sudden dismay.

'Who is doing this?' I asked.

'The SS. The Jews have to dig their own graves first, then they open up with the machine-guns, drrrrrrrrrrrrrr drrrrrr and the next group is brought for the same treatment. Ha ha ha ha ha! Serves them right, those warmongers! They wanted a war, now they're getting it! Eh!' No cruelty was apparent in his face. He described all this as if it were merely part of some football game with a score in thousands of lives. He didn't seem a bad sort of man, a good father, fond of his children and his wife. Yet he had been poisoned by Nazi propaganda which had been hammered into him for years until he had lost the power of critical thinking. The Jews were enemies of the State and it was right to destroy them, he believed.

I felt cold. What had I come home to? I kept my face straight, knowing that if I uttered a wrong word now I might be reported and that would be the end of me. Alone with Helen again, I had to tell her what I had heard.

'I wish we could pack our cases again and go back,' I said. It was too late. What I had seen as my patriotic duty had led me to the position where now I was an accomplice to terrible crimes. I had never been in favour of the war. Wrong though it was I believed that the only way ahead for a good German was to get it over with quickly, to bring some kind of peace out of it as soon as possible. The alternative was treason. Now I was forced to see I had betrayed something much more important than my country. These were crimes against humanity.

Did Müller really know, had he seen with his own eyes? He had never said that. Had such things really happened? Was it just a ridiculous story someone had told? The internal defence mechanism came into action again. Helen was shattered too at first but tried to find some hope.

'Perhaps it has happened, but only once,' she said. 'In war we know there are atrocities when people get out of control or misunderstand something. The tales become exaggerated, spread around, make everything seem much worse than the truth.' I wanted to believe it. Perhaps some fanatical SS chief had given the order to kill a number of prisoners in a moment of rage at some partisan brutality against his men. Müller had mentioned the partisans with their ambushes and lightning raids. He said they spared no German soldier if they caught one. Yes, perhaps that was it. The man liked to make himself seem important and knowledgeable by spreading the story he had heard and adding a little to it each time. After thinking along these lines I began to settle down again. Helen and I reassured ourselves. Such things could not be true. Could they? If they were, into what sort of situation had I brought her? Some thoughts are so dreadful that one forces oneself not to think them.

Felix arrived on leave after all, at the weekend. He and I had never got on well, always fighting when we were boys. A few years older than I, he would have bullied me when we were in our teens but, luckily for me, I was bigger and heavier than he was despite the age difference so I could look after myself. This made him detest me all the more. He had joined the Nazis quite early and had used his party connections to get himself elected as mayor of the village, but had joyfully enlisted when the war came. Within an hour of his arrival we were quarreling again. No matter what I had seen in the USA, I could tell him nothing of importance, he was better informed about everything, he knew people who knew. It was a relief to get away from him.

Two or three days later we went to Berlin and found a rather primitive hotel room for the time being. We were lucky to get anywhere at all for the city was very crowded. My first move was to report to the Air Ministry and the Attaché Department. Instead of the chief of the section one of the less senior permanent officers, Colonel Hühnerberg, received me. His chief was evidently not interested in meeting me even though I had just returned from the USA. Hühnerburg greeted me in a friendly fashion, asked about our journey and chatted for a little about more personal matters, my marriage and my health. The small talk drying up, I turned to business.

'So, what am I to do now?' I had expected, in a military organisation, to receive orders, not to ask for them.

'We have nothing for you! You don't really belong to the attaché service, Riedel. Let me see, I think there was something, there was a request . . . Oh, yes, I believe Schwenke asked about you. Do you know Colonel Schwenke?' I thought I remembered having met him once. He was a colonel in the engineering section and had been an Assistant Attaché in London for a while. Now I learned he had become chief of the *Luftwaffe*'s department GL-7, dealing with foreign armaments. This did sound like my area. I was told to report to him. 'Thank you for all the work you did in Washington,' said Hühnerburg, shaking my hand as I left. 'Much appreciated.' The *Attaché Gruppe* had already taken me off their list.

So much, I thought, for my report causing a stir! Perhaps I had overestimated my own importance but I was sure the facts I had given them were important. I went back to Helen and we laughed about it. What next?

I discovered that Hanna Reitsch was in town, taking a few days off from her numerous test flying jobs, about which she said little. She was much more conscious of security than others I had met. She was lodging temporarily at the Aero Club, very near the Ministry, and I took Helen to meet her. As usual Hanna was full of energy and delighted to meet Helen. We thanked her for the help she had given about our marriage and this brought back sad memories of Ernst Udet, whom we both mourned. Hanna told us nothing about the crash that had killed him, which was puzzling. Among flying folk, as a rule, any serious accident is talked about and the details gone over again and again, never entirely forgotten especially when a close friend has been killed. Here was a complete blank. Ernst, I thought, must have been flying some very secret aircraft. There was something odd about Hanna's manner. I resolved to ask someone else about Udet when the opportunity arose.

Hanna recommended some better accommodation. The hotel we were in was very shabby and grubby and the food there was dreadful. After White Sulphur Springs we now seemed to be slumming and Helen was disgusted. There was, Hanna said, a kind of country club with accommodation for visiting scientists or aviation people. She knew who to speak to and after a few words on the telephone arranged for us to go and view a small apartment. There was, when we got there, a living room, bedroom and bath, a small lawn and patio area. There was no kitchen but a central dining room where all the residents ate. The amount of food was adequate but it was very poor stuff. There was practically no fat or protein in our Berlin diet. Helen, fortunately for me, did not like butter or milk so I had her ration but despite this I began to lose weight faster even than she did.

I told Helen about the furniture I had stored in my neighbour's cellar when I had left for Colombia in 1936. We needed some of it now. Frau Lintz, Jewish, had foreseen the war when I still believed it would not happen. Was she still in her old home? I telephoned. The familiar voice answered but she sounded nervous. When I explained who I was she seemed glad to hear from me. It had been a long time.

'Herr Riedel! You were lucky to catch me. In three days . . . No, we had better meet somewhere and I'll tell you about it.'

Helen and I arranged to meet her under the clock at the Tiergarten station. She looked fairly cheerful.

'I can't stay long. My friend Herr H is home on leave just now from the Eastern Front and we don't want to lose any time while we can be together.'

I understood. She and Mr H had given up the idea of marrying. He had been employed as a singer on Berlin radio and marriage with her, a Jewess, would have cost him his career. If, that is, he survived at all.

'You see, I am not wearing the star,' she said, pointing to her left side where Jewish people by law were now required to display a yellow star with the word *Jude*. 'I have managed to dodge it so far because I do not look Jewish. I even found a job in the management of a women's magazine and I was working there until recently. But now someone has denounced me and they expect me to go to a police station to be registered. You know what it means? No more right to work, then deportation to Poland. Do you think I want to die in a mass grave, not even dead yet from the SS bullets? Covered with more Jewish bodies and some lime?' She spoke quietly without any change of facial expression.

'In three days I am going to leave Berlin and get out of Germany. There is a high official of the SS who is going to take me as his 'secretary' to France. He is one of the few who is sick of it all and wants to help me. I hope to escape into unoccupied France and disappear into the French population. So, you and I must say goodbye now. The people who are going to take over my apartment know about your things so you only need to visit them one day after I have left and you can arrange everything with them.'

She shook my hand hurriedly and left us without another word. I was able only to wish her good luck as she hastened away.

I stood dumbly amidst the bustling crowds. What I had forced myself not to believe had been confirmed. I was trembling. Helen knew I was deeply upset but she had not followed the swiftly uttered, almost mumbled German. We took the subway as I tried to recover and collect myself again. Helen must be told but what could I say now? I had brought her to this! The train we were on passed a large building which had been burned down.

'Look,' Helen said, 'it must have been bombed. How strange that a bomb should flatten just one building in the whole area! None of the others have been touched.' I knew better. Very few bombs had come near Berlin at that stage in the war. The burned building had once been a synagogue and religious symbols were still faintly visible on the remaining walls. I knew it had been burned in that dreadful *Kristallnacht* of 1938. Two Jewish women with the yellow stars were standing in the crowded carriage. They kept their eyes down, did not dare to look around or speak to one another.

Get away, get away from this country, escape, was the thought uppermost in my mind. Yet how could I do so? I conjured up a wild dream. I would get myself a job in an aircraft factory. One day I would take Helen with me, we would steal a plane and fly away to a neutral country where we could stay until the horror was over. I knew it was a dream but somehow, *we must escape.*

129

The train arrived at the station, Gleisdreieck, where we had to change lines. Two young nurses were there with two soldiers, arms linked it seemed to me in an unusually intimate way. Then I realised the men were blind, stumbling along with the girls guiding them and sitting them down in the places reserved for war wounded. The nurses chatted gaily, the men responded with half smiles but most of the time just seemed to be resigned, blank faced. They had sacrificed their sight. Put yourself in their place, I thought. What would you think of a man who now wants to run away to a neutral country before the war is over? I could think no more. Do your duty. Obey your training. Continue as best you can. Bury the fear and the pain and the horror. Survive, survive if you can.

13

Defeatism

I went to see Schwenke who gave me a position in GL-7 but I had little
work to do and was not even required to go in to the Air Ministry building
every day. There was no sense of urgency. What did not get done today
could be done tomorrow and if it wasn't done at all nobody seemed to care.
Little had changed here since 1938 when I had spent so many weeks
wandering round trying to get some sense out of the system. Here we go
again, I thought, on the Berlin bureaucratic merry-go-round!

One thing I began to feel I must do, which nobody else cared about it
seemed. What had become of my reports about American air power? If I
backed up the documents with a personal approach at the highest possible
level, I might have some influence, might even contribute in this way to a
recognition by Germany that suing for an immediate peace was the only
hope. I went to see Schwenke and explained to him what I wanted.

'Forget it, Riedel,' he said. 'The facts are well-known to Milch and the
General Staff. We know about your report. It is under examination in my
department. I can't see any point in your fronting up personally to Milch,
let alone Göring himself. It would be most unwise. Just between the two of
us, I can tell you our friend Hermann does not like to hear news like yours.
If you tell him the truth bluntly like that he turns his back, or gets furious
at you and screams with rage. I should know . . .'

Schwenke had at first treated me like an equal and a friend despite the
difference in our ranks but during these first few days he became somewhat
irritated with me since I persisted in my belief that a personal report would
be effective in alerting the authorities to the situation. Nobody seemed to
understand what was going to happen. I made the point that, unlike him, I
had little to fear. I was not a career officer and was not afraid of offending
my superiors by telling the truth to their faces.

'Don't be a bloody fool, Riedel!' he said, dismissing me. Despite this I
decided to persist. I called on Engineer Rulof Lucht, who had briefed me
back in 1938 before I went to Washington. He might listen and be able to
do something. He heard me with apparently genuine interest.

'They will not come in gradually increasing numbers allowing time to
adjust and prepare. They are building up their strength now and when they

are ready they will make their appearance with crushing superiority. Not scores or even hundreds of heavy bombers. Thousands, thousands!' This was my main theme.

'I would help you, my dear Riedel, if I possibly could. But you see I am on the point of getting out of this place myself. You evidently haven't heard. We are all resigning, myself here in the Ministry, Reidenbach and Franke at Rechlin. Why? Because we will not go on being treated like children by Fat Hermann!' He started in his usual loud voice but, realising the need for caution, toned it down and spoke more quietly.

'You probably haven't heard of our troubles. The new Messerschmitt 210 is a failure so we can't replace the old 110 which is too slow now. The Me 210 was supposed to be delivered to the front long ago. It isn't ready and never will be, it is a dog. It lacks stability, isn't safe. It is more danger to our own pilots than to the enemy. The Heinkel 177, our four-engined bomber masterpiece, should have been in service two years ago and always there are new technical problems with it. Another dog, only a bigger one. In the midst of all this our great *Reichsmarschall* Hermann appeared at Rechlin a while back and we all had to stand to attention like raw recruits while he raved at us! It's all our fault, every failure is laid at our door. We engineers are being made into scapegoats. He ranted at us, talked about sending us all off to concentration camps as if we were intentionally sabotaging everything. Well, it's too much, I can tell you. The three of us senior men have handed in our resignations to Milch. He refused them at first but in the end he has had to accept them. So you see, I am here now only as a ghost of myself!' Lucht laughed sourly. He was just clearing up to make way for his successor and then was going to work for Messerschmitt in Regensburg, as technical director. Franke was going to Heinkel's in Rostock and Reidenbach to Dorniers in Friedrichshaven. I asked, as tactfully as I could, why Göring was behaving in this way.

'It's the old problem, tension between the officers and the engineers, between the Staff of the *Luftwaffe* and the Air Ministry, personal squabbles between the Chief of Staff and Field Marshal Milch. It is only Göring's friendship that keeps Milch himself in position. We have shown him up time and again, he should have gone long ago. He has Udet on his conscience now too.' Lucht was the last of Udet's men remaining in the Air Ministry. He paused.

'Tell me about Udet's crash!' I said. 'I never heard what happened.'

He hesitated a long time.

'It wasn't a crash. Keep this under your hat. Udet shot himself. He'd been depressed, the job was too much for him and he was drinking a lot. Milch and Co hated him and his old pals, the real airmen, thought he had sold out to the bureaucrats. He telephoned his girlfriend one day to say goodbye and then shot himself. He didn't ring off properly and the poor girl heard the bang.' Shocking though this news was, it did not really surprise me very much. I had suspected almost from the beginning that something about the official story was not right. It brought tears to my eyes nonetheless.

'Let's change the subject,' Lucht said. 'Did you know that your former boss, General von Bötticher, was awarded the Knight's Cross of the Pour le Mérite? Pinned on his chest by the Führer in person!' I detected a slightly ironic tone. 'Yes, Ambassador Thomsen too, they both got it. I saw Bötticher yesterday and congratulated him. He is very full of himself just now, you can imagine! Apropos of that.

A new idea had evidently struck him. 'Bötticher is to make a personal report to the whole conclave of chiefs of the Air Ministry next Tuesday. It's a regular thing, a weekly gathering under the chairmanship of Milch. That would be the right occasion, if one exists, for you to speak. Hasn't Bötticher told you about it? He will want you there.' I had heard nothing from Bötticher since getting to Germany, and said so.

'Ha, the foxy old bugger, he wants to take all the credit for himself. That's typical of him, proud and devious with it. I've known him for years. But you should go to that meeting. Tell Schwenke I said so, he should even order you to be present. That is just about the last thing I shall do as Chief of the Engineer Corps here!' He patted his desk with his hands, laughed again, obviously happy to be leaving the intrigues behind and beginning a new career in the aircraft industry.

Quite accidentally I ran into Bötticher soon afterwards. I hardly recognised him for he was wearing his splendid full dress uniform, all gold braid around the collar and red stripes down the trousers, the bright new medal reminding me to congratulate him. Now I shall hear about the meeting, if he intends me to be there. After the usual conventionalities had been dealt with he did not mention it and seemed ready to depart. I tried to approach the topic I was worried about.

'I have been having some difficulty finding an opportunity to make a personal report of my experiences in the USA, General. I wonder if you . . .'

'Colonel Schwenke will take care of all that,' the General said, brusquely. Any request should be addressed formally to my immediate superior officer and that, now, was Schwenke. Yet he, not Schwenke had been my boss in Washington. Now Bötticher told me he was going away on leave for a few days, to Dresden where his elderly parents were still living. 'You deserve a rest. You should apply for a few days off,' he said.

I knew how he had couched his reports to Berlin, always reassuring, toning down or fudging over the impact of purely technical material.

Without ever making himself vulnerable to a charge of lying or falsifying facts he had always found ways of expressing himself that would not agitate his superiors. They in turn reported soothingly to the Führer. For this kind of diplomacy Bötticher had received the Knight's Cross. I wondered if the material I had taken such trouble to collect had ever been read closely by anyone in the higher echelons. Well, I would go to the meeting. Bötticher would get a surprise on Tuesday, I thought, as I watched him get into his waiting car to be driven away.

Schwenke raised no objections. On Tuesday I was very early and waited in the semi darkness of a long hall outside the room in the Air Ministry building where the conferences took place. People began to assemble and soon the jingling of spurs and medals announced the arrival of General Bötticher, all dressed up to take the centre spot.

'Oh, so you are here!' he said, brusquely, as he passed me. I slipped through the door behind him, hardly noticed in my civilian clothes among so many uniforms.

After Field Marshal Milch had said a few introductory words the General spoke. His report was, as I expected, a clever compromise between truths which could not be hidden and soothing remarks designed not to upset the morale of his audience. He mentioned my work as Air Attaché once, pointing me out as I sat in my corner, and for a moment all eyes turned to me. At the end of the lengthy statement Milch rose again and thanked Bötticher. Then he greeted me.

'And you too must come here one day, Riedel, to report to us here,' he said as the meeting ended. That was all. Schwenke was present and had heard Milch so it would be up to him now to see that I did get a place on the agenda for a future meeting. I was reassured and started thinking about how I would put the blunt truth to these complacent gentlemen and stir them from their habitual routines.

Now that he had been reminded of my existence, Milch invited me to a luncheon he was giving in honour of General von Bötticher in the Aero Club building nearby. There I met again my former *Lufthansa* chief, Baron von Gablenz, looking rather uncomfortable in the uniform of a general. I greeted him by his military title but he grumbled at this, 'As far as you are concerned, it's still Herr von Gablenz!' I had always liked him and felt that with him at the table I should be able to speak up without fear of reprimand.[1]

When the lunch was over I chose my time and, as a lead in to what I thought was my main point, raised a topic with Gablenz that had bothered

[1] General Karl-August Freiherr von Gablenz was appointed to the post of Chief Airforce Equipment Officer in the re-organisation imposed on Udet by Milch in September 1941.

me during the last few days. I spoke quietly to him as he sat next to me, not wanting to cause an immediate confrontation with the top brass. I had heard more careless talk. There was a scheme to fit out a special aircraft with the intention of bombing New York. It was proposed to use a four-engined Focke Wulf Condor. Aircraft of this type had been airliners but now some were being used for long-range reconnaissance over the Atlantic, shadowing convoys and calling up submarines to attack them. The idea was to equip a Condor with long-range fuel tanks and a few bombs. Stripped of everything else it would be just capable of flying the Atlantic, dropping its few small bombs on Manhattan and then it would have to ditch in the sea, almost a suicide mission. It was expected to scare the cowardly Americans and, presumably, make them surrender immediately. It seemed to me a totally ridiculous scheme and revealed utter ignorance of the reaction it would produce.

'Such an attack might scare a few hundred women and children in New York,' I said, 'but otherwise the effect would be exactly the opposite of that intended. It would create a huge wave of anger, give enormous strength to Roosevelt and his supporters and prove the isolationists wrong. To speak plainly, it would be sheer stupidity to try such a thing.' Von Gablenz listened with attention.

'It would be up to your chief, Bötticher, to pass these thoughts on to those responsible for the plan,' he said, glancing at Milch and the General.

'I don't think he has heard of the matter at present,' I said, quietly, 'and in any case the assignment has ended now. He isn't the Military Attaché any more and I am no longer in his department. And he doesn't like to swim against the current,' I added, in a whisper loud enough only for Gablenz to hear.

Thereupon Gablenz turned to Milch and asked him about it, mentioning my opinions. Milch stared at me, no doubt wondering how I had ever come to hear of the supposedly secret scheme in the first place. He then turned to Bötticher.

'What do you think about this?' he asked. Fortunately for me the General agreed with my view.

'Certainly the effect would be to strengthen the American will to fight. It would be a great mistake.' Milch shrugged his shoulders and changed the subject. Perhaps this conversation caused the plan to be abandoned for I never heard more about it. My opportunity to broach the subject of my report slipped by somehow.

Days went by and no word came that I was to present myself at the next Tuesday meeting, or the one after or the one after that. I reminded the Colonel several times but nothing was done. In exasperation I eventually decided to do what no military man ever should – bypass my superior. I telephoned Milch's secretary, Richter, and asked him to remind Milch that he had wanted me at one of the meetings. I was immediately put in my place. I should go through the proper channels. There was no chance for me to approach the Field Marshal who was vastly overworked. Once again, I was shoved aside.

A few days later I and an old friend, Fritz Pichelsdorf, were dinner guests at the home of Herr Lewinsky who was working as a liaison officer between the Japanese Navy and German industrialists. A Japanese guest, Mr Sakai, was also present. As usual these days I spoke about the growth of American air power and told them of my lack of progress in making myself understood. Fritz, who had a lot of experience and knew about all the intrigues and gossip behind the scenes, listened to me, laughed slightly and winked at Lewinsky.

'How long do you think he's got?' he asked. I was baffled.

Lewinsky replied 'Oh, I should think a few more weeks, if nobody stops him. A fortnight?'

'What are you talking about?' I asked.

'We are wondering how long it will be before they take you off to Oranienburg, the concentration camp, as a defeatist!' He had begun with a smile but as he spoke his expression became grim and I realised he meant it seriously.

'You mean, telling the truth would be called defeatism?'

'Yes, my friend. The truth is not always welcomed especially if it is disagreeable. To let you make your report public would spoil the whole thrust of the propaganda campaign which always speaks of victory and only of victory. I am sure there are people already who know everything you have to say. They have probably followed your reports. In any case plenty know enough about the world to make a shrewd guess for themselves. But these same people will not and dare not spread the word to a wider audience. It would be too discouraging to let ordinary folk know. So be careful, otherwise there could suddenly be very unpleasant consequences for you.'

'Very well, I can understand all that,' I said, after a moment. 'I wasn't proposing to shout about this from the roof tops. But surely I should be given a chance to report directly to Göring, or even to Hitler in person. They could do something about it. What I have in mind, I can't see how the huge bomber fleets can be stopped or turned back. The British couldn't stop our raids and there will be far more coming in the other direction soon. We should evacuate the big industrial cities in the Rhineland and Ruhr. I mean those people whose presence there is not absolutely essential to the war effort should be moved out. The men in the works are like soldiers at the front, they should expect some hardships. They can't require to have their families waiting at home every evening. In any case, surely they will work all the better if they know their wives and children are safe in the country somewhere when the big raids begin. That is one of the proposals I want to make. It isn't defeatism! It isn't! Is it?' Pichelsdorf and Lewinsky laughed ironically. Sakai's face remained immobile.

'Where did you get such radical ideas?' asked our host. 'You will get yourself widely disliked. You seriously want to separate wives from their husbands? You will have all the women against you.'

'I thought there was supposed to be total war! The children at least were evacuated in England.' I protested, but did not know what more to say. Did our leaders shrink from applying these stern but necessary measures? What kind of leaders were they?

Having been silent so far, Mr Sakai now spoke. He had lived in Europe for twenty years and needed no help with the language or explanation of our customs.

'It is one thing to talk freely here among a small circle of trusted friends but be very circumspect elsewhere. I am quite sure you are right and your proposals should be put forward but only privately to the men who have the power to bring them to realisation. Be very careful with such a sensitive topic. The Gestapo have ears everywhere and are daily growing more powerful. Himmler against Göring . . .' I sensed a chill in the room and conversation for the rest of the evening became very limited.

I still believed I must persist but realised I must change my tactics. The direct approach to the top, through the Air Ministry, was getting nowhere. Three weeks had passed since Bötticher had reported to the conference. I had a new idea. I would visit leading men in the aircraft industry and tell my story. Some of them I knew well already. They would understand what I was saying better than the bureaucrats and officers. They were important enough to be able to open a way to the top. After all, their plants would be the top priority targets for the coming air attacks and their aircraft would be needed for defence. It would be in their own interests to see that the word got through.

The next day I proposed to Schwenke that I should make a trip through Germany to visit all those aircraft factories I had seen in 1938 before going to Washington. I could make a comparison between their development during the last four years and the American expansion. I should be in a good position to write a report which would be of some use in guiding future plans. Schwenke agreed, perhaps because he saw it as a way to get me out of his hair for a while. The next day Helen and I were ready. She was to come with me for I wanted her to see more of Germany before it was too late.

Our trip began in the last week of June 1942. We had been back in Germany just four weeks. How many impressions had crowded in upon us! We were glad to get away from Berlin. In country districts and small towns the food was better because it could often be supplemented from the farms, but the official rations, we thought, were hardly enough to keep anyone alive.

Our first call was to the Junkers works at Dessau, a little more than 100 km (60 miles) south-west of Berlin. Helen spent her time walking and sketching in the park by the castle as I went to the plant. A new administration building of modernistic design seemed to point to a large expansion since I had last been there in April 1938. Chief pilot Kindermann was preparing to fly the new stratospheric version of the Ju 88 bomber. Before taking off he chatted to me briefly and advised me to go first to the other Junkers plants at Bernburg, Aschersleben and Halberstadt. Afterwards I could come back to Dessau to the headquarters. I took his advice and we went to Aschersleben, for this had been my home town from 1917 till 1921. It was about 50 km (30 miles) west of Dessau. The old town had changed very little and I hurried out to the factory. Here I saw the production of Junkers 88 fuselages. The wings were built at Halberstadt 30 km (19 miles) down the railway line to the north-west and the various sub-assemblies and other components were brought together for final assembly at Bernburg, which was between Aschersleben and Dessau. Thus the works were dispersed and were unlikely all to be destroyed in one raid. But it was obvious that if any one of them were destroyed the other two would be useless. Most of the work force at Aschersleben were, I discovered, foreigners, Russian or Polish prisoners-of-war in some cases but mostly deported civilians, Czechs, Poles, French. I asked if there was sabotage.

'No, it goes surprisingly well,' the plant manager answered. 'We treat our workers well and most of them are willing to do their best once they get here. Russian women are very good but the French prisoners-of-war are some of the best. If there were to be any sabotage it would show up at once because every part goes through controlled inspections. If anything were found we could trace the item back directly to the group of workers responsible. They know it.'

In Halberstadt I found the Junkers wing-building factory was housed in primitive wooden sheds. A day later in Bernburg I was shown the one large hangar where the final assembly was done. Herr Poehlmann, the manager here, had spent some years in the USA and Canada and had learned a great deal about their production methods. Under his control the work was being done well in a very limited space. Poehlmann and I talked about the American industry. I described the Willow Run development and gave him my estimates for American production during the current year. It was no surprise to him for he had enough experience in the USA to guess what would be happening there. He let his eyes rove around the shed where we stood, raised his eyebrows and looked to heaven. It was not necessary to speak.

The production methods were well organised and efficient but the whole Junkers plant was small by comparison with the American factories I knew. I remembered when we had travelled by the special train from White Sulphur Springs to New Jersey, we had passed the Glenn Martin factory. While we had been in our luxurious captivity, there had been massive changes. I had seen gigantic new shining assembly halls and sixty to seventy B-26 Marauder bombers standing outside in full view. I asked if other factories were building the Ju 88 and was told yes, there were about fourteen plants altogether including some in France but the total production figures per month made me gasp.[2] Germany's best twin-engined bomber was being produced on a much smaller scale than I had imagined. I had expected to find a vastly increased aircraft industry to compete with the American one. This was an illusion. During this visit to the Junkers factory I was once again overcome by the conviction that we should lose the war and lose it disastrously.

Still I did not give up hope. I would speak to the heads of the firm.

Back in Dessau I was taken all round. Apart from the administration block there had been no expansion here at all. I was told that this was the centre of designing and developing new aircraft types and devising new production methods. There was no serial production.

A meeting for me with the Chairman, three directors of the Company and the chief pilot Kindermann was arranged.

'How do things look in America now?' the Chairman asked. 'We don't hear very much about what is happening in the outside world. We are all so busy!'

I started my favourite theme and spoke without restraint. Let the Gestapo listen if they wished. I felt it was my duty to let these people know the dangers they faced. Perhaps, after I had finished, one of them would approach Göring or even the Führer about it. I spoke for three-quarters of an hour and waited anxiously for their reactions.

Nothing happened at first. The five men sat in silence round the table, none had anything to say, none asked a question. I supposed they all felt utterly helpless, unable to change anything and for the first time, perhaps, realising that the country faced defeat. At last the Chairman spoke.

---

[2] From 1940 to 1943 Ju 88 bomber production was about 2,000 aircraft per year, corresponding roughly to 55 to 60 per month. The total of all bomber and reconnaissance variants was 10,774 by the end of hostilities, with another 5,000 approximately of the night fighter version during 1944–5.

'Did you have a chance to tell all this to the people up there, in Berlin, the Air Ministry?' He looked seriously worried but somehow lifeless and resigned.

'No, I didn't. I am only a Captain in the reserves. General von Bötticher stood between me and the people I needed to see. He is not the man to raise these matters with the Führer, even after receiving the medal from him. The highest in the land are not going to spend time listening to the little fellow who knows what is really going on. That's the army way, you know.'

They did know. They now stared to pour out their own troubles. The army was calling up people everywhere, often taking their best specialist workers who could not be easily replaced. Key personnel from the works were out there freezing in Russia or frying in North Africa with guns in their hands while fat Party men were strutting about at home dodging military service. Raw materials were scarce, necessary machine tools could not be obtained. There were two quite uncoordinated government agencies both supposed to be responsible for allocating priorities between all sections of the armaments industry, with the result that confusion reigned.

'On the one hand there is Speer, the Minister for armaments and all his department, and then there is Göring the Air Minister and his twenty other titles and all his underlings who control everything to do with aircraft. The two lots never get together about anything. We are constantly in conflict with the submarine companies or the ones building tanks, guns and armoured cars.' So they went on. If what I had said was defeatism, what was this, I thought! The truth did not make pleasant hearing and I understood that they were quite helpless. They had only one channel of communication. It led to the very man responsible for their plight and he would not listen or accept any criticism.

Finally I was asked which other factories I was intending to visit. Dornier was next on my agenda so the Chairman sent a telegram ahead to announce my imminent arrival and recommended that their senior people should hear what I had to say.

14

Old Friends, New Despair

The Dornier plant at Friedrichshafen, to which we travelled a couple of days later, was small even compared with the Junkers concern and again I was directed away to another factory, this one near Munich where we checked into a hotel and Helen enjoyed herself for a day in the ancient city. Even though Helen and I spoke English to one another on the trains we hardly ever met the slightest hostility from other passengers. Friendly interest rather than enmity was the usual reaction.

When the time came for my meeting with the directors I was warned that Professor Dornier, the elderly chief of the whole concern, would be present but that I must not talk too much for he would never listen to a long speech. I promised to limit myself to twenty minutes. He came in, a shy, small old gentleman with an absent-minded air who, nevertheless, seemed to frighten all his subordinates. He sat after a very brief word or two, thanked me for coming and I was signalled to begin with a small bow. I forgot my promise and talked for nearly an hour but I saw that Dornier, far from becoming bored or impatient, was attending with great interest and intelligence throughout. I backed up all my figures with a careful explanation of how they had been gathered for I did not want anyone to suggest that I could be in error.

When I finished, the reaction was much the same as it had been at Dessau, stunned, miserable expressions and no words. Dornier himself broke the silence but he pre-empted any discussion and dealt quickly with one or two other issues in the Company before closing the meeting and turning to me.

'Will you drive with me back to Munich?' he asked. Soon the two of us were sitting in the back of his car with a plate of glass between us and the driver. Dornier suddenly thawed.

'It has been most interesting, Herr Riedel, to hear your report and I thank you again for coming. What you have said is no surprise to me. I know the United States and I wish there were more people in this country who understood their huge resources of both manpower and material. American ways of technical thought and planning cannot be suddenly transplanted into Europe and cannot even be imagined by the average

European. Well, I have already tried to talk to Göring about this. He listened no longer than two minutes. Then he became angry, told me I had been too impressed by the USA. Everything over there was sheer bluff, he said. He turned his back on me and let me stand there. Herr Riedel . . . I am afraid for Germany!'

I said I felt the same, after which the old man fell again into his thoughtful, apparently absent-minded state and roused himself only to shake my hand when I left the car in front of the hotel.

Augsburg next, the Messerschmitt plant, an hour by rail from Munich. I arrived unannounced and nothing had been arranged. I was being shown round by a junior employee who really did not know what to make of me. Suddenly, in one of the hangars, there was Alexander Lippisch, designer of the Fafnir sailplane in which I had broken the distance record in 1933.[1] As I had heard in the Frankfurter Hof, Alex was working on the tiny, tailless rocket plane.[2] I was in luck since one of them was being prepared for a test flight by Heini Dittmar. How good it was to see them both again! I did not mention that I been told about the flights in this extraordinary little aircraft so soon after arriving last month. What good would it have done, other than to cause him to distrust his friend? The secret had escaped by now.

And suddenly, there was Hanna Reitsch too! I was astonished almost beyond belief that I should meet all three together here without any appointment or preparation but of course they worked there practically every day just now. Hanna was also playing a role in testing these little aircraft which, I discovered, might blow up if the motor failed or the fuel, a mixture of highly volatile and unstable substances, was mishandled. The new, more powerful motor for this particular version was not ready yet. The Komet that stood there in front of us was to be towed up as a glider by a twin-engined Messerschmitt 110. The rocket plane had a pair of wheels which had to be dropped soon after leaving the ground, just like my Kranich. After releasing from the tow at a great height the aircraft would glide down to land on a skid, also like a sailplane but at God knows what speed.

[1] The distance of 229 km on 7 June 1933 was the longest flight made by a sailplane at the time but was not accepted officially as a record since it did not exceed the previous best flight also done in the Fafnir by Gunther Groenhoff by the requisite 5 per cent. Riedel later flew the Fafnir in Brazil during the expedition there in 1934.

[2] Lippisch in 1972 explained that the rocket plane had originally not been intended for military use but was for research at transonic speeds. The basic aerodynamic design had been done when he was at the DFS Sailplane Research Institute but was transferred to Messerschmitt at Augsburg when construction began and the *Luftwaffe* required it as a fighter. Dittmar's flight on 2 October 1941 reached Mach 0.84, 1004 km/h. Lippisch did not believe the Me 163, with a larger motor and very much over-weight, would make a successful military aircraft. He quarrelled with Messerschmitt and resigned from the project in 1943. (See *Air Enthusiast*, September 1972, pp. 136-50.)

After watching Heini being towed off I was able to see Professor Messerschmitt. We had known each other since 1923 when I had lived for a few weeks at the gliding school he started on the Wasserkuppe. He was designing and building sailplanes at that time, eventually to fit an engine in one of them. After our greetings and reminiscences I began to tell him why I had come and launched into my usual explanations. He stopped me and suggested I should say everything to the assembled directors at a meeting he would call tomorrow. Meanwhile he would arrange for a car to take me to see the new Leipheim plant. We would meet again at 10 am the next day in the boardroom.

At Leipheim I saw the production of the huge Gigants, the Messerschmitt 321 and 323. The 321 was an enormous glider of 55 metres span (180 feet) which had been used on the Eastern Front to carry supplies to forward areas. I recalled the flimsy contraptions that Messerschmitt, not much more than a boy like myself then, had built in 1920 with his older friend and mentor, Friedrich Harth. In those gliders the pilot had perched under the wing within a cage-like structure of tubes and had two poles to steer with. Could anyone have imagined that a monstrous thing like the Messerschmitt Gigant would come from such beginnings? It was designed to be made from simple and cheap materials, steel tubes, wood and fabric. Just a bigger Harth-Messerschmitt glider but far larger than any existing powered aeroplane! It had to be towed up by a four-engined bomber, or even a special Heinkel with five motors. They had tried a 'troika' of three Messerschmitt 110s working together, six engines in all. This had proved highly dangerous because the towing planes had insufficient power. They could hardly reach flying speed and if one should stall the whole lot would usually crash. The 323 was a six-engined version which was more successful, though terribly slow and cumbersome. The labour force in the factory was mostly Russian prisoners-of-war.

The meeting with the big chiefs of the Messerschmitt firm took place next morning and I went through everything as before. The effect was the same as with the Junkers people. Someone suggested that only a direct report to the Führer or perhaps Göring would have any effect. These people were quick to say that there should be a massive increase in fighter production, a big preparation of aerial defences against the bombing hordes. I myself stressed only the need to evacuate people from the cities. I did not believe that fighters would be able to stop the attacks. I had wondered about their rocket plane. Now I knew. It could never be ready in sufficient numbers to make any real difference.

As the conference ended Messerschmitt suggested that I ought to come to work for him on the administrative side. It would be useful for them to have someone who knew the big shots in the Air Ministry and who was used to plain speaking when it was needed. Although I was nominally an officer of the *Luftwaffe*, he could make a good case for me as a qualified engineer and pilot to be released to work in the industry which was in urgent need of people like myself. He made sure that a suitable letter would be written by the technical director, Herr Croneiss, on my behalf. For my part I was delighted at the prospect of getting away from Berlin to do something more useful and I was impressed by Croneiss. What, though, would my duties be? I was handed on to the technical manager who explained to me about the difficulties they were having with the Messerschmitt 210, intended to replace the old 110 type. I had heard some of this before from Lucht.

'It is a long and sad tale,' I was told. 'The plane was unstable and the *Luftwaffe* wouldn't accept any more after the first small production run. They had a tendency to spin in. But we have transformed it now, chiefly by adding a bit over a metre to the length of the fuselage and slots to improve the wing tip stalling characteristics. It has quite good flying qualities now and should go into production.' As we spoke, one of these twin-engined planes flew low and fast over the airfield as if to make his point for him. 'But there is another problem, not technical. Our exalted *Reichsmarschall* Göring heard about these problems because the front line squadrons were needing faster aircraft urgently to replace their 110s. From that day on Hermann demanded almost daily reports on our progress. Our production lines and tooling, everything, was all geared up for the 210 and we had stacks of components ready, but couldn't produce anything until the design had been sorted out. Well, we were just about ready to go when, a few weeks back Hermann lost all patience. He got quite hysterical and ordered that our production lines should immediately go back to produce more of the old 110. That was bad enough but even worse he ordered that all the tools and jigs and everything for the 210 should be destroyed. Herr Croneiss took it on his own responsibility to countermand this order without telling the *Reichsmarschall*. That was a big risk, you know, but it would have been absolutely crazy to do as we were told. Well, you can see the problem now. Here we are, the 210 is ready but we dare not start building it because we are supposed to have destroyed all the tools weeks ago.' So he ended, and looked at me. I understood now what they had in mind for me! They needed some naïve soul brave enough, or stupid enough, to go ahead and tell the truth even if it was dangerous. Well, I had no ambitions now beyond bringing the war to an end as soon as possible. Was this the way to do it? I would have to wait to see if the Messerschmitt firm could pull the required strings.

In the train on the way back from Augsburg to Munich I again met Dr Maerkel who had attended my talk. He was the Company's lawyer. He chatted quietly with me and agreed that the only hope was for me somehow to approach the Führer himself. This was the only way to get through all the red tape and the great difficulty caused by Göring who seemed to stand in the way of everything.

'Do you know the name Colin Ross?' Maerkel asked. I did, for Ross was a famous writer who had published many travelogues. Although not really an explorer his name was as well-known in Germany as that of Amundsen.[3]

'You should meet him,' said Maerkel. 'He will be able to help. He is one of Hitler's most trusted friends, standing outside the state machinery and with direct access. He could either introduce you personally or at least see that a written report from you reached the Führer quickly. What about it?' My hopes were once again raised and I quickly agreed to meet Ross, if it could be fixed up. I did meet him on the following Sunday at Maerkel's home, although on this occasion, in the presence of several other guests, I was unable to do more than mention lightly some of the things I wanted to talk about. To my relief he understood and invited me to his own home for a private dinner.

There he listened to what I had to say and in response to my final question agreed that he could get me into the presence. 'You know how to speak,' he said, 'and you would make an impression, no doubt of that. I am not an expert in aviation but I understand enough to see that what you have to say might have important consequences.' This sounded promising and I believed that this time I had reached the right man. He said I should hear from him soon about it and turned to other matters. What, for instance, was my assessment of the radio propaganda that was broadcast to the USA from Germany. I decided that I could speak freely. He was not a fanatical Nazi.

'The story that the Jews rule America is only laughed at over there,' I said. I had heard so much along these lines since coming back to Germany that I could not keep quiet about it. In the illustrated papers Roosevelt, Kaiser the shipbuilder, Morgan the banker and others were described as Jewish or of Jewish descent. Pictures of these and other personalities were printed, retouched to show their allegedly Jewish features. It all seemed like madness to me, sheer paranoia, a kind of obsessive search for Jewish influence everywhere behind the scenes. So I told Ross. How could such small minorities have the all-pervading influence they were supposed to have? I even quoted Helen to him. From a Catholic viewpoint she said that

[3] Colin Ross published some dozen travel books with Brockhaus of Leipzig. He is mentioned once in Goebbels' diaries as being with Hitler on 15 March 1940, a 'very likeable man'. He should not be confused with the American journalist who wrote under the same name but whose real name was Harry Roskolenko.

in times of trouble people search for scapegoats and seize on the nearest they can find or imagine. Her own family had suffered to some extent, meeting prejudice from Protestants in her home town. It didn't matter what you were, black, Catholic, Jewish, Asian, it made no difference, you would be blamed when things went wrong. I developed this theme a little and finished by saying that if American people happened to pick up such stuff from Germany on their short-wave radio, they would switch off or change to another frequency. Ross heard me out.

'You are right, Herr Riedel,' he said afterwards. 'This is a very sad business altogether. But I must warn you. If you are to meet the Führer you must say nothing of this whatever. Never try to talk to him about these things. There are two topics about which it is altogether impossible to speak to him: Jews and Bolsheviks!'

Constantly I found my hopes were too naïve. I had supposed that Hitler himself, preoccupied with matters of high policy, was above such things and could not be responsible for the atrocities we had heard of. This was a common view among the ordinary people I met. If something was obviously going wrong they would say, 'If only the Führer knew, he would put it right.' I had begun to blame Göring and some of the other high-ups like Himmler for everything, rather as my friends in the aircraft industry tended to do. Now I was being told by someone who knew Hitler well, that the trouble lay at the very top. Was our leader totally mad? Would any kind of rational argument or statement of fact have any effect, if this was so?

The time had come for me to leave. Before he showed me out, Ross spoke seriously to me again. Had I been too outspoken with him? Did he fear that he could not trust me to speak tactfully if I should meet Hitler? Perhaps he was right.

'I think we should consider your position again, Herr Riedel. There is a difficulty that we cannot afford to overlook. You are an officer of the *Luftwaffe* and you will be expected to make your report first to Göring before going to the Führer. The *Reichsmarschall* is vain and would be furious if he thought you had passed him by. He would make sure that nothing was done about it. It would be a mistake to make an enemy of him.'

So I was back exactly where I had been. Dornier had told me what I might expect from fat Hermann. I should be considered pro-American, a defeatist. Ross heard my protests but insisted that this must be the correct procedure. He would introduce me to someone who would open the way for me to Göring. That was all he would do. After I had seen him, an interview with Hitler might be possible but even if that happened, I should have to guard my tongue. It was another let-down.

In September I signed a contract with Messerschmitts which was subject to my obtaining release from my present service. This would come through eventually. Now it was just a matter of Schwenke finding something for me to do until I could leave. Remembering the contacts I had made in Washington he appointed me to act as liaison officer with the Japanese Air Attachés who needed as much technical information as they could get from Germany and who wished to arrange for the importation of war material from us. Their offensive in the Pacific had made rapid progress at first but now they were losing impetus. They must soon meet the American power.

I barely had time to explore this new responsibility before Schwenke called me in to meet General Aschenbrenner who had asked to see me. Aschenbrenner had been our Air Attaché in Moscow. I was not sure what this meeting signified and felt apprehensive but the General was a relatively young man who proved friendly and spoke to me quite informally. What had I thought of America, and what was it like to be home again? All my bitterness and disappointment began to pour out again. Aschenbrenner listened for a time, laughed occasionally and before long stopped me.

'My dear Riedel, you don't have to tell me all this!' Now he was not laughing. 'It all happened to me, exactly the same.' He half turned to Schwenke who nodded in confirmation. 'Reports, reports, reports! How many reports did I write? How many times did I try to warn them when I was visiting Berlin? It wasn't just me. Koestring, Major-General Koestring our Military Attaché, the ambassador himself, Graf von Schulenburg too. It was useless, a complete and utter waste of time. The Führer always knows better. He decided to make war against the Soviets and nothing whatever would make him change his mind. No, Riedel, do not try to report personally to the Führer. He will simply brush you off like a fly. Worse, you will get swatted! In any case, the men surrounding him won't let you anywhere near him with this story. Never mind what your influential friends tell you, you will never have a chance to speak to him. Your smooth Bötticher had the Führer's ear for a short time when you came back from Washington but he did not say what you have told me now. As he described things, there was little cause for alarm. I was there, I heard him make his report. Don't try it, my friend. Don't try it, you will only get your neck broken and it won't do the slightest good.'

After he had gone, Schwenke kept me back in his office. He and I had become quite friendly by now.

'I told you it was useless, right at the start. The staff know perfectly well that we have no reserves but it is hopeless to try to get through to our leaders. It only makes them furious and then there's trouble. You have done the best you can. Your duty was complete when you handed in your final report and you have nothing whatever to reproach yourself with. Let me tell you a bit about my own experiences. You know, in January 1941 the Russians sent a big delegation of engineers to Germany. We were supposed to be friends with them then! Well, they were taken round all our armament works, saw Krupps, I. G. Farben, the lot. One day they went all over an armoured car factory, one of the biggest we have. They saw the cars on the assembly lines in full production. Afterwards, the head man of their lot turned to our man and said "That's very interesting, but where do you have your mass production plant?" Can you believe it? This fellow was under the impression that all he had seen was an experimental works turning out a few cars for testing. That one question revealed more about their own industry than any report from the *Abwehr* could have done. In any case, the *Abwehr* doesn't get much of value from the USSR.'

Maybe this was just an ironic tale, I thought, but it had a point for me. Preoccupied with my own frustrations I had not till now given any thought to the eastern enemy. Like everyone else I had been led to believe that the Red Army was broken, short of material, losing everywhere. I still had not learned to disbelieve everything the propaganda machine was telling us.

'That's just an example,' Schwenke went on, 'but listen. The Russians themselves saw to it that we were thoroughly informed about their power, we didn't need spies. They wanted us to know their strength because they never trusted Hitler. They thought a show of power could deter him. After the delegation from their side had gone home they invited us to send a similar one to them, in April the same year. There were thirty-two of us, I went with them, under Engineer-General Günther Tschersich.[4] After all, I am the head of the *Luftwaffe*'s foreign armaments section. We went everywhere, saw everything we wanted to see and a good deal more. They went out of their way to impress us with their strength and they made no secret of why they were doing it. "You have seen how strong we are. Wouldn't we be a dangerous enemy?" The message they were giving us was as clear as that. They guessed what Hitler was thinking of and this was a plain warning.'

'Tschersich was born in Russia, you know. His family fled from the Bolsheviks and they lost everything. Of course he hated the communists

[4] Günther Tschersich, Head of Technical Planning, 'managed to acquire great influence over his chief (Udet) but placed his interest in the development of aircraft at the expense of their procurement' (Cooper, op cit., p. 29). Milch described him as one of Udet's 'evil spirits' (Cooper, p. 31). He was dismissed with the most scathing remarks by Milch on 9 Sept 1941 (Cooper, p. 277).

and most of our delegation had been picked by him. He made sure they were juniors, 'yes' men, people who would never dare to oppose him. Every evening after we had been to a factory or something, we would sit down and review the day. Tschersich always picked out weaknesses we had noticed and concentrated on them. He would not admit that what we had really seen was a growing, mighty power. He was blinded by hate and made sure that his underlings saw things his way too. When we got home he wrote the report. What came out of that you can imagine. Everything he said distorted the real picture, picked on the little weaknesses and made them huge, passed lightly over the massive strengths, encouraging our chiefs to write the Russians off. There were only two of us who dared to submit anything more realistic and it got us nowhere except into the black books. So you see, I do understand how you feel. But there's nothing to be done, believe me. I told you, lay off!'

'But wouldn't the USSR have attacked us anyway? If they were arming, as you say, what was the purpose of that?'

'Riedel, consider. Hitler wrote *Mein Kampf* when? Back in 1924! Do you suppose the Russkies didn't read it? If not immediately, then at least when he had become Reich Chancellor! And what's in there, from their viewpoint? He raged against communism. He declared the Ukraine should be part of the German empire. They were hardly likely to ignore that. You can't afford to do nothing when someone is constantly saying you should be beaten up and robbed. They had to start arming themselves once Hitler came to the top. He undoubtedly started it. Look at what their last five year plan did. It was supposed to raise the living standards of the people. Instead, they diverted huge efforts from making tractors to building tanks. Who could blame them.' Having started he seemed desperate to speak his mind fully.

'And you remember Lipetsk?' I shook my head.

'No, I'd forgotten, you weren't ever there. But does it seem to you the Soviets were preparing to attack Germany before Hitler? We got along with them fine then. Why should they have helped us to build a secret air force like that if they imagined they would have to fight us? Our diplomats in Moscow were always convinced that they wanted peace.'

'Too late now,' I muttered.

'Yes, too late. Much too late. Something else I can tell you about Schulenburg, our ambassador in Moscow in 1941. Just a few days before the army advanced into Russia he came rushing to Berlin in a desperate effort to persuade the Führer not to attack. He knew the true position. He was not even admitted to the presence! Poor Schulenburg wept in public, became hysterical and suffered a nervous collapse. He was sent back to

Moscow having accomplished absolutely nothing.'[5] Schwenke broke off here. He had a meeting to go to.

I had a letter from Colin Ross, saying he had written to his mysterious highly placed personality and that I should soon hear something about meeting Göring. I never did.

[5] Frederic Werner, Graf von Schulenburg, ambassador in Moscow from 1934, was an aristocrat of the old school. In an address to the *Wehrmacht* as early as 1937 he warned of the growth of Soviet power although later he estimated that it would take four years for the Red Army to recover from Stalin's purges of the officer corps. His despair when Hitler launched Operation *Barbarossa* was genuine. Following the Stauffenberg assassination attempt of 1944 Schulenburg, who would have been foreign minister after the intended coup, was executed with the others. Like Peter Riedel he seems to have been intensely patriotic and driven by a strong sense of duty but held in contempt the men who had risen with Hitler.

15

Heinkel's Mankiller

Unlimited co-operation with Japan had been decreed from on high and Milch ordered the setting up of the special department in which I was now to work: Armament Aid Japan. Ambassador Oshima had pleaded with Hitler for help. Despite initial delight at the effectiveness of their aircraft the Japanese knew they could not maintain superiority for long. The Pacific campaign had extended their forces to their limit.

I faced new responsibilities. The first thing I had to look at was a long wish list from our allies which made clear that they were very much in need of help. They wanted to examine several types of aircraft and aero-engines, there were some secret instruments they would like to buy. The 'Wurzburg' radar apparatus was high in their priorities and in addition they needed several hundred of our most up-to-date machine tools. It seemed to me that this war was going to be won by machine tools.

Even though Japan was practically on the other side of the globe, deliveries must be made. Small items could go by submarine; bigger cargoes would require blockade-running ships from Bordeaux or Brest on the French Coast. Both looked desperately difficult. The alternative of aerial transport was considered. The planes would have to leave from Northern Finland to follow a Great Circle route to Manchuria over the sub polar regions and north-eastern Siberia where we supposed the Soviet defences were negligible. The Japanese dared not risk a quarrel with the Soviet Union. While allied against Germany with the USA and Britain, who were also at war with Japan, the USSR was neutral in the Pacific war. The flights would have to be made by German aircraft and aircrews.

The idea of letting our equipment go in this way was repugnant to some of those I had to deal with on our side.

'Why should we give away our technical secrets to these Asians?' yelled one colonel at me. 'They will be our enemies in the next war!'

'Colonel, let's first win this war with them on our side. Never mind the next.' I would more fairly have said, 'Let's see if it is possible to win this war!' but that would have been defeatism and highly dangerous to say in the circumstances. This officer was not the only one who revealed a complete ignorance about the realities of our position. The racist doctrines poured out by the Nazi party did not help. Often I was able to overcome deliberate obstruction only by proving that my assignment was created by special order from the summit.

Working with the Japanese was not altogether easy either. Once or twice a week I would walk to the Tiergartenstrasse where the Imperial Japanese Embassy building stood. The ground floor housed the professional diplomats and the only occasion I entered there was for a ceremonial banquet given in honour of General von Bötticher. One floor up were the Japanese Naval Attachés and on the top floor their army men. Both services had their own separate air arm, an organisation similar to the USA at that period. This meant a great deal of duplication. I would spend an hour or so in discussion with their Naval Air Attachés, then had to bundle up all my papers and climb the stairs to do it all again with the army men. After a few times I suggested to both groups that we were really wasting a lot of time and energy. Could we not get everyone together? I was met with polite nods and agreement; yes, it would be better, and they would arrange it next time.

The next time came and I made my way to the three naval gentlemen with whom I had to speak, Commanders Yoshima, Iwaya and Nomaguti. I was ushered into the usual small room barely large enough for the four of us to sit at the table. I supposed they had forgotten about my suggestion but as we sat down there was the sound of feet outside and the door opened. The army Colonel Inouye came in, with about a dozen companions crowding behind. He bowed and smiled.

'Ah, not enough room . . .' All eyes turned to me in silence.

'Yes, well . . . I see . . . I'll meet you upstairs later,' I said, and the army promptly turned around and trooped out. I sensed some relief among the navy people. The two services never associated if they could avoid it. Even though we were discussing the same aircraft, the same engines, the same armament, the navy and the army would not work together with me even at this level.

Among other things I arranged for the Japanese to visit aircraft factories. One day we were at Cottbus where the Focke-Wulf plant was building the four-engined Condors. In a month Focke-Wulf produced the same number of four-engined aircraft as Ford's Willow Run factory was now turning out in a day. Two days previously Hitler had made a speech in which he talked of calling the American bluff. I had no doubt whose bluff was really being called.

In September we went to Heinkels at Oranienburg, not far from Berlin.[1] Here we saw the Junkers 88 in production under contract while the Heinkel 177, the big four-engined bomber, was being finalised. The Japanese were

[1] Oranienburg was also the site of one of the notorious concentration camps, as mentioned earlier.

very interested in the He 177 which was much larger and heavier than anything they had. While they were looking at it the Director of the plant, Herr Heyn, asked me about my experiences in the USA. After a few minutes he suggested that I should talk to him and his colleagues in the same way as I had done in Dessau, Munich and Augsburg.

'I will invite Colonel Theodor Rowehl, who is the CO of the special squadron for high altitude research, based here.[2] He has a lot of influence, and is greatly respected. Won the Knights Cross early in the war. He should hear what you have to say too.' I agreed and several days later returned to give my talk. Rowehl did not turn up, which disappointed me. The others reacted very much as I expected but I had no high hopes of anything arising out of it at this stage. I was pleased then, after all, to get a special invitation from Rowehl to have dinner and spend an evening with him and his officers. Accordingly, a few days later I travelled to Oranienburg again to meet the stratospheric fliers.

I was greeted frigidly by Rowehl himself, so much so that the young officers nearby noticed and became embarrassed. There was none of the instant friendship usually shown by pilots. As Rowehl was showing me to my seat for dinner he stopped and spoke loudly enough for everyone to hear.

'I have been informed,' he said, in the sudden silence, 'that you have an excessively high opinion of the American Air Force, Herr Riedel. I hope this is not so. I am looking forward to hearing you refute the charge.' This was too much and I was angered, answering him in an equally forceful manner.

'Colonel, I have very little to say about the American Air Force. I am an engineer and my particular task was to observe the American Aircraft *Industry*. I am not for or against anything but I shall tell you only what I believe to be the truth.' The dinner was served and eaten in embarrassment and near silence. Rowehl spoke not a word to me throughout, conversing only with the young pilot on his right who had the place of honour because he was leaving the squadron. Afterwards we were ushered into an adjacent room, some fifteen officers and myself.

'Well, you can start now,' said Rowehl, turning half away from me as if to dissociate himself from everything I said. Fifteen minutes later when I was well into my talk, he turned back to face me and gave his total attention. When I had finished he made a complete apology, saying he had

[2] Rowehl himself had suggested to the RLM that high altitude reconnaissance aircraft should be produced. The Henschel 130 A reached 43,309 feet (13,200 m), altitude in 1940. The Hs 130 A 06 of November 1943 reached 50,750 feet (15,470 m). It spanned 29 metres (95.2 feet). Although driven by piston engines these aircraft were somewhat like the later U-2 high altitude spy plane and served a similar purpose (J. R. Smith and A. Kay, *German Aircraft of the Second World War*, Putnam, 1972).

been misinformed about me. He was anxious that my message should be heard at higher levels in the service. The rest of the evening passed in better spirits. His squadron were flying extraordinary Henschel reconnaissance aircraft with pressure cabins, at heights over 40,000 feet (12,200 m).

Two days later Rowehl turned up in my Berlin office. A Colonel on active service wearing the Knight's Cross was a rare sight in these quarters.

'Come along, we'll go to see Vorwald,' he said. Major-General Vorwald was the current chief of the Technical Department. We went at once to his ante-room but there Rowehl learned that even he could not walk in to the office of a high official in this way. We did not get through. Somewhat cooled, Rowehl took me to Colonel Pasewaldt, the next man down in the hierarchy. Pasewaldt was another old acquaintance from the Wasserkuppe days and welcomed us heartily. He listened to our requests with goodwill, but in the end, what could he do? He told us he had little influence. Our effort came once more to a hopeless end. I was no longer surprised and in some ways felt almost relieved. I had done my best and was increasingly aware that I was endangering myself. Rowehl departed, much chastened. I never met him again.

General von Gablenz approved my discharge from the Air Ministry with effect from 1 November 1942. Helen and I counted the days until we should be able to leave Berlin, which was becoming an intolerable place to live though, as yet, hardly any bombs had fallen there.[3] I continued to work out my time as well as I could for the Japanese aid programme although I could not see that much was possible. Blockade-running ships were rarely successful in getting through, often being captured or sunk. Shortly before I left Berlin a large Japanese submarine did arrive in a French port. It was loaded there with valuable instruments and technical drawings because it was considered certain to reach Japan on its return voyage. We heard later that it did get through the blockade but, ironically, struck a Japanese mine outside Singapore harbour and was lost, so our material never arrived. Six months later we heard that another Japanese submarine carrying Commander Yoshikawa, who had been one my friends, disappeared without trace on its way through.

When November came I cleared my desk but found myself suddenly in a position of great uncertainty after all. Before going to Messerschmitts I was expected to renew my flying licence by putting in a few hours in some modern aircraft. I had not flown a multi-engined aircraft since 1938 when I left SCADTA in Colombia. Instead of going at once to Augsberg, Helen

---

[3] The first RAF attack on Berlin had been on the night of 25-6 August 1940, by 81 aircraft in reprisal for bombs on London, followed by five more reprisal raids in December. Very little damage was done. In 1941 a raid by 169 aircraft caused the deaths of nine people and injuries to 32, with losses of 120 aircrew. (Terraine, *The Right of the Line*, Hodder & Stoughton, 1985).

and I went to Rechlin for the flying course. After this I was expecting to go immediately as a personal assistant to Croneiss, who was now managing director of the whole Messerschmitt concern. But Croneiss had a sudden stroke which put him in hospital and while we were at Rechlin another stroke killed him. I was very sorry because I had liked him and was sure we would have worked well together. It was not clear at all what work I should be doing with Messerschmitt now.

I began again to think of ways to escape from Germany altogether. When in the air at Rechlin I thought sometimes how easy it would be just to keep flying north to Sweden or south to Switzerland. But Helen must be with me and I could not do any such thing when there was a checking instructor by my side. If we were to get away it must be by legal means. I knew that several people who had been in America when we were there were now in the German Embassy in Stockholm. Thomsen himself, the former Washington Ambassador, was now Ambassador to Sweden and the Press attaché, Hebb, who, like me, had an American wife, was there too. Schwenke, whom I still saw from time to time, hinted to me that a technical assistant for aeronautical matters was needed there for the Military Attaché. With my previous experience in Washington, who else but Peter Riedel was qualified for such a position? I showed interest and Schwenke agreed to recommended me to Vorwald. He would pass my name on to the *Attaché Gruppe* but I was not at all hopeful. They had said last year, 'We have nothing for you.' I was not even a real member of the *Luftwaffe*.

While we were wondering about this a telegram came from Ernst Heinkel at Rostock on the Baltic coast where his main works were sited. He had heard something about my talks to the other firms and wanted me to go to Rostock to tell him and his people about the USA. I had never met Heinkel and was pleased that he had heard something about me. He was one of the very few Germans in aeronautics who had never done any gliding. A few days later we arrived at Warnemünde.[4]

The familiar ritual followed, the same reactions, the same feeling of hopelessness on my part, but Heinkel would not leave it there.

'Write me a report, Herr Riedel. Put it on paper at once, as quickly as you can, and I shall take it to the responsible men. Milch or Göring must see it.' I was not enthusiastic but felt I must make the effort. We had been back in Germany now almost six months. The Americans had not yet appeared in German skies. It was not too late to prepare for them. I spent a day writing a paper which I arranged as a technical comparison of the

[4] Heinkel founded his company at Warnemünde in 1922, established the Rostock works in 1932 and in May 1937 opened a very modern plant at Oranienburg. In 1942 his design offices were transferred to Vienna-Schwechat.

American aircraft industry, size, methods of production and factory layout, against the German plants I had visited. The comparison was enough to show how utterly inadequate our response would be unless there were quite radical changes in policy. I hoped in this way to avoid any charge of defeatism, letting the facts speak for themselves. I was too naïve still.

On delivering the paper to Heinkel I expected him to read it immediately and make comments, since he had pressed me to get it done so soon. He had a new idea, however, and laid the document aside for the time being.

'I heard about Croneiss,' he said. 'What are you going to do now?'

'I still have a contract with Messerschmitt. But I don't know, maybe he doesn't want me now.'

'Would you like to come here?' He explained that following the visit earlier in the year of the Japanese naval personnel, escorted by me, he had concluded an agreement with them for the setting up of an aircraft factory near Tokyo. He would need someone on the spot there to act as his representative. Since I had already established good relations with the Japanese and had some understanding of them, even having picked up a little of their language, as well as an engineering and flying background, it seemed to him I should be the ideal person to go there. What about it? It would mean a few months training in his works first then I should have to travel to Japan by submarine or blockade-runner. It would be my job to advise the Japanese and keep him in touch with the work as it progressed.

The idea appealed to me greatly. Anything to get out of Germany, especially since the Messerschmitt job didn't look so attractive now. Of course I must ask Helen what she thought but I was sure she would go with me wherever it might be and however dangerous to get there.

Full of this new prospect we went back to Rechlin to complete the flying course. Meanwhile I got in touch with Professor Messerschmitt. He admitted that since Croneiss had died the situation had changed and he was quite willing to release me. Accordingly, I accepted Heinkel's offer. Since I was going to work for him it was obvious that while at Rechlin I should take every chance to study the big bomber, the He 177, called the Greif (Griffon), several of which were there undergoing all kinds of tests. I had already heard from several sources that things were not going well.

The basic concept of this aircraft was similar to the American Flying Fortress or Liberator, a long-range strategic bomber capable of carrying heavy bomb loads and striking distant targets, with powerful armament against fighters. The wing span was 31.44 metres (103 feet) almost the same as the Fortress but it was somewhat heavier and had slightly less engine power. Originally it had been intended to use two very powerful engines of 2,000 horsepower each but nothing suitable existed yet. Therefore it was decided to use four 1,000 hp engines arranged as Siamese twins. On each wing two engines were mounted very close together with gears coupling them to drive a single propeller. The bomber therefore looked like a very large twin-engined plane but it was not so. Because of its slim lines when the prototype flew in 1939 this heavy bomber was faster than any of the fighters of that time making it almost impossible to catch. Fighters had improved now while the He 177 had suffered a whole series of disasters.

Since the original plans had been drawn up the requirements had been increased with the intention of making this one aircraft type capable of many different functions. The He 177 was now also required to be capable of dive-bombing, launching torpedoes against ships and doing long-range reconnaissance flights at high altitudes. Hence it must fly fast and high for the reconnaissance, low and slow for torpedoing and be extremely strong for the dive-bombing. Every change meant more delays, more complications, more structural weight. The design had become increasingly complicated and there had been an endless string of failures.

After three years it was still in the experimental stage. More than thirty of the type had crashed during test flights and many crews had been killed. One of the worst problems was with the coupled engines which overheated. Most of the accidents had been caused by engine fires but nearly as many had resulted from stalling and spinning. The cause of the spins had still not been found.

I had a chance at Rechlin to compare the He 177 with a captured British Stirling bomber which stood nearby. The Stirling was a very simple aircraft designed for one purpose only – long-range bombing. In this role it was very effective and not required to do anything else.[5] Its simplicity made mass production and maintenance in the field very straightforward. The He 177 was quite a marvel of clever engineering, looking like a racehorse next to a carthorse, but it was complex, temperamental and unreliable.

When they heard of the plan for me to go to Japan with Helen, the naval people in Berlin refused point blank to let her travel by sea or under it. All blockade-runners were counted as warships and the presence of women was totally forbidden. Heinkel nevertheless told me to continue my training at Rostock and we should hope for a change of attitude later. If the Japanese pressed for it when the time came some arrangements might be made. Heinkel himself was still thinking of the possibility of flying one of his bombers at very high altitudes to Manchuria by the Siberian route. So during the first days of December 1942 I found myself in the modern

[5] The Short Stirling was the first four-engined monoplane heavy bomber introduced into the RAF, entering squadron service in August 1940. A total of about 1,630 were built as bombers, later versions being used for transport and glider towing. As a front line bomber it was considered obsolete by mid-1943, having been superseded by the Avro Lancaster and Handley Page Halifax.

administration building of the Rostock Heinkel plant. My initiation consisted in a systematic inspection of the different departments in the factory. Everything I saw confirmed the judgements I had incorporated in my paper for Heinkel. Rostock had been heavily bombed by the RAF nine months previously, over three consecutive nights. The centre of the town had been completely destroyed.[6] It was clear to me that this would be the fate of every large German town in western Germany or those near the coast.

The factory itself showed few signs of damage. The workshops of steel and concrete had withstood incendiary bombs without difficulty and the high explosives had not demolished them. A single 500 kg bomb had hit the final assembly hangar and blown several half completed aircraft to bits but the debris was quickly removed and production continued next day as usual. The most vital part of the factory had escaped damage in the raids but it was also the most vulnerable. This was the machining shop. It was in an old, wooden building and a few incendiary bombs would have destroyed it. I mentioned this to Heinkel. He knew better then I that if the machines were lost we should never replace them. The German machine tool industry had been unable to fulfil orders for months on end. The only hope was to transfer the machine shop to somewhere safer. The new Heinkel works at Schwechat near Vienna was one obvious choice but Heinkel thought it much too far away. The Heinkel plant depended absolutely on this one workshop and transporting parts to Rostock would be almost impossible. Somewhere about midway between would be much better. What about Saxony, my home region?

'Everybody wants to transfer his plants to Saxony,' Heinkel lamented. 'I believe every square centimetre of factory space there has been taken up but if you want to try, go down there and see what you can find.' I imagined it would not be possible for cities further inland than, say, Stuttgart, to be bombed. Even I was not pessimistic enough to think beyond that.

The next day I was in the beautiful city of Dresden, so far quite undamaged. Here I did find something like an effective economic administration for the war effort. Weaving was a major local industry but any factory building not producing arms was liable to be requisitioned. The officer in charge was a smooth, rather supercilious Major and inclined to brush me off but after explaining the importance of maintaining production

---

[6] The official RAF history gives the dates of the Rostock attacks in 1942 as 23/24 April (161 aircraft), 24/25 (125), 25/26 (128) and 26/27 (107). Twelve bombers were lost. Damage was most serious on the last of the four nights when 55 of the aircraft were directed to attack the Heinkel factory itself and 52 to the town. Goebbels wrote 'The Führer is in extremely bad humour about poor anti-aircraft defence ... the *Luftwaffe* wasn't adequately prepared and this alone made damage to the Heinkel works possible.' (John Terraine, *The Right of the Line*, Hodder & Stoughton, 1985).

of Heinkel aircraft and the credit that would accrue to him if he should help, he gave way.

'I will show you the last few pearls in my treasure chest!' he said, with a wry smile. I understood that we were among the last firms to seek refuge in this region, already becoming packed with relocated industries.

There were three suitable weaving mills available between Plauen and Adorf, both in open country and not likely to be bombed at night. The owners were resigned by now to their works being taken over and were relatively glad to hear that it was Heinkels who were coming, recognising the importance of our operations. As I was taken through the different departments of one Plauen mill I was amazed to see a huge weaving machine busy making what I could see was an enormous and luxurious carpet.

'Yes, this machine is something very special,' the manager explained. 'It is designed to weave carpets up to twelve metres wide. It doesn't get much use in the normal way but just now we have an order from one of the Gauleiters in the east. He wants a big carpet for his castle there.' The man said no more. He did not know me well enough to reveal his feelings but I suspected he was just as disgusted as myself. A Gauleiter in Poland could order such a luxury when everyone else was expected to cut private needs to less than the minimum. Comment was unnecessary. My choices of location were approved and the entire Heinkel machine shop was transferred with very little delay. I suppose the Gauleiter got his carpet too.

Meanwhile, what of my report? One day Heinkel called me and said, 'I have to see Milch in Berlin tomorrow about the 177. I will give him your paper.' I waited for his return, without much hope. I did not see him at all for days after he got back and he did not send for me. Director Franke had been with Heinkel at the Air Ministry and explained. They had both been savagely criticised by Milch because of the shortcomings of the He 177.

'After Milch had finished his sermon he walked to his desk to get something and there was a break. We were standing there like delinquents. Dr Heinkel whispered to me, "Should I give him Riedel's thing now?" and he pulled the papers half out of his pocket. "No, better not," he said and pushed them back again. So there you are,' Franke said, laughing. It was no surprise to either of us.

Another conversation set me worrying again about the treatment of Jewish people. It was mentioned to me one day that a Heinkel factory had been set up in Poland using both Russian and Polish prisoners as workers. We did not think of them as slaves. The foreign workers we met every day in Rostock, supplied by the Todt organisation, were not ill treated. It was true that they had no option but to work for Heinkel but to Helen and me they seemed contented and were fed at least as well as the German population. She met and was able to speak, in stumbling German on both sides, to the women folk among them as they did their shopping. Surprising numbers of them said they would like to settle in Germany permanently. Their lives at home had not been good even in peace and for the first time now they had security, regular work, shelter and food. But in the Polish factory I learned about there was a constant argument between the Heinkel managers and the local Gauleiter. Was this the same man who ordered the carpet, I wondered? The SS wanted to round up all the Jews in the place and execute them. The aircraft factory could not function without these men, who were on the whole excellent skilled workers. Did the death squads intend to sabotage the war effort? The more one heard about the SS the more barbaric and terrifying they became. But, I thought, the Heinkel management would defend their wretched work people and the insanity of a few brutes would not be allowed to prevail. I had to believe it.

To do some flying was always a relief. Now that my licence had been renewed and arrangements for the Japanese trip were advancing so slowly, when a batch of Heinkel 111 bombers was ready for delivery to the *Luftwaffe* I was often called in as a ferry pilot. The aircraft were flown from Rostock to the military airfield at Barth, only a short trip of about 65 km. I enjoyed being in the company of pilots again. I knew Heinkel's chief ferry pilot, Heinrich, very well since we had been flying students together. I knew Hermann von Oertzen too. He had been an airline pilot in South America on the route between Rio de Janeiro and São Paulo. We had much in common.

Walter Flinsch, a production test pilot, was another old friend who became very close in the next few months. He, like me, had been a *Lufthansa* pilot and now was a First Lieutenant in the *Luftwaffe*. His brother, Bernard, had been a very fine glider pilot. A small man, he had been very successful flying the tiny Windspiel sailplane built by the *Akaflieg Darmstadt* in 1933. This little gem of an aircraft had been built so lightly that one man could lift it despite its span of 12 metres (39.3 feet). I remembered how Bernard had been sitting in the cockpit one day on the airfield at Darmstadt when a powered plane landed on top of the Windspiel, smashing it to bits but fortunately leaving Bernard with only a few bruises. Poor Bernard had been killed recently when testing one of those Messerschmitt Gigants near Regensburg.

Walter himself had been a great athlete, having won Olympic Gold Medals for single scull rowing at Amsterdam and Los Angeles, though he never spoke about these events unless directly questioned. He had served on a squadron operating Focke Wulf Condor planes over the Atlantic, shadowing convoys for the U-boats and occasionally bombing the ships. All the other members of his squadron had been shot down into the sea and killed so his commander reckoned he had done his share and had him posted to a supposedly safer job. Walter had been born in New York and spoke English. He had dual citizenship and his German had a slight American accent of which he was quite unaware. The whole family had come back to Germany with their parents shortly after the end of the first war in 1918 but two of his brothers and their sister had gone back later and, he told me, the two men were now serving in the US Army. Because of our American experience and the fact that we both loved that country, we had much in common. Helen, who still had difficulty following rapid conversation in German, Walter and I spent many hours talking English in the evenings for we all lived in the small Heinkel Hotel at Warnemünde. Another young test pilot often joined us, Herbert Koenitzer. He spoke English well and enjoyed the conversation practice.

Walter told us many stories about his time in the Condors. During the Narvik campaign they had been instructed to concentrate on British submarines and warships but on one occasion when he was only a Sergeant Pilot the young and reckless Lieutenant in command of his Condor had ordered an attack on a tiny coastal ferry steamer, obviously carrying Norwegian civilians out to one of the islands. When he had realised what the target was Walter deliberately upset the bomb aimer by yawing as the bombs dropped, so missing the little ship by a kilometre. He had assured the angry Lieutenant that turbulence in the air was responsible.

Walter also told me that during the time he was based near Bordeaux his mother and an aunt had actually been arrested by the Gestapo. They had both joined the Christian Science church which was a proscribed organisation under the Nazis. He had, with the backing of his commanding officer, Field Marshal Sperrle, flown immediately to his home town and personally gone to the jail to demand his mother's release. The Gestapo had not dared to stop him, in his uniform and coming straight from active service. But his poor aunt, over sixty years old, had been sent to a concentration camp for six months.

'Walter,' I asked, 'why ever did you decide to stay in Germany? Why, when you saw how things were, why didn't you go back to the USA?'

'We were only children when we came back, and later I just didn't think it fair to leave my parents. By that time I owed everything to this country, I had even competed in the Olympics under the German flag. I was trained as a pilot here, flew for *Lufthansa*, I felt absolutely tied to Germany. When war looked like starting I did seriously consider going to the USA but I couldn't bear the idea when it came to it. There's many of us in the same situation. We opposed the Nazis from the very beginning but still felt we had to serve our country. Once the war started, one could not change sides.'

I knew the feeling.

One day Koenitzer came to me in some agitation. He was worried about Walter who was, he told me, in danger.

'Let me be frank with you, Herr Riedel. You have no idea what intrigues go on in our department.'

'Go on,' I said, assuring him he could speak as freely as he wished. I had noticed already some division within the test flying group. The chief scientist in this section was a young, arrogant fellow who threw his weight around, bullying people in a loud voice, but he never took any risks himself, always staying on the ground when anything unusual was to be done. The chief test pilot was rather the same sort of man. I remembered him as a competent but not outstanding glider pilot belonging to the Dresden *Akaflieg*. Now he was apparently always ready to send someone else off rather than flying himself.

'It is about the He 177. You know that the attempt was made to equip some *Luftwaffe* squadrons with the monster though we all knew it was not ready. There has been so much pressure . . . Anyway, far too many accidents, young pilots stalling and spinning-in. The *Luftwaffe*, Göring himself, is insisting that there have to be more stalling tests but instead of giving the job to Rechlin they have shoved it onto us here. It's our baby, they say, we have to clean it up! It is sheer madness, stalling the 177.'

I knew he was right. Small fighter aircraft and trainers have to perform stalls and spins with recovery because in operational use these are normal manoeuvres for small planes. But large, multi-engined, heavy bombers, like airliners, are designed for flying mostly straight and level and making relatively gentle turns. The dive-bombing tests insisted on by Hitler were dangerous enough and several of the prototype 177s had failed, some through control surface flutter, others simply breaking up altogether, usually killing everyone on board. To stall such a big, heavy aircraft deliberately was asking for trouble.

Koenitzer went on. 'We had our routine conference this morning. Nobody had said a word about this. Suddenly our scientific friend brought up the matter of the stalling tests and Walter Flinsch was told he was to do them. It's the chief pilot's job but he's obviously scared to death so he's picked on Walter because he knows he will do as he's told. Walter said he would do it but he wanted the aircraft fitted with an anti-spin drogue parachute and an ejector seat for him in case that didn't work. The boss got quite nasty then. "Göring wants these tests done immediately. Fitting all those gadgets would delay us," he said.'

Koenitzer was obviously hoping I could do something but I had no status or authority whatever. I thought the only hope was to persuade Walter to refuse the job. I spoke to him at length. The whole thing had been sprung on him with no warning and he should ask for the normal procedures to be followed: if his boss wasn't prepared to do these tests himself he should ask for volunteers and Walter, I insisted, should not offer himself unless they did fit the aircraft with the safety devices he was asking for. Despite my appeals and approaches made to higher authorities, Walter set about performing the tests without any special precautions. For several days things apparently went well, the He 177 landing back each time safely.

He came to see me once when half the test programme was done. 'It isn't easy but it is possible. I do it very slowly and carefully, always at a good height, 12 to 15,000 feet, gradually easing the nose up, up, up a little bit more, up, airspeed falling off very gradually, carefully, feeling for the stall, and then away it goes! Usually it just pitches nose down in the usual way and it's easy to recover. So far, if a wing goes down I have been able to get it level again with a big boot full of rudder to keep more or less straight as the nose drops. If the heap really does start spinning I reckon there will be enough height to pull out of it. If not, we'll have to jump!'

The last radio message came from 13,000 feet (3,970 m) altitude. A farmer heard aircraft engines, looked up to see the He 177 come out of the clouds spinning wildly. There was an enormous crash when it hit. Walter Flinsch and his mechanic had tried to escape. The mechanic got out but the escape hatch was in the nose of the aircraft and as he left he was struck by one of the propellers. Both his legs were severed. Even though his parachute opened he was dead when he was found among some trees. Walter's parachute never opened. His body lay on its back fifty metres from the wreck of the aircraft which had fallen near Fürstemberg. Ejector seats would probably have saved them both. Because I had known Walter so well, Heinkel asked me to telephone his family. Helen and I were heartbroken. He had been a good friend to us both, charming, thoughtful, humorous. Now he was gone because idiots in elevated positions were ignorant and cowardly.

I saw many parallels between Walter and myself. He could have returned to the USA before the war began. Driven by a sense of duty and patriotism he had done his utmost to serve Germany and had paid with his life as had his brother Bernard. He loathed Nazism, detested and despised the Gestapo, the rats as he called them. It made no sense at all.

16

Stockholm Spies

We had been back in Germany almost a year. Living in the company hotel we had to survive on the meagre rations. Other people could often supplement their diet by buying extras from farming relatives or friends in the country but we knew nobody of this kind and both of us had lost a good deal of weight. I made the best life I could for us and even bought a small sailing boat, the *Sturmvogel*, for the weekends. It needed a good deal of work to make it useable. The two of us spent some time mending, scraping and varnishing. The wild idea came to me that one day we might just set out for a little sail and go north to Sweden. It would have been crazy. If caught we should both be in a concentration camp at once even if the sea itself did not kill us. We even talked about my smuggling Helen on board a Heinkel bomber and flying it to Sweden. It was not really feasible.

Helen never did get to sail in our little boat. She caught hepatitis which made her very ill. She came through this but began to suffer from periods of breathlessness. We supposed the poor food and the cold, damp Baltic climate was responsible, as well as her recent illness. Walter, before his death, had recommended exercise.

'You need to get out on the beach and do a little trotting,' he said. Helen found she could only trot about five steps! Otherwise she did not complain of any other symptoms although the breathlessness was a nuisance. We expected it to improve with warmer weather and sunshine.

In April 1943 the government decreed that not only men but also all women under forty years old who were not already employed and who had no young family to care for, must undertake some work in the armaments industry. Helen came into this category and since she had her MA in Fine Art from Columbia it seemed reasonable to us that she should work for Heinkel in the drawing office. Heinkel agreed although she would be required to take a short course in technical draughtsmanship to begin with.

It was an official requirement that all prospective employees, which included the many French and Russian workers, should submit to a thorough medical examination before taking their job. Serious epidemics in the workforce had to be avoided. We received a very severe shock. Helen's chest X-ray revealed several shadows on both lungs and she was diagnosed as having tuberculosis. Helen bore the news with good courage, as always, but I was desperately worried for TB killed millions of people throughout the world and there was no real cure. There were no antibiotics or drugs for this disease. Even the causes were not fully understood.

It was urgent that she should get the best possible treatment. At Heinkel's personal request she was immediately admitted to a sanatorium at Amsee near Waren, about 65 km (40 miles) from Rostock. It was a beautiful place beside a lake amid low hills where women and children with lung trouble were cared for by allowing them to rest in rooms with plenty of fresh air, large windows open at all times, night and day, rain or snow. In fine weather the patients would move to reclining chairs outside on the balconies. The food was a little better. Helen used her four months there well. The sanatorium had a kindergarten. She was pleased to talk with the teacher and helped a little for she discovered that with the children she could learn German more easily than with adults whose language was more complicated.

The doctors decided to use pneumothorax to treat her. The idea was to rest each lung in turn to enable the affected places to heal. For this the lung had to be collapsed, which was done by inserting a needle and pumping air into the cavity of the chest outside the lung, compelling it to deflate and remain idle as long as the introduced air was present. The patient had to survive on one lung until the doctors believed the healing process had advanced far enough. To take the air out again required another operation and the lung re-inflated. The other one would then be dealt with in the same way. This was the best treatment available. Helen felt that the doctors, although doing the best they could and individually very kind and attentive to their patients, were driven by the need to get sick people back to work and, in Helen's case, the intention was for her to return to Heinkel as soon as possible. People who had advanced TB were expected to die of it anyway. In most cases the best one could hope for was to slow the progress of the condition.

I felt desperate and believed that Helen's only hope was for her to get away from Germany, preferably to a sanatorium in Switzerland where medical science was very advanced and there were places specialising in treating lung conditions. I supposed they would require payment in the local currency and I had no access to Swiss Francs.

While we were at White Sulphur Springs we Diplomats had continued to draw our salaries in dollars and we had no expenditure. I had left some money behind in a sleeping bank account but brought about $8,000 cash back with me from Washington. This had to be surrendered in exchange for Marks on our arrival. To retain dollars would have been a capital offence. The result was that I had no way of paying hospital bills in Switzerland, even if Helen could go there.

I had heard that one of my old acquaintances, the former German consul in St Louis, one of those who collected press cuttings for me, was now at the consulate in Switzerland. I wrote to him and after enquiries on our behalf he replied that there was a good German sanatorium in Davos which would accept payment in either German or Swiss currency. But now another difficulty presented itself. Despite her American birth, Helen had entered Germany as my wife on a diplomatic passport and she was now regarded by the authorities as a German citizen by marriage. She would not be permitted to go to Switzerland without special permission and a visa. I knew there would be difficulties about this but made the necessary applications and expected to use all my influential friends and contacts to help.

I was prepared to do almost anything to get Helen away but time went on and nothing happened. Her condition did not improve. The only hopeful thing was that it did not seem to get worse. In August I was able to move her out of the Amsee sanatorium to a private one at Todtmoos in the Black Forest, much further away from any danger of bombing and close to the Swiss frontier in case it became possible to move her quickly. The doctor who ran the sanatorium had good relations with the local politicians and, despite his Jewish wife, was able to survive by keeping out of sight as much as possible. Even Nazis might need a good doctor so it paid no one to disturb him. Unfortunately it was much harder for me to visit her now.

No doubt the word that I was becoming desperate went round. I am not sure what happened behind the scenes when Helen's visa application was being considered but one day I heard from Fritz Grosskopf of the *Abwehr* and we met again in Berlin. I suppose I should have expected something of the kind. Once before they had asked for my help in their secret work and I had refused. Now through Grosskopf they applied much greater pressure. They could arrange for the paperwork releasing Helen but nothing would be done for nothing. They knew I had sought the job in Stockholm and no one doubted my ability to do it. Well, they could fix that too but they would expect my full co-operation this time. While being formally attached to the *Attaché Gruppe* again, I would work also for the secret intelligence service, *Abteilung 1*. This was headed by Colonel Georg Hansen, under Canaris, and I should come under the Air Force Technical Intelligence division, one of about a dozen subsections. There was no alternative. If that was required to get Helen out of Germany, I would become an amateur spy.

Things began to move. Soon I was Captain Riedel of the *Luftwaffe* Engineers again and had to get a uniform. I would need it only for occasional formal ceremonies. Helen's visa came through and in the first week of November I took a few days off to move her from Todtmoos to the frontier. My second sister, Annchen, and her husband, an architect, lived permanently in Switzerland but she had a house in Germany near Basel and it was standing empty at present. Helen and I stayed there for a couple of days. Still operating on one lung she was not well and I feared for her. It would be our last time together for we knew not how long and we made the most of it although with much sadness underlying everything. I took her at last to the Basel border post. I had no visa for entry into Switzerland myself. My sister Annchen had agreed to meet her on the other side and to escort her to Davos. We said farewell and she passed through the barrier. It was an enormous relief to know that she was relatively safe and would be well cared for. Neither of us knew if we should ever meet again.

A few days later I left Heinkel. He had guessed by now that the proposed factory in Japan would never come to anything. Further plans were made for flying and shipping material there but nothing of importance ever happened.

Now I had to traipse again round all the offices of the Air Ministry and General Staff in Berlin, pack and see about getting my belongings, my little DKW car and my little boat to Sweden. I managed to arrange for it all to be transported to Stockholm.

There were regular flights by Ju 52 airliners between Berlin and Stockholm but rather than flying I chose to go by the Baltic ferry from Warnemünde to Gedser on the Danish island of Falster and from there to Copenhagen by train. I had assumed that in occupied countries a German officer could travel without formalities but I was not wearing my new uniform. At Warnemünde I presented my ticket for Stockholm with my diplomatic passport to board the ferry. There was a Danish Customs man at the head of the gangway who decided he would put me in my place. Denmark might be under occupation but that did not excuse a German from observing the regulations! I should have applied in Berlin for a Danish visa and I had not done so. It required a lot of argument before eventually I got onto the ferry. The boat and train were crowded with young German soldiers and sailors returning from leave to their units in Denmark and Norway.

I had pleasant memories of Copenhagen because of my famous pre-war soaring flight from Sweden across the Oresund Strait and my enthusiastic welcome on landing. I had won a prize of Kr 1,000 for that. Copenhagen did not seem much changed but now at night there was a curfew. I walked a little distance from my hotel in the late afternoon to a restaurant and found it crowded with Danish people, all looking better fed than their supposed conquerors, the Germans I had left behind in Berlin. Much more food was available than in Germany. I had not yet learned Swedish but German was understood well. The dinner was by far the best meal I had had since getting back to Europe.

My sleep that night was disturbed by sounds of shooting not far away. I did not come awake fully and did not pay much attention. There were many occasions now when nervous troops would start shooting, thinking they saw a raiding aircraft or something suspicious out at sea. Much later when I had access to Swedish newspapers I realised that what I had heard was a genuine street fight between German troops and the Danish resistance. The fact that there was an armed resistance movement in Denmark had not been allowed to reach the public in Germany.

On the evening of 24 November 1943 I arrived in Stockholm.[1] My previous visit at the time of the gliding expedition in 1936 had been in May during bright weather, but November evenings tend to be dull and grey and the end of the year was always a time of profound depression for me. In December 1914 my mother had died and I never fully got over the shock. Without Helen it seemed much worse. I was met at the station by one of the other assistant attachés and escorted to an hotel. Somewhere more permanent would be available before long. On the following morning I presented myself to Colonel von Heimann, the Air Attaché himself. He had been born in St Petersburg for his father had been an admiral in the Czar's navy before the revolution of 1918. The family had escaped to Germany where he had grown up and he was now a professional soldier but with very limited understanding of aviation. His wife had come from Riga in Latvia. They had lost a son in the air fighting over Britain. Heimann was well liked by all the Embassy staff. He was cheerful and easy-going, perhaps too much so. It was a relief to me that he was even-tempered, friendly and without bluster or pomposity, quite unlike General von Bötticher. He asked me what I had been doing since leaving the USA. I told him of my frustrations and forebodings.

'Ha! I know all about it! I used to be Chief of the Department for the USSR in the *Luftwaffe* General Staff. My colleagues and I struggled for weeks to prepare an assessment of the Soviet aircraft industry similar to yours for the USA. Our figures were quite well founded because after the Russian campaign had started we were able to interrogate many prisoners. In spite of the losses they suffered at the beginning we knew they were still producing and impressive number of aircraft. When I gave this report to Colonel Schmidt he glanced over our estimates. "What! So many?" he said. "I can't present these figures to the Führer's headquarters. No, Heimann we must change things a little. Here, 640 fighters per month you say?

---

[1] Berlin was by now under heavy aerial bombardment with a series of very heavy attacks on 18, 22 and 26 November and 2 December. Great damage was done but RAF losses were also heavy.

Nobody will believe it. Let's make it 300, that's better. Twin-engined bombers, 380? Say 130. You must understand, dear boy, it would upset the gentlemen if I let them see this." and he went through the whole thing in the same way! What can we do? Don't worry too much,' he said.

I was re-introduced to Ambassador Thomsen but had almost nothing to do with him afterwards. I saw him from time to time and occasionally was spoken to at the seemingly endless round of lunches, cocktail parties and formal dinners that we could not avoid.

An apartment was arranged for me on Strandvägen which as the name suggests is a way along the strand with a view over Lake Mejnade. It was one of the most fashionable and expensive areas of the city which I should never have been able to afford normally but the rent was paid by the *Abwehr*. I could entertain friends there when I chose. I settled in very comfortably. Now I had to work myself into the new job, which included learning Swedish. Fortunately I have always been able to make rapid progress with a new language and could function well enough after a few weeks.

As in Washington, each of us had newspapers and journals to read in the morning before attending a general meeting at which we reported and shared information with our colleagues. An item that caught my eye quite early was a name I knew. The Americans had set up an organisation called the Office of Strategic Services, responsible for espionage and sabotage directed against Germany and Japan. To my surprise, it was headed by 'Wild Bill' Donovan, now a General, the man I had met and spent a day with in New York in 1938 and at whose house I had been a guest. Well, I thought, he would do a good job from their point of view.

There had been other important changes in America during the last two years. There was virtually nothing of importance now to be gleaned from the kind of news clipping activity I had been used to in Washington. Obviously a strict censorship had been imposed and even with careful reading between the lines very little could be learned. The few stories that did appear were from the large news agencies like Associated Press and these had been carefully filtered to avoid revealing anything beyond platitudes and generalities. We could buy the English weekly magazines *Flight* and *Aeroplane* in the shops but nothing that could possibly have military value appeared in them now. If an aircraft type was described, the information was already months or years out of date. If not, the important details such as engine power, speeds, range, operating altitudes, armament were not included. Government handouts and reports, Congressional Committee transcripts, armament company accounts, once so readily available, were now classified documents and not obtainable. The Swedish authorities themselves were, and always had been, much more circumspect than the Americans and we could find out little about the allies from them even if they knew anything. I began to worry that before long my superiors would see that I was making no contribution of any value and would recall me to Germany. I might find myself back in some routine job in the Air Ministry or worse. That would be disastrous not only for myself but also for Helen, since I had to keep up regular payments to Davos for her.

However, I was now part of the *Abwehr*. Heimann was very much less opposed to undercover work than Bötticher had been, indeed I found he himself was actively co-operating with them and was in effect my *Abwehr* supervisor on the spot. While he must not himself engage directly in illegal activities he knew all about them and turned a blind eye. Not that there was anything I could do that could be called spying. There was nothing to spy on.

In the office adjacent to my own was Major Fritz Busch from Dresden, a round-faced, chubby fellow.[2] He, too, was nominally an Assistant Attaché and an *Abwehr* man but under a different section from myself, the *Amtsgruppe Ausland* (Foreign Branch) with the general responsibility for overseeing secret operations in Sweden.

At first Busch treated me with great reserve and I had the impression that he had been opposed to my appointment before I had even arrived. I guessed that he expected me to be an incompetent who had used unfair influence to get myself a cushy job. Perhaps in some ways I felt that this was true of myself so I was prepared for such a reaction and read it into his response to me. I realised fairly soon that the trouble was not this. I had acquired the reputation of being a great intelligence expert with some sort of network of contacts and sources in the American air forces and industry. No one understood how I had worked quite legally in Washington. Busch was afraid that I should put him in an unfavourable light if I was able to supply reams of information that he himself had been unable to discover.

I did my best to assure him that I had no intention of embarrassing him and explained that in any case I knew next to nothing of recent American developments. I had been completely out of touch for the best part of two years and I could see already that I was not going to discover anything much in Stockholm. He relaxed towards me and soon began to treat me as a friend and even confidant. He had been brought up in the Sudetenland, spoke with an accent very similar to that of Saxony, and we began to get along well. After about a month he admitted to me that he too felt we were wasting our time and was afraid that one day this would be recognised in Zossen, the bunker about 30 km (19 miles) south of Berlin where the *Abwehr* headquarters were now situated.

---

[2] It is not clear if this was the same Major Busch who, according to Leverkühn, was implicated in the *Europa* spying affair in New York.

'Peter, we can't do a thing. The Swedes don't know anything that we don't. What do the high-ups expect? This whole business is a waste of time.' He had been able to do practically nothing and was very conscious of the fact. Like everyone else he feared for his job and his future. To be recalled in his case might mean a posting to active service on the Eastern Front, which was universally dreaded. He did not have the engineering and flying qualifications that had protected me.

I had been advised by Grosskopf before coming to Stockholm that I should get in touch as soon as possible with a Dr Krämer in Busch's section. I would not, in the course of ordinary diplomatic routine, have much to do with Krämer but he was the *Abwehr's* expert on the British aircraft industry, having lived in England for years before the war. Krämer, I was told, controlled many agents both in Britain and in high positions in the Swedish Airforce. They supplied him with a regular flow of important news and he was allocated generous funds to pay and bribe them. Grosskopf had said I should be careful not to have too much to do with this man since it would tend to expose us both. All the same Krämer might be able to help me catch up on the Americans through some indirect contacts.

Busch seemed very reluctant to let me meet Krämer at all, as if he wanted to keep me away from this treasure. I supposed Krämer reported regularly to Busch but I was not introduced. One day by chance I spotted a tall, thin man in his mid-thirties with thick glass in his spectacles, going into Busch's office. One of the telegraphists, who was my best source for gossip, told me this was Dr Krämer and soon afterwards, in January 1944, I was able to meet him informally. He was very cultivated, well-spoken and intelligent with a wry sense of humour. We got along well socially on the few occasions when we happened to meet but when I tried to sound him out concerning his sources of information I found him expert at sliding away smoothly from my questions or changing the subject. On later casual meetings at the usual sort of diplomatic parties and at the reception after the funeral of a high Swedish officer which I attended, for once in uniform, I probed again, here and there. There was no result except that I developed a certain suspicion of him. When he did say anything of the American aircraft industry I guessed he was even more out of touch than I. His remarks puzzled me and sometimes I knew them to be quite wrong. After a few meetings like this I asked Busch directly about him. It was as if a dam had burst.

'Herr Riedel, that bloody man is fabricating most of his stuff. Do you know where his information comes from? From our own *Geheime Kommandosache*, top secret military reports from commanding officers about actions in the field and interrogations of captured airmen! He pesters

Heimann all the time for the latest batch of reports, takes them home for the weekend, which he ought not to do, and compiles a supposed intelligence report which merely confirms what the men at the front have already said: which enemy formation is stationed here, which aircraft they are using there, how many aircraft of this or that type are reaching the squadrons. If he can't find some detail this way, he guesses. He has an elaborate statistical system on file cards which he never lets anyone see.'

'Perhaps he is using the *Kommandosache* just to cross-check on his agents,' I said. I thought I knew something about the usefulness of statistics, indices and files.

'Nonsense. I don't trust any of it but he has impressed the people at HQ so much, telling them what they expect to be true, that he can get away with anything at all now. I have no control over him. All I can send to them myself is rubbish, stuff that any schoolboy can read. He claims to have V-men in the Swedish Foreign Office and through them lines running to Britain and the USA. How can I tell? I never meet any of these people. I'm not convinced they exist at all! And what does he do with the money he gets to pay them, eh?'

I could not offer any real advice. My contacts with Krämer and his information remained distant. I made a point of checking up on him, as far as I could. I never saw any of his reports and he showed in subtle ways that we should not discuss or attempt to exchange information. I began to believe that everything Busch had said of him was true. I was soon to meet him in stranger circumstances.

A few weeks later Busch evidently lost his temper, had a real row with Krämer and complained directly to *Abwehr* headquarters in Zossen. In April a young Lt-Colonel Klegenstüber was sent to Stockholm to investigate. He made himself known to Busch on arrival but after that we saw little of him. Busch was infuriated when he discovered the supposed investigator had attached himself to Krämer as a close friend. The two spent hours carousing, attending all kinds of parties and social functions, exploring night life in Stockholm, Krämer spending money lavishly. The visitor had been supplied with a very limited amount of Swedish currency but Krämer had lots to spare. They bought American cigarettes and French Cognac for Klegenstüber to take home and other luxury goods all unobtainable in Germany. The enquiry was apparently treated as an excuse for a kind of wild holiday. When the young man finally went home Busch was in despair.

'The *Abwehr* people do not want to know the truth,' he said. 'I was a fool ever to think I could do anything about it. Krämer's reports are passed right to the top, to Milch, Göring, to the Führer himself, because they look good and make an impression. Can you imagine what an outcry there would be if it were suddenly shown that Hitler had been served for years with rubbish cooked up by this charlatan? I don't understand why Hansen ever let things get to this point. Do you know Colonel Hansen? I thought he was an honourable man!'

I did know Hansen slightly because he was one of those officers who, in 1938, had sat at the dinner table with Canaris and the others when they were trying to persuade me to work for the *Abwehr* in Washington. He was second-in-command to Canaris now. Beyond knowing this I had had no direct contact with him but I was to meet him again sooner than I expected.

'Krämer is a clever bastard, I'll grant him that. He's got them all eating out of his hand and he's done for me!' Busch believed he himself was finished in Stockholm. Sure enough, at the end of April he was recalled. I never heard of Busch again. Perhaps he was sent to the east.

There was a tacit understanding between myself and Krämer now which in more ordinary times would have been despicable but in 1944 I justified it to myself by thoughts of Helen and my own self preservation. He let me see that he would not harm me if I did not attempt to injure him. I learned a lesson from Busch's experience. In the service of the Nazis there were many things it was better not to know.

Meanwhile Helen was in Davos. After I had waved goodbye to her she carried her suitcase the few metres into Switzerland where my sister greeted her and took her first to an hotel in Basel. They went next day by train to the sanatorium in Davos, which is about 1,000 metres (3,300 ft) above sea level with the surrounding mountains rising well over 2,500 metres (8,200 ft). Slightly rarefied air was thought to be good for sick lungs and at least the atmosphere was clean. The sanatorium, which was quite large, had separate wings for men and women but there were no children. Davos was also a well-known ski resort but the trade was depressed during the war.

To begin with things went badly. Helen was sicker than either of us had thought. I was able to speak to her by telephone but she had arrived at Davos with a high temperature and fever, more breathless than ever and feeling very ill. She had developed pleurisy and could feel the fluid sploshing around in her chest as she changed position. She was X-rayed again, confirming the diagnosis. There were injections that may have helped but the main treatment was simply to lie in bed and eat properly. Fortunately the pleurisy soon cleared up and she was able to take an interest in life again.

During her school teaching days in Washington she had developed an interest in puppetry and, while resting in bed, she was able to have materials brought to her and began again to create glove puppets, making them talk and move much to the amusement of her fellow patients and the medical staff. The radio kept her up-to-date with news. There was a library with books in English but Helen was fascinated to find a German translation of Mark Twain's *Huckleberry Finn*! She had never read it in English for she did not much admire Mark Twain. Thinking to improve her German, she began to read it and was highly amused because the numerous Americanisms had been translated literally, rendering them totally meaningless yet she was able to guess what the original had been.

As usual, come wind or snow, all the windows and doors were open and, except in the most extreme weather, patients spent their afternoons, well wrapped, lying or sitting outside on the balconies. When she was strong enough Helen was encouraged to take gentle exercise, walking around the ward to begin with, venturing a little further out when the sun was shining and she felt stronger. Now she was able to meet some of the other patients, making friends especially with an English-speaking woman of Latvian origin who had married a German. Like Helen, she had been allowed to come to Davos for treatment, leaving her husband behind.

Before long Helen was fit enough to begin painting again. The view from the sanatorium was splendid with the Davos Lake and surrounding mountains. She had never lived nor attempted to paint in a mountainous region before and her first efforts, she said, made the scenery look like great loaves of bread. She learned to do much better. There was another painter, a man, whom she had met once before in Rostock. He, too, was at the sanatorium for treatment and was helping to pay his fees by selling his works, even holding a small exhibition in the town. From him she learned a good deal and actually bought one of his paintings.

Gradually her health improved, although she was still breathing on one lung. I was able to correspond regularly and we spoke sometimes by phone. Twice, once soon after she arrived there and once again at Christmas, I was able to fly down to visit Davos to see her briefly. I cannot truly say that these were happy occasions for, although glad to see each other again, our time together was very brief and it was hard to see any clear future for us.

In Sweden I made contact again with some old friends, the Leube family. Anne Marie who had been at school with Annchen, had married Kurt Leube. They had left Germany years before the war and become Swedish citizens, living now in Malmö. I visited them whenever I could. He had become very prosperous, owning several factories, and hearing of my difficulties getting enough money to Davos for Helen he offered to help financially. 'If I keep the money I shall only have to pay more taxes!' he said. I did not like to accept his offers but assured him if I ever needed help I should not hesitate to ask him.

17

The Final Solution

My life was becoming complicated and uneasy. I was required to make routine trips to Berlin about once a month, reporting in person to Schwenke and Grosskopf. They looked forward to my visits for, travelling as a diplomat, I could bring a few Swedish luxuries with me, schnapps, grenadine and other items, but it was depressing. Things in Germany were deteriorating despite official attempts to keep up a bold front. Berlin was being devastated now. The propaganda machine was still fully functional, pouring out tidings of mighty V weapons that would bring final victory. I believed none of this although I did know of some developments like Lippisch's little rocket plane. I could not believe that such things could turn the enormous tide that was rising to drown Germany. In the east there was defeat after defeat although we were told of re-groupings, strategic withdrawals preparatory to a new offensive and other such rubbish. If the British and Americans invaded in the west they would be thrown back into the sea. Did Goebbels really think anyone believed this? It was a great relief to get back to Stockholm each time.

Without Helen I was desperately lonely. At official and unofficial social functions, as an apparently single man I became something of a target for the numerous attractive women who came with their husbands or men friends to these parties. Their men seemed to pay them little attention and they were bored. They found me interesting, I was flattered and easily susceptible. Swedish attitudes to sex and marriage were very much less inhibited than those my grandparents would have respected. Sex and love are not the same thing to me. Helen understood my needs. She knew I was not inexperienced when I met her, I had told her of that passionate affair with Doris in Brazil as long ago as 1934 and I still thought of her often. There had been other, casual liaisons in Colombia. Not long before I met Helen I had become very fond of Joan Burberry in England. I had visited her at her home and asked her to marry me. I believe in ordinary times she would have accepted but in the end she refused, perhaps because she saw war coming and knew how difficult life would be if she married a German at such a time.

At an Embassy party on one occasion I was standing at one side feeling very gloomy and alienated, not part of the festivities at all, when I was approached by the charming wife of a Swedish Airforce officer. She tried to draw me into the throng but I hung back. Why was I so gloomy, she asked. I told her Helen was sick, Germany was going to be destroyed and everything was going to hell.

'Oh,' she said, 'I would like to make those sad eyes happy.' Her husband was rapidly getting very drunk and it seemed he would soon be unconscious. She and I went to my apartment. After that one night I did not meet her again but there were soon other women.

After a while I settled down in a stable relationship with Caroline, or 'Ninnie' R. She was a divorcée who came from a Swedish aristocratic family and had many friends in Stockholm society. I first met her through my contacts with the local representative of *Lufthansa*, whose Danish wife was a friend of hers. It was an open secret that there were special flights by very fast Mosquito bombers carrying ball-bearings from Sweden to Britain. The Mosquitoes belonged to British Overseas Airlines, BOAC, and had civilian registrations. The official reason for their flights was to carry mail but there was not much of that. In their adapted bomb bays they had capacity for more than a ton of cargo. The *Lufthansa* man telephoned our office when a Mosquito was about to make a flight, usually too late for anything to be done about it and I never heard that one had been intercepted by the *Luftwaffe*, although one crashed near Stockhom in July 1944.

Ninnie was kind to me and we met whenever we could. Before long I was spending much time in her apartment. She had a close friend, Märta K, whom she had known since school days and whose family held controlling interests in one of Sweden's largest industrial companies. From time to time I met members of the firm since a good deal of material, especially the ball-bearings, was still going from Sweden to Germany for the aircraft industry. The German and British planes meeting in the skies to fight often depended on the same Swedish products. The executives were invited to our Embassy parties. The two women and I had many pleasant times together. I did not hesitate to confide in them my belief in Germany's defeat and described the state of affairs in Berlin and other cities under the bombing raids. This greatly upset Märta because her husband Rolf was German, a *Luftwaffe* lieutenant in charge of an anti aircraft 'flak' battery near Hamburg. Like so many expatriates, when war came he answered what he regarded as the call of duty. During the summer of 1943 Hamburg had been practically destroyed in a series of utterly devastating air raids by both British and American bombers. Huge fires had swept the streets generating their own howling winds in firestorms. Many thousands of people had died. He had survived so far but she feared for him and was desperately anxious to get him out of

Germany altogether if she could. He would not desert his post. She was determined somehow to get him back.

Things were changing among the upper echelons of the *Abwehr* although what it meant to us in Stockholm was not clear. Canaris, we heard through the rumour mill, had fallen out with Hitler because he totally failed to predict the massive amphibious landings on 21 January by American and British troops at Anzio on the west coast of Italy. There were other rumours and gossip, so fragmented and unreliable that I could make little sense of it. It was obvious only that the *Abwehr* was in disgrace. In February a directive bearing Hitler's signature announced it was to be reconstructed.[1] All intelligence services would in future come under Himmler. I did not like the sound of this for it made us virtually a division of the *Gestapo*. Canaris, we heard, had taken a long leave and was in effect replaced by Colonel Hansen. It seemed at first not to change anything for us so far down in the hierarchy.

At a party in April we were standing around with our cocktails as usual. Among the guests were the Finnish Naval and Air Attachés. I had been introduced to them as a *Luftwaffe* Engineer Officer. The Finns were fighting with us against the Soviet Union but in that curious state of affairs there was no war between them and the Western Allies, indeed they had been directly supported in the winter war of 1939-40 by Britain and the USA and still regarded them as friendly nations. It had only been Hitler's attack on the USSR that forced the Allies together and gave Finland a chance to strike back at the traditional enemy.

At this party the Finnish naval man came up to me quietly. He remarked that he and his colleagues were on good terms with the British and Americans. They were often invited for dinner with the Attachés of those nations. A common topic of their conversations was the Red Air Force. Despite the so-called alliance the Russians never passed on any information to the Americans about their own aircraft and their capabilities. The traffic was all one way, British and American aircraft were being supplied to Russia but nothing returned, not even goodwill. I listened, not sure at first where these remarks were leading. He came to his point.

'You *Luftwaffe* people know a lot about the Russians, you are fighting them every day. You have captured and tested some of their planes, know their capabilities. We know a little too but nothing like your side. How about an exchange of information? We could be intermediaries, you see. We can talk to you here, like this, and next week we shall be chatting with the Americans. It would be very easy!'

[1] Hitler's directive was dated 12 February 1944.(Heinz Höhne, *Canaris*, Doubleday 1979, p. 554).

'You mean we should pass information to the Americans at the expense of the Russians?'

'Don't look so surprised! Think about it. You know perfectly well, when this lot is over the Americans and the Reds will be at each other's throats. If you want to trade with the Yanks, I expect there would be something for your side in it.'

I knew I could not ignore this. On my next trip to Berlin I told Grosskopf. He was instantly enthusiastic.

'Great idea, wonderful, we'll do it! We are losing the war. It won't do us any harm to have some friends on the other side. I'll talk to Hansen. He'll want to see you.'

Almost immediately there followed a very private meeting in a small room in a suburb of Berlin, not far from Johannisthal. Grosskopf took me there to meet Georg Hansen and, when I went in, there was Krämer too, with his supposed high level Swedish agents and connections. They listened to what I told them. There was some discussion about the pros and cons before Hansen finally decided.

'Well, it depends on what they would give us in exchange. But in principle I will authorise you to respond and see what happens. You must tell your chief, Attaché Colonel von Heimann, that I have authorised it. He must know about it for your own protection. These two officers,' he indicated Krämer and Grosskopf, 'are also witnesses.' I understood that I should be playing a difficult role in this and might easily be accused of making traitorous contact with the enemy. If so, these men would be ready to testify that I had acted under orders. There was no record of the meeting, nothing on paper. I was to follow up the suggestion to see what it might involve, no more at this stage.

I told Heimann. 'Oh sure, there is a whole stack of secret deals like this. They're going on all the time!' he said, rather lightly. 'It's mostly tripe, you know. Go ahead, see what they say!' I met the Finn and indicated that we were prepared to hear more.

He said 'Mr Riedel, I will give you a phone call after I have talked to my American friends again. Then one day you should come for tea with us and we can take the next step.' It seemed harmless enough.

Serious events were at hand although most of the time we in Sweden were little more than spectators. Rome fell to the Allies and four days later on 6 June came the long expected landings by American and British forces in France. Their progress at first was slow but propaganda from the German side could not conceal the fundamental facts. The attackers had not been thrown back into the sea. As if to counter the effect of this news the first of the secret weapons came into action within a few days – the V-1 flying bomb, which was supposed to destroy London within a few weeks, forcing Britain to seek an immediate armistice. They did not sue for peace. The Red Army began a massive advance, there were enormous German casualties and by the end of June almost all the Soviet territory that had been in German hands was retaken. The Russians pushed on and in July captured the Polish town of Lublin. At the time it was just another name on the list of places overrun by the huge armies. Germany now was fighting and losing on all fronts, in the east, in Italy and in France.

The Finnish Attaché telephoned to invite me on a Thursday afternoon at five. I had expected to get some kind of indirect message but instead he took me in the dusk to a tall apartment house a few blocks away. We climbed up to the fifth floor. There were no lifts. At a door on the top landing he pressed a bell button, said 'Goodbye' and set off immediately down the stairs, leaving me standing there astonished and somewhat alarmed. This was not what I had expected. Perhaps I should run down the stairs too!

The door opened quickly and a man appeared. In good American-English he said, 'Mr Riedel, welcome, how is your wife, is she getting better?' He knew all about me! I was face to face with an American secret agent. I was taken in to the apartment, given a comfortable seat and a whisky. He wore civilian clothes and told me his name was Svensen. He was, or pretended to be, a representative of a famous American cosmetics company.

'What can I do for you,' he asked, after a few minutes. Did he not know already why I was here? I explained as best I could but was feeling far out of my depth. I outlined what the Finnish officer had suggested. Further than that I had no idea what might happen. It seemed that man sitting opposite me was quite taken aback.

'Oh!' he said, 'This is a very touchy area, politically. I can't decide anything of this kind myself, I have to hand it on higher up. Leave it with me, I'll get back to you when I have an answer.'

That seemed to be that but, on an impulse, I said, 'By the way, I know your chief, General Donovan. Give him my best wishes!'

'What? You know Wild Bill?'

'Yes I do.'

'How come?'

'I met him in New York when I was there before the war,' I guessed Svensen didn't really believe me, 'and in Washington, I visited his home as a guest. I knew his daughter Patricia too, went out with her once. She took me to a young folk's party. Of course I know she was killed in that awful road accident in 1940. I was very sad about that. I was in the Embassy then. But please, give Donovan my greetings.' Svensen said he would do so and would be in touch. It would take a little time.

Late in July the Swedish papers were full of the German Generals' attempt on Hitler's life which failed and led to the arrest and executions of those involved or suspected of being so. Admiral Canaris himself, former head of the *Abwehr*, was among these. If we had doubted it before we were sure now that there had been a bitter and violent struggle for power within the German hierarchy and Canaris was one of the losers. Hitler himself and Himmler, the *Gestapo* and the SS, remained very much in control and anyone connected with the *Abwehr* itself must now be under suspicion. I heard no more of Hansen but news filtered through that he was found to be involved in the conspiracy and had been arrested.[2]

I was not the only person who could see where things were going. Early in the spring of 1944 we had been visited in the Embassy by Major Golcher of the *Luftwaffe* General Staff. He was chief of the *Attaché Gruppe*, responsible for allocating all Attachés to our various positions. He had some official rationale for his visit at that time but what he was really doing then was studying the lie of the land and deciding if he could organise himself out of Germany. Heimann had made himself vulnerable by occasionally voicing mild criticisms of the government and he was, perhaps, too casual in his attitudes. Golcher, aged only 34, had a young family. He put them and his own personal safety first, which, in such desperate times, was not really blameworthy except that someone else must suffer. In mid-August he recalled Heimann and appointed himself to the Stockholm position. To become Air Attaché was no promotion but it had the advantage of getting him and his family out of Berlin to a safer place. We in the Embassy regretted Heimann's departure but manoeuvres of this kind were becoming almost commonplace and I was not in any position to criticise.

When I was called again to meet the American OSS man he told me, politely enough but bluntly, that the proposal was turned down flat. Even the slightest hint of such an exchange would put strain on the American alliance with the USSR. Stalin was already intolerably suspicious. There was no possibility that such a thing could be kept secret. The Russians had sympathisers everywhere just now and the information would reach them immediately. It was all off, indeed it had never been 'on'. I was prepared to depart at once.

But Svensen said, 'Hold on a moment! Don't you want to hear the rest? Wild Bill sends his best wishes and asks how you are!' So he did remember me! I sat down again.

[2] Hansen was interrogated by the *Gestapo* on 22-23 July and as a direct result of his statement Canaris was arrested the same day. Hansen was shot within a few weeks. After long imprisonment, Canaris was executed on 9 April 1945, three weeks before Hitler's death in the Berlin bunker (Höhne, op cit., p. 570).

'That is very kind of him!' I said.

'He understands your situation, asks after your wife, and so on.' I told him that Helen was improving now and was finding life in Davos quite comfortable. I was able to correspond with her regularly. Svensen turned the conversation back to the war.

I admitted to him that I saw no possibility of Germany winning and now understood clearly what kind of regime we were working under. I admitted I did not wish for victory any more. My chief concern was that peace should come quickly with the least possible damage to my country and its people. Was I ready to change sides, work for the Allies, he asked. To do what I could to bring the inevitable end sooner? I could not do it. I still felt bound by duty to serve my country.

'That will be serving your country. You must face it, we are going to win the war and our troops will occupy Germany. That's how it is going to finish. The sooner it happens, the easier it will be for your people.' I understood this but it was not enough. I could not bring myself to go over to the Allied side.

'I expect,' Svensen said, 'the Western Allies will take the western part of Germany and the Russians will take the rest.' I nodded, miserably. My birthplace in Lower Saxony would be occupied by the Red Army.

'You know, apropos of that, there is one thing that does concern Wild Bill and you could still help us without any commitment. We won't ask you to do anything against your conscience but you could give us some advice,' the agent said. 'We pick up talk of so called "werewolves", which is a code name for a proposed Nazi resistance movement. We'd like to know how much there is behind these stories. I guess there are sure to be some maniacs who will want to go on fighting. We can deal with a few fanatics but will there be general support among the population? If so, that would be very much more difficult. What do you think about it? Are the ordinary folk still behind Hitler and his gang? I can tell you, our troops are still having a hard time, the fighting is very fierce.'

My immediate reaction was to say that the ordinary Germans I knew had long ago had enough of war and of the Nazi party. Soldiers will do their duty, as they see it, and the traditions of the German army were still strong. They would not surrender easily. But like me, they only wanted the war to end and for something to be saved out of the wreckage of Germany.

'We'd be very interested in anything you could say about this, Mr Riedel. Perhaps you need to give it some time. Write a report for us on the likely reaction of the German population under Allied occupation. Will they go on resisting? I'll see that Donovan gets it.'

I left, deep in thought. Hansen was probably dead by now, Heimann was back in Berlin or where I did not know. Perhaps he too was disgraced and under arrest. The two senior men who understood why I had approached the Americans, who had authorised it, were no longer available to speak for me. I did not know what had become of Grosskopf and I did not trust Krämer. Dared I continue with these contacts?

The question of what was to happen when the war ended began to preoccupy me. I thought long and deeply about what Germany would be like under occupation. The 'unconditional surrender' which the Allies were demanding worried everyone who had heard the phrase because we did not know what it meant. What would they do to us? Would there be a terrible revenge for the things that our side had done? *Delenda est Carthago!*

Was there anything I could do, say or write that would reduce the harm? Could my contact with Donovan, so long ago as it seemed now, be turned to some use? I began to work on a draft of a statement that I might send to him. It would be my own work, of course, nothing to do with my official position in the Embassy. The *Abwehr*, still less the *Gestapo*, must not know of it. I wrote and re-wrote, hesitating, sometimes destroying the pages I had scribbled but always coming back to try again. The draft document grew longer but I was not satisfied and I hesitated and hesitated about it. Should I throw it away or pass it on to Donovan? Would he ever read it if I did send it? Could I trust anyone?

Supposing that Helen would have to stay in hospital for a long time even after the disintegration of Germany, I worried about what would happen to her when all German services collapsed. I could not expect to continue receiving a salary and the sanatorium was very expensive. At best I should be unemployed and impoverished, at worst held prisoner for how long I did not know. I must ensure Helen's safety as far as possible. I had brought her to Germany which had probably been the indirect cause of her illness. One day Ninnie and I went sailing in the *Sturmvogel*, which I had at last made serviceable and was able to use sometimes. Out on the water, well away from any listeners, Ninnie spoke to me about Märta and her husband, Rolf. Märta was feeling as desperate about Rolf as I was about Helen. He was stubborn and refused to desert, determined to stay at his post as the catastrophe of defeat came closer.

He must be brought safely to Sweden in some way that would allow him to preserve his honour. Could I help? For instance, could I arrange for Rolf to be ordered to take an appointment in Sweden? It would then be his duty to come home. Under pressure from the Allies, Sweden had officially stopped exporting engine parts to Germany but we in the *Abwehr* were working to get round this official embargo. A delegation of Swiss business-men would come to Stockholm and place large orders for the same kinds of material. The stuff had to travel through Germany to Switzerland but it would get lost somewhere, it might even be listed as destroyed in a bombing raid! It would, of course, find its way to the Daimler Benz works and other important plants. The Swiss would be well paid for their trouble, the Swedish company could claim innocence providing no direct contact with Germany could be proved. Märta's family were important industrial executives. Could I persuade my bosses that Rolf would be useful to us in the Swedish branch of the *Abwehr*, simply because he was married to Märta? Rolf could be our channel of communications, through her, with the Swedish manufacturers. At least I could pretend so. I realised that this idea originated with Märta herself. She had asked Ninnie to make the first approach.

What it came down to was that if I could arrange Rolf's post accordingly, Märta would pay 15,000 Swedish Crowns, enough to keep Helen in Davos for two years whatever my own fate. I agreed, but stipulated that the money should not be paid directly to me but to Ninnie to hold so that she could see it went to Davos when the need arose, no matter what became of me. My relationship with Ninnie was without jealousy or mistrust and I felt confident that she would use the money as I wished. I approached Golcher and obtained his permission to go via Denmark to Hamburg to see Rolf. I reached Hamburg and was completely appalled at the devastation I saw in the city, worse than Berlin even though it had been more than a year since the fire raids. I explained what would be expected of him and at the same time Rolf was presented with an ultimatum by his wife. If he refused to accept this chance, she would divorce him under Swedish law and he would never see her again. He accepted the appointment and not, it seemed to me, very reluctantly. Accordingly, in due course he received his orders and was expected to join us in the Attaché's office in November.

In the third week of September a large envelope arrived on my desk, addressed to me by name but with no return address on the back. Inside was a typewritten pamphlet headed *Committee of the Union of Free German Officers in the USSR*. We had received such leaflets before. They purported to be written by German army officers who had been captured and who, since 1943, had decided to ally themselves with the communists. Generals von Seidlitz and von Daniels and others of lesser rank were involved. As a rule we dismissed the contents as propaganda from the Soviet Legation in Stockholm and they were thrown away.

This one was different. When the Red Army captured Lublin they had found on the western side of the town a huge SS concentration camp, called Majdan Tatarski, abbreviated to Majdaneck. It was a death camp of more than 660 acres extent. The leaflet included horrifying photographs taken by the Russian commission of enquiry and gave the facts soberly. There were seven gas chambers and a crematorium for the corpses. The camp had been in use since 1941. Huge numbers had died there, either by starvation and untreated sickness or by hanging or in gas chambers. Jews were the vast majority but thousands of Russian troops had been killed as well as large numbers of almost every other European nationality, anyone who had offended the Nazis in any way: Poles, French, Italians, Belgians, Dutch, Czechs, Greeks, Serbs and Croats. On the last page was given a date on which Heinrich Himmler had visited the camp. There was no room left for doubt. I knew now with awful certainty that the stories I had heard, the rumours of mass shootings, were far less terrible than the reality. I had tried for so long to believe that Germans could not do such things.

I was in despair. I dared not mention this document to anyone and no one said anything to me about it although I knew several other officers in our Embassy would have received it, when I did. Even to admit that we had read it would get us into trouble.

The Moscow government made sure that the same facts reached the Western news media. A few days later the American magazine, *Time*, dated 11 September but not on sale in the Swedish newsagents until several days later, carried the story. The American reporter Richard Lauterback told how he had visited the camp with other non-Russian journalists. An item which stuck in the memory was his account of a shed containing 820,000 pairs of shoes taken from the victims before their execution. The total figure of those who died was stated to be 1,500,000, there were heaps of human ash to be used as fertiliser for crops.[3]

I made up my mind. I could no longer work for the German government. I finished and typed my letter to Donovan, in English. The typescript was dated September 24th. It was too long and wordy but it was the outpouring of a tormented man. Having written it, I still hesitated. How should I get it to Donovan?

[3] The date and page reference to *Time* magazine is correct.

18

A Letter to America

Stockholm
September 24th 1944

Dear General,[1]

May I return the greetings you were kind enough to send to me and express at the same time my thankfulness for your attitude of goodwill towards me.

Please permit me to come to my theme without much introduction: the question of German co-operation after Germany's defeat. I would like to say a few things about this.

I am speaking on my own initiative. No organization stands behind me. I have got no authority from anyone to write to you about this question of future co-operation. What made me think of you was first the kindness you showed me when I had the honor to meet you in the U.S.A. Besides you knew pre-war Germany. You have studied it. You had German friends and you seemed not to have any prejudices against us.

Therefore, I was longing for a chance to talk to you before it was too late, as a self-appointed representative of the misled, patient, hard-working and suffering German masses. My heart ached each time I came back to Germany and I had to see these worn-out over-worked people patiently and obediently plodding on, without hope, without love for war or any more for Hitler. No chance of escape from the big prison they voted for themselves. They were as badly deceived as were you foreign powers. Now they have to go on, driven either by fear of Himmler or the sense of duty towards their country at war.

---

[1] All footnotes to the letter, except this, were appended to the original. The wording and spelling here follow the final draft. An earlier draft with many minor corrections also exists. Phrases not translated include *Kraft durch Freude*; strength through joy, *Volkswohlfart*, social welfare, *Kranken und Invaliden Versicherung*, health insurance, *Vernichtungslager*, extermination camp.

The reference to 'Vansittart ideas' is to Baron Robert Gilbert Vansittart of Denham, a British diplomat who visited Germany and met Hitler in 1936. He became an extremely outspoken critic of Nazi Germany and a vitriolic opponent of appeasement. He was dismissed by Chamberlain but in retirement wrote savagely in denunciation of all things Germanic.

This duty towards our country keeps most of us going on and Hitler shields himself behind it. Can one desert one's country in war because it is run by gangsters? That is the question most Germans will still answer with 'no'.

We face a disasterous end soon. What constructive could be done now?

Permit me to tell you what I experienced and felt since I came back from the U.S.A. in May 1942: that America has the biggest chance to find co-operation of the little man in Germany after it is all over. I experienced how nice everybody was to my American-born wife, who could hardly speak one word of German, when we arrived. How eagerly everybody inquired about America; how frankly they all acknowledged your superiority in many respects. After people had had a chance to hear from me more about America than they had heard in the last ten years they often admitted that the American way of living and doing things was better than their own. Even the boldness and discipline of your daylight attacks are presently discussed by the little man in Germany with a hidden admiration and without personal resentment or hatred.[2]

The little man in Germany has pinned his last hope and faith on America. Many Germans have dared to discuss privately with me the impending defeat. When the future aspects seemed utterly hopeless and disastrous, most of them expressed the hope, that America would not permit things to go so far. I beg you not to disappoint this hope too badly. The German people do not expect love and kindness, but they hope for decent treatment from you, severe as it might be.

One day you Americans will have to deal with the little men in Germany. I am one of them. I know you and I know them. I am interested in the fate of the German people, because of the old law that blood is thicker than water. On the other hand I am very fond of America. I am tied to America by being married to an American girl. In the past it has been my greatest desire to end my days as an American citizen.[3] War has forced me to take the road of duty towards the country of my birth.

My people are facing the greatest disaster in all their sad history. I am standing in between the two camps. What to do now? Please permit me to continue this self analysis. You may consider, that all Germans who would like to co-operate later are faced with the same problems as I. Therefore one can quite well generalize the ideas, which I prefer to describe from my personal point of view.

[2] Machine-gunning of civilians from the air. Fortunately it seems to have stopped. Its continuation would have created real hatred.

[3] I inquired about American citizenship in July 1940 at Lawyer Howard Le Roy, Washington D.C., 14th and G-Street. He still has papers about this.

I am facing a decision in three alternatives: Should I choose to cooperate

1. In Western Germany, occupied by the Anglo-American forces or in
2. Eastern Germany, under Soviet rule or
3. Should I choose to seek refuge in Sweden?

I mention this third alternative because I want to make it clear that I do not feel myself hopelessly bound to the fate of the German people. I have no more close relatives or any personal friends in Germany. My name as a pilot might give me the chance to begin a new life in Sweden as a free man rather than as a subject in a country ruled by foreign powers. I mention this because it might be necessary to prove I am not pleading so much for my own sake as from the sincere desire to help bringing a lasting peace between Germany and America or the Anglosaxon world.

After Germany would be occupied by Allied troops in the west and Sovjet troops in the east there seems not to be a chance for any German to choose his own way. Still our own bad experiences during this war showed us that one cannot rule a nation by force alone. Even the conqueror will need co-operation and it is only the question if one wants Quislings or decent people to co-operate with.

The German people of the lower classes might tend more to the Sovjet Union. The Sovjet Union can promise to treat them more as new members in their community of workers and farmers than as enemy aliens. There might be quite a number of people in the class of intellectuals and former officers, who might see a better chance for survival of the German race within the frame of the Sovjet Union. Such tendencies are created by the fear that Western nations might follow Vansittart ideas. Such people are not necessarily irresponsible desperados but men who love their people more than the class they belong to.

On the other hand Nazi propaganda has created a general fear of Sovjet Russia. How much there is reason for it remains to be seen. For most of our people there is enough despair accumulated to make them indifferent to under which flag they will continue to live, if they only could live decently again. Especially the Nazi-educated youth might easily turn to the some-how familiar form of Sovjet-government if there would not be any future for them under Anglosaxon rule. Here I see America's biggest chance to be the real winner. There is no general hatred yet of America and England. No bombing attacks, no Göbbels propaganda has been able yet to create this hatred.

You can beat up a man in a fight, you might imprison him for his misdeeds, you might make him poor and work hard. He will not hate you for that. War is war and awful things have been loaded on the conscience of the German people. But humiliate a man who is your prisoner; let his family starve, while they are in your hands; expose him in his helplessness to the revengeful cruelties of his neighbours and you will implant a terrible deep hatred. A hatred born out of despair. A hatred which would prefer to see himself rather drowned together with the responsible ones in the big Red flood than continue a dishonoured slave-existence.

Oh, that America should see her chance! Not only our soil, our cities and plants have been plowed open by your bombs, but our souls too. We are sinking to the lowest level of hope, we are ready to grasp the straw in the rising flood of disaster, we, the little men of Germany. We know that you America, beat us, not the Sovjet Union. Your strength backed them all. You have the responsibility for the future peace!

The Nazis are done for. Our whole leading class has failed, including the arrogant narrow-minded officers cast. The most awful crimes of the Nazis (Lublin) are still unknown to the German masses.[4] Most of us tried not to see this horrible spot on the German name, when we heard rumours of these unequalled crimes. Most of us were horrified, not for fear of revenge, but from shame. When conversation comes to this subject one avoids the other one's eyes. After a horror-stricken pause follows the question: 'How is it possible to find German men to do such things?' Pardon me – this is no arrogance. But every nation tries to think itself being composed predominantly of decent people.

German newspapers have never published descriptions of the often sadistically cruel methods of the *Gestapo* applied in trying to hold opposition down in occupied countries. To give an example: the deportation of all Norwegian students to Germany never was made known to the German people. No decent German approves of these *Gestapo* crimes when he hears of them. War propaganda has created the impression as if such things were done with the knowledge and approval of our whole nation and that one should punish all Germans for that. Public opinion in the world has concluded that cruelty is inherent to the German character. It is difficult to counteract the effects a longlasting propaganda campaign has created. I only want to point out two examples to counteract:

First: Do the American people have the impression that American citizens of German birth or extraction have shown worse characteristics than the other ones? I myself have found that USA judges the German immigrant mostly as an orderly and law abiding citizen.

Second: Men choose their professions according to their inclinations. Therefore I think that people who have chosen to be *Gestapo* agents are predominantly of two types, political fanatics or sadistic madmen. On the

[4] Best propaganda against the Nazi Government in Germany would be to make the Lublin crimes known to the German masses by, for instance, throwing down leaflets giving the mere facts as published in *Time Magazine* 11th September 1944, page 17, with the heading 'Murder. Inc.'

other side the German army is formed by the average German. When I followed the American newspaper-reports about the conquests of Norway and France in 1940, I never found any report about atrocities on the part of the German soldier. On the contrary as long as the occupied countries were under army rule, things seemed to go along quite alright. Only after the Nazi Civil administration took over, trouble started.

Would it be fair to let a whole nation suffer as punishment for the crimes of some fanatics?

What I am aiming at by writing these lines was trying to prove that the German people could be quite easily won over by telling them vividly and plainly what crimes have been committed in their name. This would be a much better safeguard against the danger of Nazi organisation going underground. But in my opinion this counterpropaganda should be left chiefly to the Germans, who think like I do.

Let people like me, who know both sides, go to work and destroy the basic ideas of the Nazi irreligion, above all the fundamental dogma: *'Die Juden sind an allem Schuld!'*[5] Let us prove to our people how Hitler's madness showed itself foremostly on this point. Let us destroy Hitler's prestige slowly and logically, not by mere counterpropaganda, which paints everything black where even I still could see some good. Even though people are now fed up with Hitler because he led them into disaster, they will always remember his good performances of pre-war times. A number of well-known Americans have gone on record like William Knudsen with his: 'Germany is the miracle of the 20th century' when he returned from Europe some time before the war.

Nothing will conquer underground organization easier than decent treatment and soft-spoken, logically destroying critic of Hitler and his mad ideas. Leave it chiefly to Germans to paint him to our masses as an ambiguous personality, genius and madness mixed, with madness slowly getting the upper hand. This will logically explain the cause of his career and our fate. I am sure that this would lead to more success in fighting the Nazi ideology than any other propaganda methods. Before Hitler's ideas have died out in the German hearts, they would not be open to accepting democracy. You should give the medium time to get the mad magician off his subconscious.

But what do I mean with decent treatment? Very little from your point of view. Our people live on the very minimum level of existence compared with Western nations. What is filling the twenty-four hours of their day? Twelve to fourteen hours' work with additional hours to make the distance between home and workingplace. Food just enough to keep going. Nothing

---

[5] The Jews are behind all the trouble.

to buy. Home destroyed. Family scattered or destroyed through evacuation, war duty, bombs, or death on the battlefield. No hope for the future.

People who have sunk so low in despair will appreciate enormously if one gives them the slightest hope. They will be contented with very little.

First of all: don't let our people starve. Don't let our masses intentionally or by gross mismanagement suffer from hunger. Do not listen to revengeful voices, who would like to see that happen. I know we have no clean record everywhere. In Poland and with millions of Russian prisoners of war awful starvation have happened. There is reason to suspect that such starvation happened partly with bad intention. On the part of the Nazis. When you are going to punish the responsible ones, we will wholeheartedly help you so that they should get their thousandfold deserved punishment. Please hold against the revengeful voices the acknowledged fact that your troops were surprised not to find a starving Europe during the recent invasion, and I know that they will not find it either in the rest of Europe to be liberated. Greece and sometimes Norway went through bad times of hunger and scarcity, predominantly because of being dependent on grain imports.

Secondly: keep order, be it with iron fist against everybody who opposes. Let the few good things the Nazis set up continue: the present rationing system with the obligation for the farmer to guarantee the nutrition of the nation. The new agricultural legislation, which gives the farmer guarantees against being dispossessed by unscrupulous bankers. The general Labour service of all young people with its equalizing effect on social prejudices. Let the German Labour Service camps be run by American C.C.C. camp officers. This would give you the best chance to get educational influence and prevent secret military training. The social organizations like '*Kraft durch Freude*', '*Volkswohlfart*' and the '*Kranken-und Invaliden Versicherung.*'

Our people are accustomed to be governed by stern authority. You will have no difficulties with them – if – if order means also protection against violence, insult and humiliation from whichever side, be it from your own forces or from the revengeful chauvinists among your allies. If some Germans have learned to hate Frenchmen and Poles, they have in mind humiliations under the French occupation[6] and Polish atrocities committed against German minorities[7] in 1939.

Help both our neighbors and us to forget our hates and resentments by holding us apart. You are welcome to do this holding apart for many years

---

[6] French Rhineland occupation 1918 to 1932. Negro troops policing the Rhinelands, assault on women and many humiliating incidents.

[7] In the first days of September 1939 8,000 men, women and children slaughtered by the Polish mob in the frontier area.

to come. It would be the only cure of this evil and it would give you the chance to

Third: educate our people to be politically grown-up members of Western civilization. I know we are not and many of us feel the same. I meant this when I said that our souls are laid open. They have been bombed and battered open, the soil of our souls has been worn loose by worries and sorrow, by blood, tears and sweat just the same. No more self-confidence, no more trust in our own ability to lead ourselves. Spared dishonorable treatment the little men of Germany will be very eager to accept new ideas and outlooks.

The average German's state of mind today is expressed by what a successful German aircraft manufacturer said to me a few days ago after we had been discussing things along these lines: '*Das Deutsche Volk hat auf der ganzen Linie versagt*'.[8] In sad variation to the German revolutionists Scheidemann's triumphant words, November 11th 1918: '*Das Deutsche Volk hat auf der ganzen Linie gesiegt*'.[9] The man who said this was no pessimist in general outlook. He simply stated what we all feel innermost.

We begin to see our weaknesses which would have made us unable to succeed on England's place even if victory should have given us a chance. And here too may I plead to leave it to us Germans, who agree with you about the necessity of re-education. One accepts easier criticism from relatives than from outside one's family.

We begin to see our inherent faults: militarism, misinterpreted Nietzsche ideas, byzantine bowing and subjecting oneself to the self-imposed authority, overemphasized selfconfidence, born out of an historic inferiority complex and lack of civil courage. Preference to bullying, instead of soft-spoken insistence helped by appeals to reason when leading people. The tendency to see the guilt for our own unhappy history not enough where it lies: at our own door. Had our ancestors better not been fighting each other thirty years for slight differences of how to pray to our Lord! Had our different tribes better unified at the same time when England and France were formed by originally opposing tribes. We should learn to see the blame for our troubles in history and in present times more in our character than at our so-called outside enemies. What I mean is the fatal German tendency to loose oneself more than 100% to some onesided idea and trying to verify such radical ideas by all means. Be it on the field of politics, religion, socialistic experiments or race prejudices.

The latest and worst example to this German extremism was the gruesome '*Vernichtungslager*' near Lublin, where thousands of Jewish

[8] The German people have failed on the whole line.

[9] The German people have won on the whole line.

people fell victim to the insane antisemitic ideas of Hitler. All Germans who will hear of these unheard of crimes will feel the same reaction I felt when I heard rumours about it in June 1942. I began to despise Hitler for this because he made me feel ashamed of being German, whenever I thought about this.

The persecutions of the Jewish people under Hitler had taken these violent forms only after the war started. He had promised to annihilate the Jewish people in Europe if they would 'manage to get the war against Germany started'. He put his insane theory into terrible praxis.

As one result one can state that Antisemitism is on its lowest point in Germany now. The hatred of Hitler and his crimes against these unfortunate Jewish people have made many regret that their resentment of some Jewish mistakes had formerly led them to give approval to Hitler's antisemitic teachings.

Well, there are generations to be re-educated along those lines but let *us* do it together with those of you who inspire confidence in their goodwill to our mislead unfortunate people. Never doubt that many of us who know a little more of this globe than stampsized Germany will gladly help you.

If there is a bad spirit found in our country, it is to be compared with the spirit of a mono-maniac, who has been living too long time secluded in the attic, loosing himself into onesided ideas and suddenly appearing in the streets running amok. Running amok with the conviction of the maniac that he alone is right, that his ideas are superior, won out of abstract thinking. To make it clear: I do not say that this is the spirit of all Germans, but it is a disease to be found among people of a certain nationalistic and antidemocratic educational background. This bad spirit dies fast in most every infected German soul, when the soul is aired long enough under the sun of advanced foreign countries like the community of English-speaking nations. Let us try to 'air' the future leaders of Germany long enough in this seductive climate of fine balance between personal freedom and governing authority as found especially in the U.S.A.[10]

Fourth: permit me to say: let our tribes stay in one unit, colony, dominion, nation or whatever name you are going to give the new Germany. This is the only purely political proposal of my letter. The reasons are very simple.

The roots of this desire of unification have grown deeply in every German soul. Hitler's following grew enormously when one saw him unifying all German speaking people into Greater Germany. It meant something different to different people. Some saw the chance for power politics, aggression, enlargement on expense of our Eastern neighbours.

[10] There is only one danger: that the student might prefer to stay forever in this climate.

Hans and Mrs Wolfram with Peter Riedel after the Breakfast Club meeting, California 1939.

Peter with executives of the Stearman Aircraft Company, Wichita, Kansas, in 1939.

Walter Flinsch.

Stockholm: Strandvägen, 1995.

Stockholm: Strandvägen in 1995. The apartment was at this end of the street.

Stockholm: Långholmen prison on the green island, taken in 1995.

Långholmen.

Cell door in Långholmen.

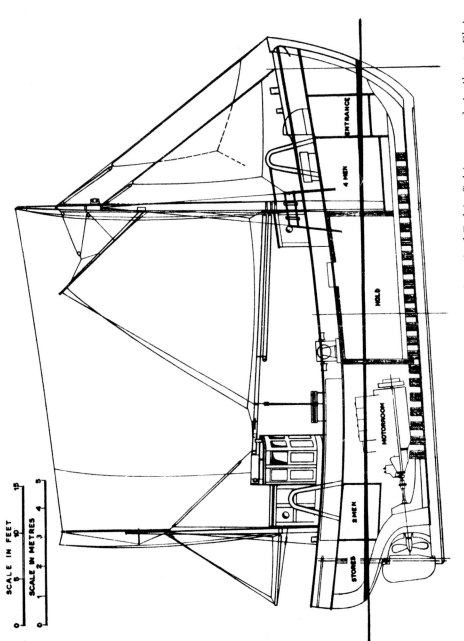

A typical Baltic fishing vessel similar to *Elvie*.

FINE HEREFORD CATTLE

Rancho Montoso

MAGDALENA
NEW MEXICO

June 2 11 1939

We were all tickled pink to welcome you, friend Peter Riedel, and your fine glider and we wish you would stop off a while with us.

Art Myrland
Gretchen Myrland
Rene Reeves
Frank Williams
Jesse Potter
Rose Chase
J. J. Sullivan

The letter from *Rancho Montoso.*

Casablanca, Place de France in 1948.

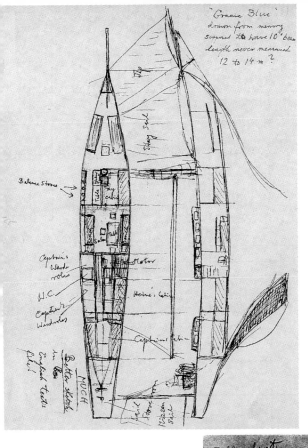

The plans of *Gracie Blue* drawn from memory by Peter Riedel.

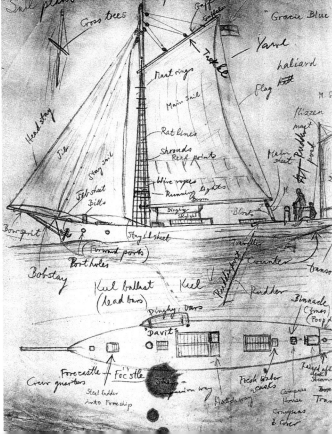

Captain and Mrs Nicholson in Las Palmas.

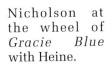

Nicholson at the wheel of *Gracie Blue* with Heine.

La Guaira, Venezuela, in 1948.

Many more, like I, were satisfied by the mere idea of seeing all German-speaking peoples unified within a common borderline. An age-old and quite understandable dream had come true. Its age is proved by the Kyffhäuser saga.[11]

We have fought and suffered together during this war, all Germans from Wien to Hamburg, from Sudetenland to Saar, including Danzig. Please let us stay together as a beaten people during the coming years of being your warden and later as a cured member in the family of nations. You will take the wind out of the sails of German nationalism, its main desire being satisfied.

If this is fulfilled there will be basic agreement from our side to your political solution whatever it might be: take over our government and decide complete disarmament for many years to come! We, the people, will only be thankful. Most of us do not like to be soldiers. Militarism was bread by evil spirits and militarism itself educated evil spirits into German youth: byzantinism, uniform craze (to counteract one's inferiority complex), arrogance hand in hand with ignorance, splendor instead of spirit, self-indulgence and intolerance instead of free discussion. Go and erradicate these evils and we will gladly help you too.

With above I do not mean to insult the German soldiers of all ranks, who fought and died in two wars. They were mostly civilians at heart, and only did their duty to the bitter end. But there is plenty of reason and lots of material accumulated to justify if one would destroy at once and for all the prestige of the German General Staff officers – of this clique, of this concentrated extract of personified Prussian militarism. I have experienced their weaknesses, their vanity, their reckless judgement about the enemy and his strength, their '*Geistiger Hochmut*'[12] their lack of courage towards their superior, which showed itself expecially by the frequent omission to report unpleasant truths to Göring and the Führer.

Fifth and last: please help to solve the problem of overpopulation by human means, not by crowding evacuated men, women and children into a too small German space, left either to starve or to kill themselves for lack of chance to make a living.[13]

[11] Kaiser Barbarossa, who drowned crossing a river during the Crusades, is supposed to be living in a big cave of the Kyffhäuser mountain until the German dissension should end. Then he would come out again and be the Kaiser of all Germans as before. All the longing for political unification is expressed in this very beloved saga. There was no imperialism hidden in the Kyffhäuser cave. All-Deutsche and Nazis added this later.

[12] *Geistiger Hochmut* = spiritual arrogance, not necessarily the plump arrogance of the stupid.

[13] In the years after 1918 statistics proved that on the average 30,000 people a year died by suicide.

Let us help you by propagandizing and putting into effect reasonable birth control to stop overpopulation in the future. After years of rebuilding Europe, when the hatred against the German people may have died down, there might be a chance to solve the problem of European overpopulation by organized emigration into the still thinly populated areas of this globe. Even if this would mean enormous investments, the world might be saved from spending some day again much more for destructive purposes. All problems need sweat, but not necessarily blood and tears for their solution.

Once our people are convinced by telling them the facts, that Hitler wantonly started this war, they will accept when you make them work long and hard to make good what was destroyed in economic values. If that is our punishment we will be able to say to ourselves: 'We brought this upon us. Big spots on the German name have to be washed away. We recognize this necessity. Let's go to work'. That would not give the feeling of slave labour with its inherent feeling of resentment.

Today after being war-propagandized nearly twelve years, the greater part of our nation does not see yet the warguilt as much on our side as you and I do. Our people have to be proven by telling them hard facts, by telling them the truth about Hitler's systematic preparation for war under the excuse of defensive measures. The German masses did not know how little armed the democracies were when war broke out. This fact is known only to the few who like I had the chance as Military Attaché to find out about your military unpreparedness. We had always been told that an envious England and U.S.A. were arming rapidly to attack us in good time. So when war broke out most of our people believed it a preventive war and most of them believe this still today.

Dear General, these are my ideas to the question of Germany's treatment after the war. There will be many Germans who will be willing to give wholehearted co-operation from the very day the war ends. In all modesty I want to point out that this our co-operation could only be expected if our conscience allows us to give it wholeheartedly. If you want Quislings, you will find them plenty I am afraid. There are a great number of potential 'Quislings' among us. But they will not be of much real help. We had a chance to learn this lesson. If you want our help, please see to it that at least the desire for food and decent treatment may be fulfilled. If you want to win over the German masses from wrong idols and ideas to your way of thinking you might later take the sting out of our defeat by considering the other three proposals.

A man with self respect cannot help the invader who treats his people unjustly even if he sees the guilt of his own side. 'Severe but just rule' announced your posters in the town first conquered on German soil. We are willing to accept this.

Give the decent people among us a chance and they will gladly help you to remove the ugly remnants of Nazism, first by destroying the culprits and later, in a slower process, by derooting it radically out of our hearts.

Sincerely yours,
P. Riedel

19

Hanna Amidst the Ruins

The letter was written, but what now? I held it back, talked about it to Ninnie. She was sympathetic. I tusted her and Märta completely, and did not hesitate to reveal my feelings.

At about this time, under pressure from the Allies, Sweden stopped sending the ball-bearings to Germany. Immediately a delegation of Swiss businessmen came to Stockholm and placed large orders for the same kinds of material. Our Embassy, of course, knew what was behind this. The stuff had to travel through Germany to Switzerland but it would get lost somewhere. It would find its way to the Daimler Benz works and other important plants. All this was discussed with Ninnie and her friend.

Early in October I went to Berlin in the usual routine manner. I took with me the Russian pamphlet, relying on my diplomatic status to ensure I would not be searched. It went in my baggage with the usual few bottles and special gifts. On landing at Tempelhof after the flight from Stockholm I saw more signs of bomb damage everywhere. The streets were desolate with ruined houses and other buildings. Schwenke was in his office as usual but a bomb had made a huge hole in the Air Ministry building. He could see what I was thinking and told me sadly that German aircraft losses were more than the industry could make good, let alone the casualties among aircrews. Fuel was running out. Yes, many enemy aircraft were being shot down but they kept coming. In a single raid of half an hour as many as six or seven hundred bombers, even a thousand, would unload their enormous blockbusting bombs, 2,000 or 5,000 kg each, or thousands and thousands of incendiaries. Everything I had predicted was happening.

He took me in the rain to lunch in the *Haus der Flieger* near the Air Ministry. This had been the luxurious headquarters building of the German Aero Club and at one time was the meeting place of the Prussian parliament. Pools of water stood about in the entrance hall and there was water dripping constantly everywhere inside as well as out. Schwenke told me that what I saw was the building after it had been repaired by special order of Milch. Without this work it would have been quite uninhabitable.

The restaurant was more or less intact and full of men in uniform but I glanced into a smaller room to one side which was reserved for officers in the company of ladies. There was Hanna Reitsch. She was the one bright spot in an atmosphere of deep gloom. We embraced like brother and sister and sat together to catch up on our news. Like everyone else, she was depressed but when talking she became more her old, optimistic self.

Hanna, soon after the last time I saw her in 1942, had been very severely injured in an accident when test flying the rocket plane for Messerschmitt. One of those damned drop-off wheel dollies had jammed! Her skull was fractured in six places. After extensive surgery and five months in hospital she had a long convalescence in a sanatorium near her home in Silesia. Only those who had known her very well before would have seen, as I did, the signs of facial reconstruction that had been necessary. It was August 1943 before she was fully active again but as enthusiastic for flying as ever. She was, if possible, even more dedicated to her dangerous work than before. She had been on a flying tour of the Russian front, piloting General Ritter von Greim to visit troops in advanced positions, some even who had been surrounded by the Red Army and who were fighting to survive their encirclement. She had been under fire and was warmly welcomed by the soldiers. Despite all the devastation around us she still believed a final victory was possible.

I was disturbed to find now that she had made friends with Heinrich Himmler, head of the SS and the *Gestapo*, now also Minister of the Interior with special responsibility for combating defeatism. During her long spell in hospital he had written admiring letters to Hanna and sent her gifts. These had continued arriving regularly for months. Despite the misgivings of her mother and other friends, when she was up and about again she had called on him and was impressed by what she saw as his high intelligence, culture and good taste. After this I found it difficult to talk to her about him. Himmler, she believed, was a kind, good-natured man, very correct in all matters of etiquette and to her quite compassionate and charming. He had told her to pass on to him at once any criticisms she heard of him or his organisation so that he could correct false impressions. Whereas before, Hanna had been a person whose total honesty and frankness I had greatly admired and with whom I could always talk freely, now there was a severe constraint between us. I had to tell her what I knew.

Later I called on her in her apartment in the Aero Club. I took the Russian pamphlet with me and threw it onto her table.

'There's your friend Himmler for you! See what he's been doing? Read that!'

She looked at it, began to shake with rage and became almost hysterical.

'Do you mean to say you believe this rubbish? In World War 1 they said that Germans had hacked off the hands of children in Belgium! You believe that? It's obviously enemy propaganda, not to be taken seriously.'

We were like brother and sister and we could also fight like brother and sister. I too became furious. I told her of what I had read in *Time*, an account by an American who could have had no reason to accept communist distortions. Where did she suppose the 800,000 pairs of shoes came from? We shouted at each other until we were both exhausted. In the end, when we had calmed a little, I said, 'Hanna, OK, if you can prove that it's not true, I will try to believe you. Show it to Himmler, see what he has to say!'

'I shall, I shall!' she swore. Himmler was such an honourable and kindly man she did not believe there was any danger in such a course. I begged her to say only that I had read the article in *Time* magazine and in the foreign newspapers to which all Embassy staff throughout the world had access.[1]

Back to Stockholm. I had a sense of approaching personal crisis. Could I ever bear to go back to Berlin? Would there be a Berlin to go back to?

One morning a few days later I was called urgently to Golcher's office. With other senior officers he was studying a lengthy teleprinter message which had come through.

'Read that!' said Golcher, handing the paper to me. It was a highly secret document which had evidently been decoded before we could read it. Couched in terse language it stated that a Captain Gerdes of the *Luftwaffe* who had been working as a test pilot at one of the experimental units near Berlin, had deserted from his post and stolen a new Junkers 88 night fighter. He had flown to Sweden and gone down in the forest somewhere near Oskarshamn in the south of the country, on the eastern coast. The pilot had been injured in the crash and was in hospital. It was likely, though whoever sent the telegram was apparently not sure, that the Ju 88 was fitted with a new secret radar instrument intended to track bombers and it must not be allowed to fall into non–German hands. Gerdes too must be prevented from passing on the information which he knew through his work.

The orders that followed were clear and alarming. A representative of the Air Attaché must immediately go to the crash site and establish whether or not the radar gear was in the plane. If it was there, if possible the aircraft

[1] There is some doubt about what actually took place on this occasion. The account here is a likely interpretation. In an account (handwritten by Peter Riedel in 1946) he did not show Hanna any document but only told her of what he had learned. He knew that even to speak of such matters might lead to his arrest. She refused to believe him. Hanna herself wrote that he 'threw a booklet on the table' for her to read. In a tape recorded interview in 1992, Peter stated that he did show her the Russian pamphlet, as he evidently said also to Hanna's biographer, Judy Lomax. Hanna did approach Himmler who reassured her. She said later that it was not until after the war that she discovered Himmler had deceived her (H. Reitsch, *Fliegen mein Leben*, Deutschen Verlagsanstalt, 1951 (translated as *The Sky My Kingdom*, by Lawrence Wilson, Bodley Head ,1955); J. Lomax, *Hanna Reitsch*, John Murray, London, 1988).

and the instrument must be destroyed. If not possible the exact location of the site must be fixed with a precise grid reference preparatory to immediate action by armed parachutists who would be dropped at the site, even if this involved fighting with Swedish guards who might be in place. The final sentence was the grimmest. Captain Gerdes had been closely concerned with the development of the new night fighter radars and was in possession of important secrets. Not only the radar instrument itself but also Gerdes himself must be eliminated before he could be interrogated.

'Well, what do you say to this?' asked Golcher. I knew that in my capacity as engineer officer I should be the one to go to Oskarshamn. I did not mind that but the implication that I might have to prepare for an armed attack on a neutral country and, worse still, somehow try to slaughter a man who was, apparently, lying unconscious in hospital, was very frightening.

It was made clear to me that I was not expected to make any attempt on Gerdes' life, for which I was grateful. I don't think I could have done such a thing but Golcher and the others discussed the matter.

'I have phoned Fincke. It's a job for him,' said Golcher. I knew that Fincke, nominally an Assistant Commercial Attaché, was our local *Gestapo* man.

'But the man is in hospital! They won't let anyone near him, he will be under guard surely,' I said.

'My dear Riedel, Fincke has people at his disposal who would attend to it if they were well paid. Swedish people. He can organise it.'

I did not find it easy to hide my disgust. Here was Golcher, a senior *Wehrmacht* officer, calmly considering the cold blooded murder of a helpless man.

The Swedish papers carried news of the landing already and it seemed likely our reaction was too late but I was ordered to go to the place and see if I could destroy the aircraft and its contents. As for the man himself, I prayed the Swedish authorities would take good care of him. I did not believe his action had been deliberate treachery. He had been ordered off on a test flight, had realised his chance to escape the war and simply headed north. I might have done the same myself, given the chance. It probably had not occurred to him that he was presenting valuable secret equipment to a foreign power who might allow it to be inspected by British and American technicians.

Before leaving I asked for a description of the radar device I was required to look for. Another telegram arrived overnight. The thing would have stencilled code on it, SN-2, and would be of such and such dimensions.[2]

---

[2] The SN-2 was the latest version of the Lichtenstein radar fitted to night fighters from February 1944. Unknown to Riedel and, presumably, the German Air Ministry, an intact Junkers 88 with this equipment complete had landed at Woodbridge in Suffolk on 13th July. (R.V. Jones, *Most Secret War*, H. Hamilton, 1978, p499.)

My journey had to be approved by the Swedish Air Ministry who ensured that I would not get up to mischief by providing me with an escort, Captain Sefeldt, who took me with him next day first to Nässjo where we had to change trains. Here on the station platform waiting for a train in the other direction we met an armed guard with a German prisoner. It was not Gerdes. This man was a sergeant mechanic who had, against his wishes, been carried off in the Ju 88 and dumped in Sweden by his pilot. The sergeant had not realised what was going on until he found himself in the crashed plane surrounded by trees. He was to be sent back to Germany at once but I was able to speak to him briefly and he gave me a better description of the device I was to look for. He was not quite sure whether it was fitted in this particular aircraft since it had not been part of his job to operate it. Sefeldt and I went on by rail to Oskarshamn, then a long way by army vehicle on forest roads and at last a twenty minute hike through dense woodland to the small clearing where the twin-engined Junkers lay, badly damaged but not burned or, as far as I could see, interfered with since its sudden arrival. There were a couple of bored guardsmen there.

With Sefeldt keeping close by I clambered into the wreck. Most of the equipment was familiar. All the standard flying instruments and engine gauges were there as usual, the radio gear looked normal so far as I could tell. But there was a grey varnished box with a milky looking glass screen and a mass of small electrical cables coming from it. I had not seen this sort of thing previously. Sure enough, SN-2 was marked on it together with other code numbers and dates. The secret gear was there all right but with the young Swedish officer present there was no chance at all of my destroying it or the aircraft. I asked, knowing what the answer would be, if I would be permitted to remove something as a souvenir, and take it away. The answer was of course no, Sefeldt had his instructions too. There was nothing more I could do other than return with him to Oskarshamn.

What about the pilot? The driver of the army truck that took us back told us that the man had not been seriously hurt but had slight concussion so they had taken him to hospital in Oskarshamn. We learned that soon after arriving there he had slashed his own wrists to kill himself. This was not because he blamed himself for losing his way and landing in the wrong country. On the contrary. The German Consul in Oskarshamn had visited the hospital to cheer him up and said 'Never mind old chap, we'll soon be sending you back to Germany. It won't be long!' Gerdes knew what awaited him if that happened and had decided to end things immediately. He had been saved from himself and now the true position was understood it had been explained to him that he would be interned if he chose.

There was no chance at all for me to do anything more. I must report back to Golcher. On the return journey to Stockholm I was able to establish friendship with my Swedish escort, Captain Sefeldt. I did not know it at the time but this contact was to prove very useful to me later.

Things had moved on while I had been away. The Air Ministry in Berlin had seen sense after all. There was no more wild talk of parachutists landing in the forest. The aircraft would be scrapped by the Swedish army when they got round to it and the grey box would go with the rest. Its special importance would probably not be realised and to make a great fuss would only draw attention to it. They were prepared to take a chance on that rather than risk a much greater catastrophe, war with Sweden.

Golcher seemed relieved too. He now told me of another, rather similar crisis which had happened while he was in command of the *Attaché Gruppe*. The Messerschmitt 262 A was new fighter bomber, powered with jet engines. Even the existence of such engines was considered a topmost secret. I had only recently heard of their existence myself. The Me 262 was quite unrelated to Lippisch's little rocket plane that Hanna and Heini Dittmar were still working on. A prototype Me 262, lost in bad weather and with very limited fuel supplies, made a forced landing on a Swiss airfield and it was quickly hidden by the Swiss somewhere under cover in a hangar there. There was near panic in Berlin. A troop of SS men was immediately organised to make a surprise attack by parachute, blow up all the hangars on the field, to make sure of destroying the one containing the hidden Messerschmitt, and fight off the Swiss Army for long enough to do this job. Afterwards they could let themselves be shot to bits or surrender, it didn't matter providing the secret plane was destroyed. Everything had been made ready and only the final order to go ahead was awaited. That the longer term consequences might have been to bring hitherto neutral Switzerland into the war against Germany apparently concerned no one.

Fortunately the Air Attaché in Bern and his Swiss equivalent in Berlin were able to come quickly to a more rational solution. The Messerschmitt would be returned without anyone looking at it closely or mentioning its existence thereafter. In return the Swiss Airforce would receive a dozen new Messerschmitt 109 fighters which they had long had on order but which had never been delivered. Golcher told me this story to convince me that military attachés were not so useless in diplomacy as we might sometimes feel. Incidentally he was also telling me that there were some hot-headed idiots in positions of high authority in Berlin.

Berlin worried still about Gerdes, the pilot of the Ju 88. Once recovered he might decide to tell what he knew in a deal for better conditions during his internment. I did not want to know what *Gestapo* Officer Fincke might be planning but after a long inner conflict I resolved on a line of action. It was not disloyal to the deeper values I held and which, I believed most ordinary German people held too, if they were allowed to give them expression. I had established friendly contacts with some of the higher ranking officers in the Swedish Airforce and I went quietly to see one of them who I was sure did not sympathise with the Nazis and who would not betray me. He did not really need much explanation once I had outlined my fears to him. He would pass the word along. Gerdes, he said, would be well looked after.[3]

---

[3] Gerdes did in fact survive and years later Peter Riedel encountered him briefly in Windhoek, SW Africa. He did not attempt to make any personal contact.

20

Treachery

'Something for you!' About 9 am on 16 November after my return from the crashed Junkers the secretary laid the telegram on my desk in a slightly odd way and looked at me as if she had something to convey. I knew her well and liked her but she seemed suddenly very serious. She said nothing more. I was to report at once to Berlin. Such an order was a little out of the normal routine but not entirely unusual. Most often I would choose my own time for the monthly trip but occasionally I was called in early for some reason. I assumed Schwenke had some instructions for me or perhaps wanted more details of the Ju 88 incident. Gloomily I began to prepare for the journey. I had a few things that must be done before leaving. About an hour later a second telegram arrived. This was odd. The girl stared hard but silently when she delivered it. Did she know something I did not?

'*Captain Riedel to report to Berlin to discuss the sale of fifty-five Daimler Benz motors to the Swedish Air Force.*' Trade was not within my area of responsibility and I knew nothing of any dealings. Did we even have fifty-five DB engines to spare? It was surprising that anyone in *Luftwaffe* HQ should think it necessary to advise me why I was wanted. The General Staff normally do not explain to a junior officer why he should report. The orders are issued and that is that, as a rule. One jumps when one is told to jump. Two telegrams within the hour, to Captain Riedel? I cleared my desk.

The conviction came to me that if I returned to Berlin I should be arrested. There were ample reasons. I had made a nuisance of myself when I came back from the USA, with what they probably considered my defeatism. I had spoken freely to Hanna and although I was sure she would not have betrayed me deliberately, she was close to Himmler and other high ranking men. In all naïve innocence and believing as she did in Himmler's good nature, she might have said too much. Anyone associated, however distantly, with Canaris' old *Abwehr* would be under a cloud now. As one of Hansen's men I would almost certainly be under suspicion. Lately, worst of all, I had truly been in touch with the enemy having had several clandestine meetings with Svensen and having written that long letter to General Donovan. If discovered, any one of these things by itself could have led to my arrest for questioning. Taken together they might mean swift execution.

I had a small two-stroke car as a runabout and drove to my apartment and packed a suitcase. If I was under observation, so far I was behaving as expected. There was one man in the Embassy I trusted, Hebb, the Press Attaché whom I had known when he was doing the same job in Washington. His wife was an American girl who came from Denver. I found him and showed him the two telegrams. He asked, 'Are you going?'

'No. I shall go to General Nordernschørt.' He was chief of the Swedish Airforce. I believed that I must approach him personally rather than any lesser officer or official. There were, in the Swedish armed forces and bureaucracy, some who would regard what I was going to do as outright treachery and would arrange my immediate deportation to Germany. I had heard of a German soldier who had been treated in exactly this way after he had deserted and escaped across the border from occupied Norway. He would certainly have been shot on his return. Hebb understood. We would keep in touch, discreetly. He would arrange for the property and furniture I had left in the apartment to be cleared and stored until I could find somewhere for them, and let him know. Then I went to see Ninnie to tell her what I intended. She took it in her stride and agreed to come with me to the Air Ministry building immediately after we had lunch.

About 2 pm we arrived outside the new Air Ministry building which was in Gardet, the so-called garden of Stockholm. While Ninnie waited in the car I was shown to General Nordernschørt who knew me already, and of my American wife. He shook my hand. We spoke English because my Swedish was still not perfect. When I explained he realised that by coming directly to him I was seeking his protection.

'Herr Riedel I understand you and sympathise. There are limits to what I can do but I will see to it that you are not interned or deported. You will have to go to the Foreigners Commission. I take it you have somewhere to live? Money?' I had saved something from my salary, enough to go on with for a while if I was careful.

'We need to call in some help,' he said. 'You should go to see Ragnar Kasparsson. He is an influential member of the Foreigners Commission and his son edits the government newspapers, *Morgen Tidningen* and *Afton Tidningen*. If you talk to him he will be able to present your case in a sympathetic way to the public. It will be a kind of insurance, so that people will know who you are and why you need to remain in Sweden. I will let them know you are coming. It isn't likely then that anyone will act officiously.' The General wished me farewell and I left his office.

Ninnie and I drove at once to see her old school friend Märta with whom she shared everything. As soon as her maid showed us into the room the woman became quite pale and looked shaken. Ninnie explained in Swedish what I was doing. Her friend seemed to pull herself together and showed sympathy but I was sure something was wrong, more than could be explained by her surprise. She was altogether more upset than seemed reasonable. We discovered that her husband, the Hamburg flak regiment Captain, was in Stockholm, although, she said, he was not at home just now. I supposed he was on leave and wondered if he decided, like me, not to return. But it transpired that he had been appointed to the Embassy staff as an Engineer Assistant Air Attaché. That was what I had been until a few hours ago! It dawned on me that a bargain had been struck: this woman's knowledge of my contacts with the OSS in exchange for her husband's official posting. Later, from Hebb, I learned that she had reported to the *Abwehr* that I had been regularly passing reports to the OSS and was being paid for them at $20,000 and $30,000 each time. The story had even been passed on to my former Japanese contacts. It was totally untrue but I was in no position to argue any more. I was branded a traitor.

In fact, the new Engineer Attaché followed my example within a few weeks, walked out of the Embassy and did not return. The difference for him was that he had a wealthy and influential wife.

Ninnie and I returned to her place and I moved in temporarily with her. I arranged to meet the journalist Kasparsson and told him my story. Among other things I mentioned the Ju 88 in the forest and warned that I knew the *Abwehr*, now in effect a part of the *Gestapo*, would like to kill the pilot Gerdes which could easily be done if somebody walked into his hospital room with a knife. Kasparsson nodded.

'There are enough Swedish Nazis who would do it too. They might even give him a pill which would kill him more quietly.' The paper carried this story, with my own part in it only mentioned.

My German diplomatic passport and immunity were of course cancelled at once. With no papers I was stateless. I was required to go to the *Utmännisches Kommission* (the Foreigners Commission) to register there. Thanks to Fritjof Nansen the famous explorer, who had done a lot of good work for international travellers after the first World War, the Swedes were able to issue a temporary document called a Nansen passport, valid for a single year. I was issued with one but apart from giving me a certain legal status within Sweden it was useless for travel at present. There was nowhere I could go as long as the war continued.

The *Abwehr* knew of my association with Ninnie and there was no secret about where she lived. Within a day or two of my defection she received a disturbing message for me through Golcher and Hebb. The *Abwehr* had taken Helen out of Switzerland and were holding her hostage! If I wanted her to survive I must surrender myself immediately to them. For a short time I was shocked but after a little thought realised that they hardly had time to organise anything of this kind. It might be a trick. Perhaps it was even a sort of warning from an unknown friend, like that second, inexplicable telegram which, whoever sent it, had in fact given me an important hint.

I went at once to the Swiss Embassy and was able to speak directly to their ambassador. He tended to scoff at the story and was somewhat offended, assuring me that no such thing as kidnapping a patient from a sanatorium and 'exporting' her would ever be allowed to happen in his country. I made him see how worried I was. Davos was not very far from the German border, Helen liked to walk by herself and set up her easel in quiet places. It would be easy for someone to pull up alongside her with a car, chloroform her and get her across the border. The ambassador agreed to make immediate enquiries. I then telephoned directly to Davos and, to my vast relief, was able to speak to Helen herself. She assured me she was perfectly safe so far. I told her the situation and that she must leave the sanatorium immediately and hide, no matter what her doctors said. She must find somewhere else to live secretly and there was no time at all to be lost. She promised to do so. Within a few hours the Swiss ambassador told me that Helen was safe, had indeed left the sanatorium and was now living in an hotel in Davos while somewhere safer was found. I must accept his word that she would be under protection as long as she remained in his country.

Helen found a convent in Davos where she could live very cheaply and privately. Soon she went by train to Zürich and called at the American Consulate. She was entitled to a full American passport and applied for it. In August there had been American landings in the south of France and German resistance had almost collapsed there. The Allied troops were advancing everywhere and the frontier with Switzerland should soon be open. Helen had maintained contact with her family in Terre Haute and with her American documents would be able to go there. Her lung trouble was much improved, although still only one lung was inflated.

This had been a foul trick. I had less sympathy than ever now for the German cause and for my former colleagues. On November 20th I approached the American Embassy and asked for US Air Force Colonel Hardison, their Air Attaché. I gave him the letter I had written for Donovan, with a brief covering note to explain why I had not dared to send it to him before. Hardison promised he would give it personally to 'Wild Bill' at the next opportunity.

My defection from the German side was well-known now. Moves were made by the German Embassy to have me extradited for court martial. It came as a shock to discover that Rolf and Märta K were testifying against me, reporting my contacts with the Americans and saying they knew that money had been paid to me. Were they trying to protect themselves from accusations of corruption? It was a disgusting way to repay me for the help I had given them. I remembered Märta's unusual reactions on the day when I arrived in her apartment with Ninnie. I guessed now that she, or Rolf, had already betrayed me then and that was why those telegrams arrived when they did. In fact I had not received the money from Märta since Ninnie had paid it into her own account. It could never have been proved to have come to me. General von Uthmann, the Military Attaché, nevertheless published widely the story that I had been an agent of the Allies all along and that I had been paid regularly for my reports to them.

I could not stay with Ninnie now. I did not doubt the *Gestapo* would find some way to deal with me if I did so and Ninnie's continuing friendship with the woman who had betrayed me created difficulties too. With the flood of refugees who came in from the Baltic States as the Russians advanced, accommodation in Stockholm was impossible to find.

Officially now I was known as a traitor to Germany. I did not doubt the *Gestapo* would find some way to deal with me if I remained visible in Stockholm. It would be safer to go into hiding, although the Swedish, authorities required me to inform them where I was. I needed to earn some money. Helen depended on this too. The owner of the garage where I had had my little car serviced regularly, when told of my problem, suggested I should go to Enköping about sixty kilometres north-west of the city where a friend of his, Larry Lund, ran one of the Hans Ostermann Company chain of garages. Lund had a vacancy for a mechanic and although the pay would be small it would keep me going. Things would be easier there in all respects, accommodation was available and cheaper than in the city, and it was much less likely that anything nasty would happen to me. I went to have a look, got the job at Ostermann's and found myself an apartment. I had my furniture transferred there at once and moved in on 18th December, with my Nansen Pass now in my pocket. I was glad to find work that would give me some practical experience of a kind which might be useful. I had little faith in my ever being able to work again as a pilot and my old academic engineering degree did not count for much now. I wanted to correspond with Helen but realised I should be careful about this. It would take only one letter to be intercepted and my whereabouts would be revealed. I got in touch again with Sefeldt, the young officer who had escorted me to the Ju 88 crash, and he agreed to provide me with an accommodation address. I wrote to Helen and explained that she must send her letters to him in future and he would forward them. Otherwise, it would be far too easy for the *Abwehr* to find me.

The winter of 1944–5 came with long, dark nights and short days. I lived frugally and almost secretly in Enköping. I became very friendly with my boss, Larry Lund, and he invited me to his home to meet his attractive wife, Else. They were of Norwegian birth. The three of us dined together often, had small parties in my apartment and talked together a great deal, improving my Swedish.

I was visited by William T. Carlsson from the US Legation. He knew of my previous contacts with Svensen and that I had written to Donovan. I talked freely to him. Declared a traitor by my own people, there seemed nothing now to prevent me helping the Allies. I was sure, all the same, that there was nothing of significance I could reveal that he did not already know. The names of my contacts in the *Abwehr* were passed on but this seemed to me worthless information. I even offered to help with Allied radio broadcasts to Germany, to try to tell the truth about the SS war crimes of which the public were still largely ignorant, and of my own experiences of the utter folly of the Nazi leadership. This, he said, would be of little use at this stage, the war being nearly over anyway. I had no direct knowledge of anyone, other than Himmler himself, who had been responsible for the cold-blooded slaughter in the camps. I told him how I had enquired about American citizenship in 1940. He would do what he could for me, he said. Nothing was promised. After he left there were occasional telephone calls from him with specific queries which I was usually unable to answer.

Richard Boord from the RAF invited me to visit him in an office in the British Embassy in Stockholm.[1] I went twice, told him what I could, and what I had seen of the bombing in Berlin and Hamburg. I answered all his questions freely.

Helen waited. I had little money to send her now. Her illness was much improved although she was still only breathing on one lung. As the war staggered on towards its end it began to look possible that she might join me and we might eventually be allowed to become Swedish citizens. Neither of us had ever raised the question of whether our marriage could continue but after this long and difficult separation it was not clear what would happen. I had nothing whatever to offer her now, little money, no secure home and very doubtful prospects. It seemed to me my best hope now was to stay in Sweden and try to make a new life, possibly continuing to work for the Ostermann organisation which had an aviation division. Soon Helen went by train to Zürich and called at the American Consulate. She was entitled to a full American passport and applied for it, intending

---

[1]Richard Boord had previously worked in Air Intelligence, analysing the results of RAF bombing attacks on German cities. (R. V. Jones, *Most Secret War*, H. Hamilton, 1978, p386).

to leave when the frontiers opened. In August 1944 there had been American landings in the south of France and German resistance had collapsed there. The Allied troops advanced and reached the Swiss border. Helen had maintained contact with her family in Terre Haute and with her American documents would be able to go there, if she chose, or come to Sweden.

I made contact with my friends in Malmö and Kurt Leube came to Enköping to see me. He found me messing about with my boat. His offer of financial help was made again and now I had to say I might need it. I made friends with a young Finnish girl, Maritsa, in Enköping. When Ninnie telephoned me one evening, Maritsa had answered so Ninnie knew I had another female friend and she was furious. I knew I should not hear from her again. She maintained her friendship with Märta and Rolf, despite their conduct. The money from Märta that was meant for Helen would never be available now. In a way I was glad, for I had begun to feel ashamed about that whole affair.

In February I read of the Yalta conference of the three great men, Churchill, Roosevelt and Stalin. The outcome as presented in the papers filled me with horror. It seemed to me the worst possible outcome. Carthage was to be destroyed. Pomerania, Silesia and Prussia, the whole of East Germany was to be taken into Poland to compensate for the loss of the eastern half of that country to the USSR. Half of East Prussia would be in Poland, the other half in the USSR. The Sudeten Germans would be ejected from Czechoslovakia. The remainder of Germany was to be carved up into occupation zones by the great powers, the Russians advancing to the Elbe in the north, far beyond Berlin, and beyond even the Elbe in the south. I felt sure that once in occupation, the Red Army would never withdraw. Austria too was to be separated from Germany and divided in two by the occupation armies. Hordes of refugees from the east, millions and millions would be forced into the war-devastated land between Elbe and Rhine and there they would starve to death in what must become a huge concentration camp. In my pencilled diary I wrote that the great powers, in punishing Germany, were going to commit the same crimes as Hitler but on an even larger scale. The occupation armies would become supervisors of a mass death camp. I could not bear the thought of returning to such a Germany.

A phone call came one evening, out of nowhere. The caller gave no name, asked only one question. Where, at this stage of final collapse, did I think Adolf Hitler might take his final refuge?

'How in God's name should I know?'

'Never mind, where might he be? If not in Berlin, or Bavaria, where?'

'Could he be in the *Abwehr* bunker at Zossen?' It was the only thing that came into my head. The caller rang off. Of course Hitler never was in Zossen.

Now, in my misery, there was Else. Once again, the Swedish casual attitudes to sex showed themselves. When Larry met Maritsa he and she became very interested in one another. Else, meanwhile, had become keen on me so there was a kind of casual swapping of partners. After a while Larry and Else separated, he taking the Finnish lass into his home. Else found herself a housekeeper's job with an elderly Norwegian man in Stockholm but came to see me often.

The day we had all waited for so long came at last on 8 May 1945, the end of the European war. The relief I felt was muted by the knowledge that Germany was in chaos from end to end and there were, as I had expected, hordes of refugees from the east, forced to live in camps. I had no home. Any friends I had were either dead or would regard me as a traitor. For the time being I survived where I was. I began to understand, however, that I could not rely on remaining in Sweden. It was generous for the authorities to offer me refuge from the *Gestapo* during the war but I was no longer threatened with instant execution. From the Swedish point of view, if I did not choose to go of my own accord, when my one year passport ran out they would deport me to Germany. There was no reason why I should remain in their country. They had more than enough refugees, Estonians, Latvians, Lithuanians, Finns, Poles and didn't need any Germans. I would certainly be wanted by the Allies for further questioning along with other former German legation staff. I read of de-Nazification tribunals, prison sentences and detention. Even innocent officials were being held in prison and submitted to long periods of interrogation. The Allies were preparing for a massive International Military Tribunal to be held at Nuremburg. No one knew what would happen there, what kind of justice or vengeance would be meted out. The phrase 'war criminal' was on everyone's lips. What did that mean? No one knew. Nothing would make me volunteer to return to Germany. I continued to work in the garage, began to hope that I had been forgotten.

Weeks slipped by and no one disturbed me. Else came regularly and was my consolation. She was with me on 12 July when we had a small party. A Swedish glider pilot, Charles Birch-Jensen, who had met me when I was demonstrating soaring in 1936 and made my crossing of The Sound by soaring to Copenhagen, had discovered I was in Enköping and came to see me with his girl-friend. In the midst of our small celebration there was a knock at the door of the apartment. A telegram from the Foreigners Commission was handed in. The decision had been made. I must report next Saturday 18 July 1945 at 5 pm, to be transported on a special ship back to Germany!

If I went back to Germany would anyone believe my story? Might I even be handed over to the Russians? Halle, Aschersleben, the little village of

Dehlitz were all under Red Army occupation now. They might have heard of the double-crossing proposed by the Finns. I could not face the prospect of returning there.

Then, I realised, the other passengers on the prison ship would be my former colleagues from the German legation, Golcher, Uthmann and others who now regarded me as contemptible. Among them would be some fanatical Nazis who would see to it, if they could, that I did not arrive in Germany at all. I should have an accident on the ship, my body would be dumped over the side. Even if this did not happen it seemed certain that I should be put in a concentration camp with them all when we arrived in Germany. I should not last long there. Shaken and terrified, I sat with my head in my hands.

'Don't go, don't go!' said Else. She had come to care for me more than I realised.

I had only until Saturday afternoon to sort things out. I went to Stockholm to the Foreigners Commission and asked, if I was to be deported, to be sent to Germany separately from the others. This was useless, there was no sympathy now. The arrangements had been made. I got in touch with the British and American legations, begging to be sent to a prison camp where I could be held in safety rather than to the same one as the others in the German diplomatic group. Some of the officials I spoke to made no secret of their hostility and distrust. Why should they care what happened to me? They probably thought of me as an opportunist who had, too late, tried to change to the winning side.

I decided to avoid deportation. I should have to go into hiding, but where? Enköping was impossible now.

'There must be something we can do,' said Else, 'Don't go! I'll find somewhere you can stay, but it will take a few days.' Birch-Jensen also promised aid.

In Stockholm I went to see the editor of a flying magazine I knew slightly, thinking he might be able to help. I explained that I needed somewhere to stay very privately for a time. He could offer nothing but as I was leaving his female secretary came with me, ostensibly just to show me out, but at the door she held me back and whispered quietly. 'I can give you the keys to an apartment I have. It's on the south side of the lake. No one will know, you can stay there, just a day or two until you find something else,' she said. 'My man friend might come in. He's Polish but speaks Swedish. If you don't say anything he won't ask!' She told me the address and thrust the keys into my hand. That, I suppose, was the moment of decision. I went to the place and let myself in, feeling like a burglar, but no one showed the slightest interest. For the time being I was safe. The hour for the boat to sail came and went. Now I was running from the law. I phoned Else.

On Monday morning, with my cheque made out to cash, Charles Birch-Jensen went with Else to my bank and drew all my money out of the account there, by now reduced to less than Kr 2000. It was somewhat risky for them to do this, but we guessed the police would not yet have organised any thorough search for me although my failure to appear at the appointed time had been noted and was even mentioned in the newspapers. My original departure from the German Embassy had made a little story and this was an interesting new development for the reporters.

I remained in the borrowed apartment until Else came and said she had found a better place for me. I should share a room with a head waiter.

'He doesn't know your nationality. I told him you are an Estonian who is writing books.' Indeed by now I was writing a book for I had decided I should try to put into writing everything that had happened to me since I took the job in Washington! I was introduced to the waiter and moved in with him, agreeing to pay half the rent. He was out at his work nearly all day and into the evening so I could get on with typing on my small machine. The apartment was in Slussen, a fairly rough sort of area but not very far away in distance from Ninnie's place. I dared not go out much but when I needed exercise I would take an evening walk.

Things went along well enough for a while until the waiter came home one afternoon and said 'I'm going to have a party next week. I've invited friends. One of them is a policeman.' Was he just trying to get rid of me? I didn't know. In a panic I called Else.

'I'll have to move! A party with a policeman is not a good idea!'

She quickly found me another place in a country area where I should be on my own but it cost more money, there was a lease and rent to pay, food to be bought and my reserves were melting away. I should have to find some other way to survive before long.

Charles Birch-Jensen came to see me and told me that Thomsen, the former German ambassador, had, during his time in Stockholm, bought himself a farm. This would have been illegal from the Nazis' point of view but he had arranged it secretly, showing a woman friend's name, Ulva Wiman, on the title. It was north of Stockholm in the forest. Thomsen was not likely ever to return so Mrs Wiman was the legal owner now. She lived in Stockholm and used the house, Apelbol, only as an occasional weekend or holiday home. It stood empty most of the time and she did not go there in winter at all. When Charles spoke to her about me she told him Peter Riedel was welcome to stay at Apelbol. She would be quite glad to have someone looking after it when she was not there and it was most unlikely I should be discovered. I was enormously grateful and travelled there alone by train. It was a snowy evening when I arrived. She picked me up from the station and took me to the house. Thomsen had been much liked by the local farming people and to explain my presence she said I was a relative of his. One of them was managing the land though I supposed there was not much to do at this season.

I had told Charles before of my hopes to get away from Europe and settle in the USA, or anywhere I could get in providing it was not Germany. We had discussed the difficulties. The idea of illegal immigration had not been far from my thoughts. I should need some sort of papers, wheresoever I went. I speculated about the possibility of a false passport. Charles told me that his sister, Elisabeth, worked for the Swedish Foreign Office and had recently been posted to their legation in Berne, Switzerland. If I could provide him with a suitable photograph he would send it to her and see if she could get a blank passport with the photo correctly mounted inside. Then if I ever needed it I could fill in the details. Charles treated the idea rather lightly but I gave him the photograph. To my astonishment, he came to the farm before Christmas and presented me with the passport and my picture in it correctly stamped, the rest being blank. Elisabeth had managed it for me, though I had never met her. Well, I thought, I shall keep it. Who knows, it might come in handy one day.

I stayed at the farm until the spring. I was totally alone most of the time, heating the house with logs cut from the surrounding forest and burned on an open fire. There was a lake, where, when it was sufficiently free of ice, I fished with rod and line. I gave fish away to the farmer when I had more than I needed. His family were glad to get it without any effort on their own part. Otherwise I ate potatoes and canned food which Else, Birch-Jensen or Ulva brought from time to time. I paid my share and managed. It was almost idyllic.

I met, unexpectedly, a half-wild solitary woodsman who had a kind of dugout house and a bicycle to move around on. He invited me to call on him and from time to time I did so, walking to his place on forest footpaths. My Swedish was imperfect and he himself was not very articulate so we spoke slowly to one another and got along well. For long periods he was my only human contact. On one occasion when going to see him, I was confronted by a huge bull elk which frightened me. I withdrew until it moved away.

The idyll came to an end in March 1946 when Ulva decided she could not afford to let the place stand empty and leased it for high rent to a man who wanted to use it at weekends. She expected him to let me stay on as caretaker but when he arrived he turned me out and locked the doors. Fortunately that was a mild spring night and I spent most of it walking about. Eventually I lay down in a sheltered, dry spot and dropped off to sleep, to be awakened at dawn by a female elk walking by. She galloped away in fright when I sat up. Ulva came and let me into the house to collect my few possessions. I went back to Stockholm to find Else.

Else's employer, Mr Muskand, was a lonely widower in his sixties. He was willing for me to stay in his house as Else's friend but he had two adult daughters who after a couple of months discovered I was there and did not like the arrangement. It did not take them long to guess who I was. On 4 June 1946 the police were at the door. They were very polite, almost apologetic.

'Herr Riedel, we're very sorry but we have to arrest you. You have to go back to Germany. Maybe it won't be so bad.' They took me and I spent a night in a cell in the main police building in the city. Next morning I was in Långholmen prison. I was treated, not as a criminal but as someone who had no right to be in Sweden and should be deported, but they did not seem to hurry themselves about this. I came to understand that at least I should not be send to the Russian occupied zone if I did not wish to go there. I should be kept in jail until I was handed over eventually to the British.

21

Boat People

At least I could now write openly to Helen and tell her where I was. If she
wanted to see me ever again she could now come to Stockholm and would
be allowed to visit me in jail. I should not have been surprised if she
decided to forget about me, but faithfully she came. Our reunion was
extraordinary but we still had terrible problems. I was, after all, in a cell.
Whenever they chose, the Swedish authorities could ship me over the
Baltic and, as far as I could tell, there might be more jail waiting for me
there. Helen found lodgings with the Schindeler family, who lived in a
small house in Stockholm and were very kind to her. Still she was breathing
on one lung!

In Långholmen prison[1] with me were many like myself who did not wish
to be sent home, who knew that they faced death if they should ever be
forced back there. They were mostly Estonian, Latvian and Lithuanian,
their countries having been overrun by the USSR as a result of the
Molotov-Ribbentrop pact. Great numbers of people from the three Baltic
States had been rounded up and sent to labour camps in Siberia, places
probably almost as bad as the Nazi concentration camps, although they had
never installed gas chambers. People in the Siberian camps died of
starvation, overwork and bitter cold, or were sometimes beaten to death
as punishment. There was brutality and cruelty but not the cold-blooded,
organised slaughter. When the Germans in turn drove the Red Army out in
1941 these fellow prisoners had understandably volunteered to fight on the
German side. As with the Finns, the Russians were for them the only
enemy! Now their homelands had been totally absorbed into the USSR.
They could not return. It was reassuring in a way that they were being held
here in reasonably good prison conditions, rather than being simply loaded
onto ships and sent on the first stage of a long trip to Siberia.

Whole families were escaping as best they could, sometimes rowing
across the Baltic in open boats or smuggling themselves on fishing vessels.
The Swedish authorities did not wish to be needlessly cruel. But neither

---

[1] Långholmen prison is now a hotel. The original cells with steel doors are still used, but
with some rearrangement and decoration the buildings have been made very pleasant. That
it was once a prison is made much of in the advertisements.

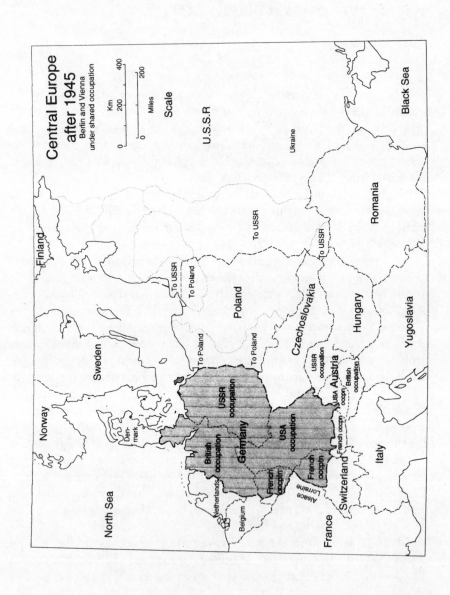

Central Europe
after 1945

Berlin and Vienna
under shared occupation

Scale

Miles

Km

0   200   400

0   200

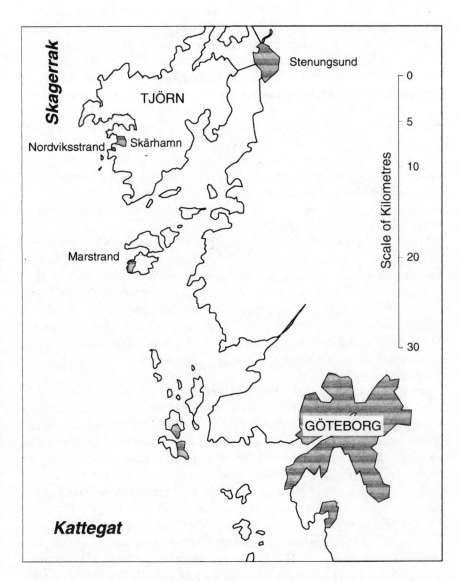

did they want to keep looking after illegal immigrants who had arrived by these means or in some other way. Most were innocents who, through no fault of their own, had lost everything and needed to start a new life somewhere, but the arrivals might also include escaping war criminals of the foulest kind. Assisting the escape of anyone who might be wanted for questioning by the Allies was not desirable. In a sense the Swedes were caught in a cleft stick. So were the refugees.

217

From the other prisoners I learned that there was an organisation for getting people away from Sweden. Most countries in the world had strict immigration laws but Venezuela, they believed, was short of skilled people and was willing to issue entry visas easily and quickly to almost anyone from Europe. They would not ask too many difficult questions. Refugees from the Baltic States were forming groups, pooling all their resources to buy boats, fitting them out and sailing quietly away aiming eventually for Venezuela. They said the porter employed at the Venezuelan Embassy, an Estonian himself, was the person with the necessary contacts. This was interesting but of little help to me since I expected soon to be put on a ship to Germany. Deportation came closer every day and I dreaded the time when I should leave Långholmen. Life in the prison was tolerable, there was regular food, we were warm enough and there was a good library. Helen came to see me regularly.

Then there was a stroke of luck, though it must have been bad for other people. A full year after the end of the fighting, Germany still had a desperate food shortage and lack of housing for many thousands of the population. The British occupation authorities were struggling to feed and shelter the population and still more refugees kept coming in, especially from the east. The Swedish government was asked to send no more deportees. I would not have to go back to Germany! My three months legal detention must finish on 4 September and they had no recourse but to release me!

But what should I do now? I was still stateless. With Helen I went to the Swedish Minister of Interior who knew all about me from his files and the newspaper reports. He was able to renew the Nansen Pass and give me a foreign visitor's permit but this would not be valid beyond 30 November. He would not help me to get away from Sweden, neither could he permit me to stay. I took it to mean that I must get out of his country any way I could and he didn't want to know how I did so. This was all very well but I feared the Allied powers would treat me as a prisoner-of-war.

I went next to the Venezuelan Ambassador, who also knew about me. One way and another I had acquired a reputation. We spoke in German for his parents had emigrated from Germany before he was born. My case was difficult, he said. Giving entry visas to refugees from the Baltic States was one thing but a German, especially a former Military Attaché, was rather different. There was in effect an international blockade in force and he could not afford to offend the Allies. There would be no official help this side of the Atlantic anyway.

I might, however, be able to join one of the Estonian refugee boats. The Estonian janitor in the Embassy, when approached, put me in touch with Arnold Vassila, an Estonian now settled in Stockholm and living in

Enskede. His nephew Valter was preparing a small vessel, the *Elvie*, and the three of us met in Arnold's apartment. They had a captain ready, Voldemar Weskimeister, aged 27 and an experienced sailor. He was at present seeing to the boat which was being re-fitted in a tiny harbour, Nordviksstrand near Skärhamn on the island of Tjörn, 40 km north of Göteborg, facing the Skagerrak, the straits between the northern tip of Denmark and Norway.

'We have 16 berths, it costs Kr 1,000 for each person. There is food and fuel to be found apart from the purchase of the boat and the work that must be done.' But again, my unwanted reputation had gone ahead of me. I spoke about my difficulty with the passport. He winked.

'There is someone who can take care of that,' he said, and gave me a phone number.

'But Mr Riedel, everybody knows about you. To allow you on the boat involves us in a greater risk. For you, it will be Kr 2,000.' It was more than I could possibly afford. Perhaps I could borrow it?

Humbling myself I approached a wealthy business couple I knew slightly. Mr Koehncke had originally been a Hamburg German, now naturalised. They had been very friendly towards me when I was at the Embassy. When I explained they gave me the cash with scarcely a moment's hesitation. The loan meant little to them and in my situation I was glad to take it, though not sure I should ever be able to repay it.

I telephoned. Yes, filling out the blank passport would be possible. He had experience. I had a friend Stig Nilsson, of about my own age and appearance. He agreed I could use his name and background details. We bought rubber stamps for modification and Helen, with her artistic touch, contributed. We worked on the booklet to make it look somewhat worn. As far as we could tell when finished, the passport looked genuine. My accent was still not good but I was ready to explain, to anyone who asked, that I had German mother. That, at least, was true. I repaid Berg Jensen for his help by giving him my little boat that had been idle all this time.

So at last I was ready and eager to get away. 'But,' they said, 'the boat isn't quite finished yet!' I waited with Helen at the Schindeler's, it seemed for a long time although it cannot have been very many days. At last the telephone call came. I was to go to the tiny harbour, Nordviksstrand, on the west coast just south of the Norwegian frontier. On the map I could see it was a rocky, inhospitable coastline. I supposed they would leave harbour and put out directly into the Skagerrak and the North Sea. Helen and I parted again. I promised to write to her regularly to tell her where I was and she would reply. She saw me off on the trip by suburban train at first, then by bus. She went back first to the Schindelers and then to friends, the Leubers, in Malmö where she remained waiting to hear from me.

When I reached the rendezvous, still the boat was not ready. More had to be done on the motor and they had not finished putting in the bunks. The boat was called *Elvie*, small, perhaps 20 metres (66 ft) long and 5.2 m (17 ft) wide, seeming nearly as wide in the beam as it was long, shaped almost like a walnut shell! It was never intended for anything more than drift fishing close to shore. The bunks, newly installed, were arranged in two small cabins, six in the front, eight in the rear, with two more in the wheelhouse above the deck. There was an elderly one cylinder engine, not in good condition, and it was possible to hoist a single small sail on a stumpy mast at the rear. There was no such thing as a radio or any means of communication. How far could sixteen of us possibly sail in such a craft? To Venezuela? That would be impossible. We might get somewhere by creeping along the coast. I had no alternative now but to go along. The hull was solidly built, as far as I could tell. Fortunately I did not probe beneath the rusty sheet metal that plated the bows.

I had a few days to get to know those who would be sailing. There were eleven men and five women. The captain was an Estonian of twenty-five years of age, Wally I called him, who fortunately knew enough Swedish to get along. He understood navigation and was equipped with a sextant and chronometer. Among the passengers most extraordinary of all was Helge Rosvaenge, the famous tenor and Wagnerian opera singer. He was Danish by birth and had a fine reputation which had been his undoing. Hitler loved Wagner and Rosvaenge was the singer he most liked to hear. It was not Helge's fault that he was commanded to perform for Adolf many times and became his favourite. Now, although innocent of any political involvement, he was contaminated. Nobody in Europe would employ him. He brought with him his *de facto* wife, an Estonian, Valentina. He was, like the rest of us, almost penniless now but he had been able to arrange a concert tour in Spain. Our little *Elvie* was the only way he could find to get there. Under Franco, Spain was the only country in Europe where hatred of everyone connected with Hitler was not automatic.

There was another male singer, Krumitsch, a bass from the State opera in Riga. He was built like a great bear and spoke some German. There was a Swede, Hans Bergwall from the island of Jotland, who had left his wife and was escaping with his girl friend, Ingrid. Then there was a South African, Paul Berjois, an experienced sailor and expert mechanic who was the only one of us who was leaving Sweden with a fully valid passport from his own country. He too had his girl along and meant to marry her. Paky was Hungarian, an electrical engineer. Everyone was, in one way or another, running away. The other seven were all Estonians or Latvians with whom I had no common language. I did the best I could with their names: Wladislav, the brothers Ilmar and Edgar Thomson, Magi, Karlis and two women, Leila and Lya. They were doing nothing illegal by getting themselves away from Sweden but my passport was a forgery. As soon as we left the Swedish coast I should be vulnerable.

At last we sailed and I had expected we should head out immediately westward. No, the skipper must first follow the coast south to Göteborg and put in there to get some maps. It didn't matter to the others. They hadn't realised how afraid I was of being recognised. We arrived at the wide mouth of the Göta river and turned in. The waterway grew narrower and suddenly to my horror a police boat pulled out from the shore, sailed a parallel course and then began to edge closer and closer, instructing us to heave to. Our motor was cut. I was sure I would soon find myself locked up again, but this time for a real offence, possessing a false passport! How could they have known I was on board? Had I been betrayed again? I had paid more than two thousand crowns for nothing and now was worse off than ever.

I went into the cabin and lay on my bunk waiting for them to come and get me. The captain, with all the passports except mine, talked to the police. I could not hear what was said. Orders were given. This is it, I thought!

The motor of our boat started again, chug, chug, chug. 'It's all right, Nilsson, you can come out now!' someone shouted. The police boat sheered away. They had been informed by telephone or radio that some Nazi collaborators wanted by the Danish police had just fled from Denmark in a fishing boat and might be heading for Göteborg. We were going up river and our *Elvie* looked likely to be the one so they had stopped us. Our skipper proved that we had come from a Swedish harbour in the north and all our people were legal. When we tied up in the harbour I didn't dare leave the boat at all and hid in the cabin. The others went on shore cheerfully and came back in ones and twos. Wally bought the maps he needed.

Late in the afternoon we set off again and stopped at anchor for the night at the river mouth. It was rather windy and the sea looked rough so the captain decided to wait till early morning. We didn't in fact get going very early since there was, already, something that had to be repaired but we got underway at 11 am. Chug, chug, chug we went against the wind, very slowly out into the Kattegat in the afternoon.

Darkness came early and we were making very little progress. The wind freshened more and more, directly from the west. Now the waves developed white heads and we found ourselves in a terrifying storm. Everybody except the captain and Helge became dreadfully seasick, the boat was flung about violently and I was sure we would soon be destroyed. My flying experience helped me to resist the sickness but this was far worse than anything that I had ever known in the air, even in gliders on the roughest soaring days. Those of us capable of standing worked the pump in rapidly changing shifts but before long one of the sick ones crawled out to say that water was rising in the cabin.

Berjois realised that the pump wasn't working. Krumitsch, the bear, helped him to lift it out of the hole in the deck and Berjois took the whole thing apart. Sick as he was and soaked by the seas crashing over us, he just spat overboard and carried on working. Astonishingly, he got the thing all together again and the two of them lifted it back into its hole. We pumped crazily and the boat stayed afloat.

We saw some lights flashing but did not know what they were. We knew there were various islands and were afraid of being blown onto the shore and wrecked, but there was little anyone could do about it. Then at two in the morning, with unbelievable rapidity the wind fell, the seas became less, the white caps disappeared, we were rolling in a swell and the danger had passed. The young captain had been at the wheel all the time and was totally exhausted. Someone else must take his place and I was glad to do so. We had survived. Chug, chug, chug. When dawn came we could see a coastline and the little *Elvie* crawled into a fjord. It led to the Danish town of Åalborg. My passport was accepted as genuine and my Swedish accent sounded perfectly all right to the Danes. It had been, we read in the papers, the worst storm in those waters for fifteen years. A fishing trawler and crew, a much larger vessel than ours, had been lost, other ships had been damaged and had run for shelter.

Helge was particularly happy to be in his own country and took us all to a restaurant, but he must get on to Spain so he intended to stay with us. We rested over night, did a few small repairs and recovered from our sickness. I was shocked when, in an idle moment, I looked more carefully at the *Elvie*'s bows. Under the metal sheathing the timber was obviously rotten. I could push a knife blade into it with hardly any resistance. Yet it had not torn away in those heavy seas!

From Åalborg we could sail right through northern Denmark without going to sea. Chug, chug, chug we puttered away, following the narrow fjord which eventually opened out into the broad Limfjorden, a large lagoon with a narrow exit to the North Sea. We had no need to fear storms here.

Chug, chug, chug . . . and then silence. The motor stopped and could not be re-started. Berjois looked at it and took off the cylinder head. Nothing to be done without a full workshop. The *Elvie* drifted in the lagoon. There was a small triangular sail and mast at the rear which was intended only to keep the boat's head to the wind when drift fishing. We hoisted the sail and tried to steer but in nearly flat calm it was useless. Before long we grounded on the mud of the Limfjord. Fortunately, a

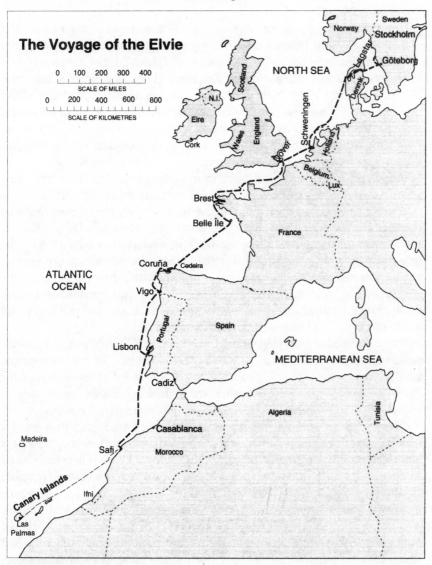

The Voyage of the Elvie

SCALE OF MILES
0 100 200 300 400

SCALE OF KILOMETRES
0 200 400 600 800

NORTH SEA

ATLANTIC OCEAN

MEDITERRANEAN SEA

Sweden
Norway
Stockholm
Göteborg
Scotland
N.I.
Eire
Cork
Wales
England
Dover
Schweningen
Holland
Belgium
Lux
Brest
Belle Île
France
Coruña
Cedeira
Vigo
Portugal
Spain
Lisbon
Cadiz
Algeria
Tunisia
Madeira
Casablanca
Safi
Morocco
Canary Islands
Ifni
Las Palmas

beautiful diesel yacht with two masts was in sight. The captain saw our problem and stopped. It was a trading vessel that sailed round all the fjord towns. A young lad aged about 12 rowed over to us with a line, which we used to haul in a towrope. The yacht pulled us off the mud and towed us back to Løgstar where there was a machine shop. Two of our Estonians were very capable machinists and over a period of several days they were able to make a new connecting rod for the engine to replace the broken one and fit it so that it would run again. It seemed as good as new.

223

Chug, chug, chug, off we went again. The delay and repairs had cost money but all went happily now. We got away from the fjord and out into the sea in fine weather. The sun shone, dolphins played around us, we sunbathed, laughed, tried to learn Estonian, Helge sang a little duet with Krumitsch, chug, chug, chug across the Heligoland Bight. We joked about this pleasant little cruise which wealthy folk would pay a fortune for, and the entertaining company. The Friesian islands loomed up on our left, we were able soon to turn south-west and were approaching the English Channel. We kept close in to the sand dunes of the Dutch coast, passed Den Helder, Zandvoort, and were near Schweningen when it happened again. Chug, chug . . . pop, BANG! We were without the engine.

Up went the sail and with the breeze fortunately we scratched our way towards the harbour. As we got closer we saw some official in uniform waving frantically and shouting too but there was little we could do. The tide must have been coming in for the current swept us into the narrow space between the short pierheads and into the harbour. There we anchored. The harbourmaster had expected us to run aground and block the entrance but the *Elvie* had a very shallow draught and we had come safely over the mud banks, riding in on the tide.

For me it was a worrying hour. I was sure the Dutch would have my name and description on a list somewhere. By now the Swedish police would have missed me and probably passed the word along: look out for Peter Riedel! Along came a rather tough looking bobby on a bicycle, requiring all our passports. He took his job seriously, inspected us all thoroughly, went through the documents. He was distracted from me by his concern about the Estonians who, as far as he understood things, were a kind of Russians and might be communist subversives. When he learned that we were fully intending to leave his country at the earliest possible moment he relaxed and left us. But now, the engine! Our engineers dismantled it and took it ashore for the necessary work which, again, would take several days. The replacements they had made in Denmark had not broken but, as often happens, fitting new parts to an old machine had been too much for the rest. I kept myself out of sight as much as possible but had to take a walk on shore occasionally.

In the town Krumitsch was amazed to meet a woman singer he knew, Valja von Siberts, also from Riga. It turned out she had even worked on some occasion with Helge Rosvaenge in an opera, though in a minor role. During the war she had been employed by the German occupation authorities on a Dutch radio station as the compere of a classical music show. She had no politics and had not been accused of traitorous collaboration by the Dutch since she had never been a Dutch citizen. Even so she had little future now in this country and could certainly never go back to Riga. She believed the Russians would soon occupy the whole of Europe and was anxious to escape before that could happen. She was far from the only person who thought in this way. So, Krumitsch said, why shouldn't she come with us? What was more, she could bring some money with her which would pay for the repairs to the engine. That decided it. She would come and there would be seventeen of us in the cockle-shell.

Despite having come so far, I began to feel thoroughly miserable, sinking into one of my dark depressive phases. Here I was, in a ridiculous but very dangerous situation with a crazy bunch of strange people, on a rotting little boat, puttering along the coast of Europe, breaking down every so often and imagining that some day we should arrive in Latin America. How in God's name had I got into this mess? The euphoria of just a few days ago had gone. At each town we passed I had written briefly to Helen using our agreed cover name. Late one night in Schweningen, full of sorrow, I thought of Else. I wrote a short note to her, hoping she was well, no more, and posted it next day to her home address with the old Norwegian widower. Why did I do such a thing?

When at last we left Schweningen there were five women and twelve men. In our very cramped accommodation there were many embarrassments and tensions. Now, to my dismay, we headed across the Channel to Dover! Why, I asked, must we do this? For me it was putting my head into the lion's mouth. The Estonians and Latvians knew that in London there were shadow governments. They were anxious to have their nationality recognised by these semi-official bodies, to get passports from them if they could. They wanted also to find out if any of their lost family members had survived and there might be news of them in London. The women in the party had been married and did not know if their husbands were alive. They needed to find out in case there was a chance of a reunion. If not, proof of death would free them to re-marry some day. So, to Dover we went across a rolling sea which made some people sick again. As we approached the harbour entrance our captain steered between the most obvious pierheads, not realising that several block ships had been sunk there deliberately when the German invasion was expected in 1940. People on shore waved and shouted, pointing to the other entrance, but all oblivious we chugged away and, because the *Elvie* was so small, she passed over the wrecks and into the calm water. Now everyone turned to me.

'Nilsson, you speak good English. Will you deal with the passports man for us?' I went hot and cold by turns but could not refuse. The others knew so little of the language that there would be a great fuss and probably a long delay if it should be left to them. Better to get the business over quickly. I had some confidence in my passport now because it had passed the Danish and Dutch inspections.

The officer came on board and went through everything. He was a cheerful sort of fellow but did a thorough job all the same. He had a book with a long list of names, which he checked carefully against each passport. I shook inwardly, guessing that Peter Riedel would be there! But now I was Stig Nilsson, a Swede, and he did not challenge me. We had decided to say we were bound for South Africa. He did not conceal his doubts that we would ever get there but said if we did so I should send him a postcard. I did take a note of his address, which he laughingly gave me. I hardly realised it but this was where our little party began to divide and argue. The question was, where were we really intending to go?

For the time being, then, I relaxed and while the captain organised the necessary excursion to London for those who needed to go, I dared to venture on shore. I reminded myself of the taste of some famous British foods like Welsh rarebit, which I enjoyed, and fish and chips wrapped in yesterday's *Daily Express* and a scrap of greaseproof paper. Food and clothes rationing was still in force so I could not buy much and in any case I had very little money. A pick-up truck with four German prisoners in faded uniforms came to do some sort of work on the pier. How they came to be prisoners still so long after the end of the war, I did not know. A British soldier with a rifle was guarding them but he handed the gun to one of the prisoners and scrambled onto our boat for a look round and a chat.

At last the party re-assembled. Nothing of any importance had been found in London but at least our Baltic companions had made themselves known, registered their names and obtained some papers, though what they were worth internationally no one knew. Off we sailed again in good weather across the Channel, chugging steadily along the coast of France, threading through the Channel Islands without landing and on to the coast of Brittany, putting into Brest. We had to stop here for fuel, cautiously finding our way in despite a slight fog. Now it was the turn of one of our Estonian women to see us through the passport controls. She had lived in Paris, spoke excellent French and was good looking too so the young officers who inspected us were distracted and did not seem to worry about us too much. During the few hours we were in the harbour I took a walk around, seeing the massive concrete pens built for the U-boats but which were now derelict. Another German prisoner in old uniform was wandering about sadly. A non-smoker myself I nevertheless carried cigarettes which, in post-war times, had become better than currency. I gave him the packet but did not stay to talk with him. That would draw attention which I did not want. I wrote my letter to Helen and posted it.

On we went, along the coast for some way, passing the high cliffs where I remembered the famous Captain Le Bris had tried to fly a glider in 1868. Based on the design of the wandering albatross it flew without a pilot several times but finally crashed. It was a fine experiment.[2] Should I ever fly a sailplane again, I wondered.

A storm arose and we took shelter in good time in a small harbour on Belle Isle. The weather held us there for four days. We were well into the winter of 1946 now. During this time we explored the island, hiring bicycles, enjoying another strange kind of holiday. I met another young German soldier working for a local farmer. This time I felt free to stop and talk, telling him that I had German mother but not revealing too much.

Once again we were off, the captain relying on a period of calm before another Atlantic storm swept in from the west. Instead of keeping to the coast he cut straight across the Bay of Biscay, which was risky but all went well. In the middle of the night we saw lights and when dawn came we found ourselves amongst a Spanish fishing fleet. They were surprised to see us and encouraged us to do some fishing ourselves. We soon had more fish than we could use. The high, green coastline was within easy reach south of us. The fishermen told us we had been mad to cross Biscay and that another big storm was coming. We must get to shelter. We followed them in to Cedeira, a small village with a very good harbour almost at the extreme north west corner of the Spanish peninsula. No one took any notice as we came in but a couple of the young fishermen visited us, full of curiosity and questions though they were not officials. Foreigners were almost unknown here. Eventually the local policeman arrived on his bicycle and came on board. He said we must go to La Coruña, forty kilometres along the coast where there were proper customs and immigration controls. He would let them know to expect us. Meanwhile, the weather was becoming very bad, we could go on shore providing we did not leave the village. I was able to use my Colombian Spanish with him and he became very friendly. Later we went to the only inn and sat with the fishermen who were prevented from going to sea by the storm. They were bored and glad to have some exotic strangers to talk to, though making little of any language but their own dialect. I had difficulty making myself understood even in Spanish, but managed to explain that we were looking for a new start in either Latin America or South Africa.

---

[2] Le Bris was a sea captain who flew his first glider, towed aloft by horses, in 1857, with himself on board. He crashed and broke an ankle, subsequently confining his trials to unmanned, ballasted gliders.

22

Casablanca Interrogation

The storm kept us in Cedeira for three days and then we chugged away for La Coruña. I dimly remembered a history lesson. This was where a British army in the Napoleonic wars had been forced back by immensely superior French forces but had managed to sail away in orderly fashion and so live to fight again. It had been a sort of former day Dunkirk! We entered the harbour, where we were expected, and anchored where directed. The inspection of our documents was apparently casual, we were welcomed almost royally and invited to call at the yacht club as guests. People who spoke English and French hastened to meet us, though the Baltic languages and Swedish defeated them. I did not try German on anyone.

Now we were in several kinds of difficulty. We needed fuel for the *Elvie* and food stocks were low. Our money, even when pooled, was next to nothing. We could not proceed but neither could we stay. What to do?

One of our new Spanish friends, the president of the yacht club, was a retired army General and had the inspiration. We must put on a concert! We could take money at the door. He had never heard of Helge Rosvaenge before but took our word for it that he was a great singer. There was Miss von Siberts and Krumitsch from the Riga opera! Somewhere in the town they could find a pianist and a Spanish singer who would be able to help and give things a local flavour. He knew someone, a young man married to a Swedish girl. What more did we need?

In no time the General sent a young, multilingual student who found a local cinema hall where the manager was prepared to rent the place to us for a nominal sum. He took us to see Maestro Brahe, a very good pianist who had fallen on hard times because he had opposed Franco in the civil war. The Maestro was highly delighted at the prospect of a performance with Helge. I myself had Spanish so could act as announcer and master of ceremonies. The General himself handled the publicity and gave information to the local press.

Helge had not performed formally for a long time and insisted on some rehearsals. I went with him and the other singers to the Maestro's small room where he had his piano and I learned for the first time what a really powerful operatic voice is like. Contained in this small space I thought the windows would be shattered but the Maestro was thrilled. Nothing so good had ever been heard in La Coruña in his lifetime.

The concert was an enormous success with packed audiences and we made what seemed to us like a lot of money even after paying the Maestro and the young Spanish boy for their efforts. We were asked to repeat the performance and did so, with similar results. I was cautious when I met the Swedish wife of the local singer in case she should notice my distinctly poor accent. Fortunately I did not have to speak to her in Swedish. She heard me announcing the items to the Spanish audience but my accent then would not have seemed out of place. We fuelled up the boat, stocked up with food, and sailed on to Vigo where we planned to try another concert or two.

Vigo turned out to be a much less attractive town, more industrial and gloomier but also more wealthy. The yacht club was more luxurious and because of the recommendations from our previous hosts we were warmly welcomed. Again we arranged some concerts. The Maestro and the young Spaniard came over land to take their parts and I was again the announcer. It all went very well. We made 13,500 pesetas. Wealth indeed!

There was, for me, a slightly sinister happening here. I heard of it only later from one of our boat people. I had to announce the name of the Catalonian composer Isaac Albéniz and, not knowing any better, mispronounced it in such a way that the audience hooted with laughter. I learned my mistake and corrected it but I was told afterwards some man had come up to one of our people and said 'Who is that fellow? He sounds German? Why is he with you?' The answer, Stig Nilsson, a Swede, seemed to satisfy the enquiry but before we left Vigo several of us noticed an elderly man, stocky, walking about the harbour, better dressed than the typical waterfront idler and taking more than a casual interest in our comings and goings. He did not approach any of us to speak but just looked. Nothing happened. Spain, I thought, would take no action against a German and our next port would be Portuguese Lisbon. Nothing to worry about.

The divisions within our own group were worsening. We were approaching the point where we would have to make some important decisions. In Göteborg we had noticed a rather fine Finnish yacht which, to our surprise, had been moored in Dover too when we arrived there. It turned up again in Coruña and Vigo, by which time we had made friends with the people on board who were bound for the USA. They had a few spare berths and were offering passages. I could not afford to pay what they demanded but Helge wanted to sell his share of the *Elvie* and go with them. We could not afford to buy him out. Bergwall suggested that we could go on to Lisbon and then to Cadiz for even more singing, to raise enough cash for all the shares to be paid out. After this those who wanted to continue with the *Elvie* could do so, but he, Helge and anyone else would head for the Americas. I would have been content with this for I could not see the *Elvie* ever being fit to cross the Atlantic. The arguments became quarrels. Valja, who had joined us in Holland, became especially vitriolic. She hated the cramped and difficult conditions on the boat and it became difficult to tolerate her constant complaining. She had managed to quarrel with the other women. She would be glad to disembark anywhere and I would have been glad to see her depart but she had contributed all her own money and did not want to see it vanish over the horizon. The Estonians, in the majority, were for South Africa and resisted the idea of any further delays. They did not see any need to stage more concerts. We had fuel and supplies and should get on with the woyage. In the end there was an unhappy compromise.

Helge now left us with his girl and Valja von Siberts. He needed go to Madrid and Barcelona for the concert tour he had been planning. He might rejoin us in Cadiz to put on another concert to raise more money but he would stay behind in Spain when we left. The idea occurred to me that we should have spare places on the *Elvie* and might find more passengers to help with payments. I was not sorry to see Valja go.

Off we sailed for Lisbon and reached there with no serious problems although there were arguments. What should be our destination? Was it Venezuela? I think we all knew that was not possible in the *Elvie*. What about South Africa? That looked more feasible, a coastal voyage along the African coast with somewhere to run to if the weather turned foul. But what sort of coast was it? Nobody had any experience. It would not be like Europe with fishing villages and facilities every few miles. Long stretches of empty land, no guaranteed welcome anywhere.

The Portuguese authorities were not unkind but very firm. I remembered the last time I had arrived here as a member of the diplomatic party in May 1942. How different things were now! Each of us was interviewed by an apparently friendly officer in civilian clothes. I was the last to be called in to him and to me he spoke fluent German, which made me uneasy. I almost expected him to say, 'You are Peter Riedel, aren't you?' but he did not. Instead he let us all go and wished us a good trip. We would be allowed to take on food, fuel and water but we must not stay. Only one of us, Wally the Captain, was allowed on shore but since he spoke no Spanish I was permitted to go with him to the post office to collect mail. I was disappointed that no letter was waiting from Helen.

At sea again. It was 9 December 1946. Now the arguments between us really developed. Where next? The argument became quite fierce. At one stage Hans Bergwall attempted to take a vote by going round the whole party with a list of our names and requiring everyone to vote. He tried to brow beat us into agreeing with his own view that we should go to Cadiz where Helge would meet us and there would be more concerts and more money, perhaps some paying passengers. Ingrid was the first to give him her vote. He shouted and swore like a Viking until he accumulated a few more. Others were for pressing on immediately to the Canary Islands. Bergwall's anger burned out in frustration. Looking further ahead, Wally had bought maps in Lisbon and was seriously thinking of plodding along the African coast to reach Walvis Bay. We should put in somewhere in Morocco on the way to Las Palmas. He was captain, he could navigate, he would have his way. It was agreed that we should get to Las Palmas together but from there it became clear our ways would divide.

Chug, chug, chug. Europe faded into the distance behind us and suddenly I felt enormously happy. Whatever happened now, I had broken free of a continent I had come to detest. As we passed the straits of Gibraltar a large freighter, the *Robert McBurnow* out of Portland, Maine, sailed heavily by. We waved and shouted but as far as we could tell there was no one on deck and the bridge was deserted. Chug, chug, chug. Our sail was hoisted to help us along a little in a light ENE breeze, making about 6 knots. The sun shone, we lounged on the deck. Wally took a sun reading at 16.37 with myself counting the time for him. I noticed a large flock of gulls, perhaps more than a hundred in a group on the water and many more circling, wings motionless, round and round overhead, soaring, gaining height. There must have been a hot current from an undersea volcanic eruption or something of the kind, producing a warm up-welling and heating the air above creating a thermal in the atmosphere. The gulls were soaring. If only I could be up there with them in a glider! Karlis and Lya quarrelled in Lettish for half an hour. Lya was sick of the journey and the boat and everyone on it and wanted only to get on land and stay somewhere. We passed Casablanca, barely visible on the horizon. The nearest point of land was El-Jorf Lasta and we turned in towards Safi, French Morocco.

At the entrance to the port was a powerful red light and we entered to anchor as the evening fell. A boat came out to us and we were told to stay on board until morning. Someone would come then to check us over. It was 12 December.

In the morning two officials in civilian dress came, at first in a very relaxed mood. Our Estonian French-speaking girl answered their questions. Who were we, where were we going? Such a motley lot? All these nationalities? Stupidly, as I found out later, she said we were tourists. Tourists! In a scruffy little boat like this? Tourists? In French Morocco? FRENCH Morocco!

They supplied us with water and fresh food. We had to hand in all our passports and we were allowed on shore but must not weigh anchor.

Tomorrow we should come to the police station to collect our passports.

They came early next day with a boat big enough for all of us, took us to the immigration office and proceeded to hand back the documents one at a time. They left me until last. I knew, as I stood there waiting, that I was in trouble. All my relief at leaving Europe was swept away and I was in the blackest depths of misery before they ever came to me. December, December. Oh mother!

They had telephoned for instructions and Casablanca had some word about an unknown German, tall, passing as a Swede. An escaping war criminal? An SS man? I was handcuffed. They took me to the police station, gave me a seat and the questions began. There were, in addition to the civilians, two men in military uniform. I knew my only hope now was to be completely truthful. They would be able to check my story and confirm it, even, perhaps, to the extent of asking Donovan if he knew me. At least they would be able to confirm that I was never in the SS, had never been in a position to commit crimes against humanity.

'Gentlemen, there is no need for this. My name is Peter Riedel. I am German.'

'Voila! La confession!' They produced a lengthy form. At the head of it I saw the words *Criminal de Guerre*.

For the rest of that day, I was interrogated by a succession of people, almost hysterical, raging at me, accusing me of lying every time I spoke. I was a dangerous fellow who ought to be shot out of hand. At times I feared they meant to do it but I stuck to the truth all the time. There was only one thing where I lied. This was about the blank passport. I must not get Berg Jensen's sister Elisabeth into trouble so I must not tell them where it came from. I said Helen had faked it for me. Later I had to admit the truth about this too. The black and terrifying day ended at last. I was totally exhausted. Then I was handed over to the local police chief who, for the time being, was to put me in prison for transport to Casablanca tomorrow and further interrogation. He was to give me a meal first and then was expected to clap me in a cell alongside the local petty thieves and among the bugs and lice. As I ate, he talked quietly to me, asked me about myself before the war. I told him of my glider flying and soaring, mentioned that on one occasion I had flown from the Wasserkuppe to land in France near Romicourt at Grancourt Belair.

'Ah, Monsieur! Je suis de Grancourt Belair!' He was delighted that I knew the place and I was even able to name the factory where he had once been employed in the small town. After this he became much more friendly and instead of throwing me into a cell, allowed me to sleep on the desk in his office with a guard outside. It was cold but at least it was clean, that night of 17 December.

Next day I was taken to Casablanca. My handcuffs were kept on. We stopped once on the road at a café and the guards left me outside while they had their snack. I needed desperately to get my trousers down in the latrine but my hands remained cuffed behind my back. Somehow I managed it.

Soon I found myself in the military prison in Casablanca and the questioning began again, detailed, increasingly penetrating. They were harsh but not deliberately cruel. I was aware that others in the cells nearby were treated much worse. I heard terrifying things sometimes and I believe at least one person died in that prison while I was there. But I had resolved to tell the truth without reservation and hoped that as long as I did so I should not be beaten or tortured. I insisted that I was neither a war criminal nor a Nazi, that I had had a position in Washington, had friends like Bill Donovan, and an American wife. I had even met General Marshal and General Arnold on more than one occasion. If anything should happen to me there would be questions.

The man who took charge of my case was Messieur G. Desameriq, *Inspecteur Chef* of the BST, *Bureau de Securité du Territoire*, the French Counter Intelligence Service in Casablanca. He was, throughout, reasonable and well behaved and I began indeed to like and respect him. But how the time and the questioning dragged on. I was distraught to learn from a fellow prisoner, a German, that he had been held in this same prison for two years on vague suspicions of espionage. He had actually deserted from the German army. When his case was finally heard he was sentenced to five years hard labour for entering French Morocco illegally. Another man he told me of had slashed his wrists in despair and had been saved only when a guard saw his blood running under the cell door. I wondered seriously about doing the same thing, only making a better job of it. But, even as I worked out the possibilities, a bit of sharp flint snatched from the ground in the exercise yard or glass from a broken bottle, I knew I did not mean to do it.

In January BST officers sent specially from Paris, arrived. The verbal abuse was at times unbearable. I was questioned for hours, then there were delays while my story was checked as far as it could be. The suspicions revealed seemed to me ludicrous and even crazy. Once again I feared for my life or sanity. Hovering in the background were two silent figures about whom there was an air of menace. I was sure that if I had given any indication of holding something back they would be turned loose on me. After a while, fortunately, the questioners seemed to realise that no force was necessary and these creatures disappeared.

'I didn't hear what you said! Say it again!' It went on and on and on. I became furious but tried to remain calm and to answer everything I was asked. The questioners suggested that I was a member of a secret conspiracy of the *Abwehr* to set up an underground Nazi movement, to help Quislings and SS men to escape from Europe. Helen, Else Lund, other Swedish friends, even Carlsson the American Ambassador in Sweden, the entire crew of the *Elvie*, all these were all part of this network. My apparent defection from the Embassy was a fake, a cover to hide my real purpose, the *Abwehr* had helped to hide me in Sweden, the money I had used to pay my *Elvie* fare was provided by the *Gestapo*.

All logic was lacking but if I said so they merely became more furious. I must have been a Nazi, how else could I ever have been appointed to the Washington position? That post before the war must have been a cover for more sinister operations. I insisted the BST would never find my name on any list of party members, which they were supposed to refer to. Of course not, they said, it would have been an undercover operation from the start. In vain did I point out that military personnel did not have to be party members, Bötticher himself had not been so. A soldier is posted wherever his superiors choose. The FBI themselves knew me well, I even gave them names of some of the agents who had trailed round after Helen and me on our honeymoon, told them about Morgan at White Sulphur Springs. No use. I was a saboteur! So on and so on. They went away from time to time but came back with a different line of questions. Days stretched to weeks.

'Now, Paul Leverkühn. Your cousin by marriage. You were very friendly with him, were you not?'

'I knew him. Renate and he divorced in 1939 or 40, I think. I met him only once or twice.'

'You are lying. The leading *Abwehr* man in Turkey?'

'Nonsense! Leverkühn an *Abwehr* man? Was he?'

'Don't pretend you didn't know that! One of Canaris' senior officers, since before the war!'

'I didn't know that. That can't be true!'

'Of course it is true and you knew it all along. Your cousin! How could you not know?'

'I had no idea. I met him, at Donovan's party in Washington. I told you all about that. He and Donovan were very friendly. Paul was never a Nazi. The last I heard of him he was sent as Consul to Tabriz, a diplomat.'

'Sent by Canaris, yes, to spy out the southern route for a German army to capture the Russian oilfields! Then he went to Ankara. Didn't you hear that Leverkühn's assistant in Turkey defected to the allies? There was a great fuss about it. You must have known.' Now he mentioned it, I had heard something of the kind but didn't know it was anything to do with Leverkühn.

'And he is free now in Germany, this *Abwehr* man even dared to act as defence counsel for some of the criminals at Nuremberg! Disgraceful, the

Americans let him go! It is all a pretence. Leverkühn too is involved in this underground organisation. Through your relationship with Leverkühn you became part of the network.'[1]

'No. It's nonsense.'

'You are a liar. You are in a league to save Nazi criminals.'

'Nonsense, nonsense, nonsense!'

When I had left the *Elvie* I gave what money I had from the concerts to Hans Bergwall, expecting the French would take it all from me. However, they were very correct and assured him that I should be allowed to keep it and would need some to buy small favours in the prison. It would be lodged with the BST officers but I should be allowed to draw on it at any time, receipts would be given and all would be properly done. They were as good as their word but to begin with I was charged for meals, a dollar each time. Someone was cheating but fortunately one of the guards told me I was entitled to proper food from the barrack kitchen. I was still allowed to write regularly to Helen, who, when she heard of my plight, decided she could achieve nothing by waiting in Sweden. Letters from her reached me, sometimes after a week but occasionally taking longer. They were all read by Desameriq and mine to her were also read and censored.

On 6 April Helen arrived in New York and travelled home to Terre Haute a few days later. She went immediately to her own family doctor. He examined her, took X-rays, and expressed utter amazement that she was still operating on only one lung. The pneumothorax had been in place from the time she entered the Amsee sanatorium, in May 1943, until April 1947 – four years! Helen explained that each of the doctors who had examined her after she left Davos had not known her history and were reluctant to do anything that might aggravate her condition. So they had done nothing! His first action was to re-inflate the collapsed lung.

Now there was a new diagnosis. The doctor's son, it transpired, had been in the medical corps in the Pacific. Helen did have a lung disease but it was not tuberculosis. Somehow, somewhere, she had contracted a rare fungoid infection which had been properly identified for the first time quite recently among soldiers in the Pacific war theatre. These men, like Helen, had reported sick with breathing problems and were found to have shadows on their X-rays. They too had been diagnosed as having TB but some research had been done and the new disease discovered. Fortunately, with rest and treatment the trouble cleared up and eventually all signs disappeared except for some scar tissue. With her lungs both functioning again she improved rapidly.

[1] Leverkühn was defending counsel for Marshal von Mannheim at the Nuremberg war criminal trials, 1945–46.

I was taken to the barber one day. For the first time I saw the streets of Casablanca. In my cell I had often heard the music at night from a nearby club and young people dancing. Now I saw where it was and envied the youngsters who were free to go there when they chose.

'You will not be released until you have told everything, every detail!' I told everything but I was not believed. Every name I mentioned had to be checked, if there was one I had forgotten I had to remember it. If Helen, in a letter, mentioned something I had not, there were questions about that. When the men from Paris were not there, Desameriq continued quietly, in a gentle fashion but insistent, probing, considering, smiling, picking away at my story.

'Who was Wendt? Was he a German agent?'

'Wendt?' Where had they got that name from? It was in Helen's latest letter. 'Oh, they were a family, man, wife and two daughters. They were friends of the Schindelers with whom Helen was staying while she was in Stockholm. When I was hiding in Stockholm, before they put me in Långholmen, I had an apartment for a while and it stood empty after I was arrested. When Helen got to Stockholm she arranged for them to take over the lease. The address was Midsommerkransen, Tångvågen 19 B.V.'

'You haven't told me everything. There is a Mrs Wendt here.' They had my little red address book! I wish I had thrown the damn thing into the sea.

'Yes, I did know some other people called Wendt. There was a Mrs Wendt in the Embassy in Sweden, I think I met her about twice. She was German, aged about 28. She had to go to hospital with TB, like my wife. I was sorry for her. I may have put her name in my book. A divorcée. That was only her married name, of course. And there was another. His name is there too, he was Professor von Wendt, a Finnish citizen, I had some slight contact with him while I was in the Embassy.'

On and on. I more than half expected that Helen herself would be questioned by the FBI and I should have been glad if they had done so. Then perhaps someone over there would do something on my behalf.

Helen was never questioned. She was angry with me for giving myself away and angrier still with the French. Apparently my silly little note to Else, posted in Schweningen, had alerted them. One of their informants, I suppose, asked her casually 'Have you heard from your friend Peter lately?' and she, being an innocent and unsophisticated girl must have said something like: 'Oh yes, I had a letter from off the boat when he was in Holland last week!' That would have been enough for them to guess where I was and what to look out for, a broken-down boat making its way along the European coast with a load of refugees. They had missed us at Dover and at Brest.

Helen was right to be angry, I had been stupid but in moments of depression one does things that are regrettable. I had to excuse myself too for telling them about Elisabeth in Switzerland and getting her into disgrace. The BST were sure my false passport had come from the *Abwehr*. I had to convince them otherwise and only the truth would do. I was sorry for the girl who would never forgive me but it was too late now to do anything to help her. I believed my arrest in Safi had come about because of a request by the British. The Swedes did not care but the British knew I had been on the loose in Stockholm and had vanished. In Spain we had made quite an exhibition of ourselves. I guessed the man we had noticed watching us was an agent, British or French, or just a paid informer. The authorities in Vigo would not have been interested in stopping us. With the French it was different. Even then, Desameriq told me later, they might easily have missed me. They were on the lookout in Casablanca but we had chug-chugged by them to Safi where things were much less organised. Only the silly woman describing us as tourists had made them look twice at us.

At last, towards the end of February the security officers decided I was harmless. The interrogations stopped. My story had checked out and they were satisfied. Desameriq brought a bottle of wine and we had what amounted to a small party in the cell. Even so, I was not a person they would entirely ignore now. He himself might be completely convinced but in Paris they would leave my file open.

Did it mean my release? No, Desameriq apologised. I should be transferred to the civil prison because there was still the other matter. I would be charged for using a false passport! No use my protesting that the officers had compelled me to leave the *Elvie*. If they had not hauled me off her I should never have entered Morocco. I had not intended to land in French territory at all! It made no difference. I had a forged passport, I could not deny I had used it in Denmark, Britain, France, Spain and Portugal. The new stamps inside proved it.

23

Guilty Until Proved Guilty

The civil police came for me, I was duly handcuffed and taken in a jeep with a couple of other prisoners to a beautiful building in French Colonial style with a fine plaza in front. In a side office was the Attorney-General, a tall, grim, black-eyed man of thirty-five or so. I was just one of several others who had to be processed. He took the papers and, without even looking at us, said 'Sign here, OK, sign here, OK, and here. Next! Sign here, OK, here, OK, here. Next!' We had been formally charged and under French law were guilty until proved otherwise. Then they drove us in the jeep to the civil prison which was quite a distance away in the old part of town. It looked from the outside like a big corporate building in light yellow mud-coloured brick. We were first taken to a place where a uniformed guard sat on the ground, the prisoners being marched up to him one by one. We had to empty our pockets and surrender everything we had, which wasn't much.

Internally the prison was laid out like a big star. There was a tremendous section for the Moroccan prisoners. The men on that side were sitting in groups under the palm trees. It did not look unpleasant but resembled a sort of open air zoo. In the European sector they kept not only white people but all the educated Moroccans and the Algerians. In theory Algeria was part of France so although these were dark skinned and of the Moslem faith they were classed as European.

I was in very low spirits as I was shown into to my cell. Here was a small man who bowed to me and said 'Lachmann!' He was from Strasbourg and spoke German fluently. He was Jewish but had not been recognised as such by the Nazis. Perhaps to avoid any possibility of being investigated by them he had been too eager to collaborate and when the Americans had entered the town he had fled and managed to reach Morocco. There he had been arrested. I had the feeling that his arrest had little to do with his collaborative activities in Strasbourg but probably to do with money that had been missed, but he did not enlarge on the matter. He proved a genial companion, a little older than myself. Whether or not I believed his story, what he said soon after my arrival depressed me further. I had supposed that I should soon have my court hearing and be released because I had been three months in jail already.

'False passport? That's nothing, three months!' said one of the men who had arrested me in Safi. I might get a short prison sentence or perhaps they would let me off with a fine. After all, I had not landed there by choice!

I had not reckoned with the French system. Before there could be a trial I must be questioned by the *Juge d'Instruction*. After the recommendations of the *Juge* I should go before a magistrate, when they got round to it.

'I have been here already eighteen months and I haven't got to court yet. Not even to the *Juge d'Instruction*,' Lachmann said. It might be a couple of years before his turn came, at the rate things were going.

No more incessant questions but no freedom either. How long should I be here? I resolved not to let myself rot in despair. I must make the most of my experiences, learn from them if I could. I was allowed to buy pen and paper, drawing on the small reserves still held for me by the BST. Every week I wrote to Helen and she wrote equally often though her replies were still sometimes delayed. One that she wrote at the end of May did not reach me for a month. I was sure all her letters were still being read before I saw them.

I smuggled a secret letter out of the prison via a sympathetic trooper, addressed to Helen's father in Terre Haute so that it would get through without being opened. I begged her to get in touch with anyone who could help me, Donovan, Carlsson, General Arnold, Hoover, anyone, anyone at all. I suggested that she should contact the British Embassy in Stockholm, or Washington, or here in Casablanca to get them to request my immediate transfer to their jurisdiction in Germany, or to the Americans in Frankfurt, or almost anywhere out of French hands. I would rather be in a British prison in Germany than where I was at present. I wrote directly to the lawyer Le Roy, in Washington, seeking his help and reminding him that I had once enquired about naturalisation. I asked about the possibility of American citizenship on account of having an American wife. I had a reply in due course and his firm offered to act for me in future but there was nothing they could do at present. An application from me in present circumstances would get nowhere. Perhaps all my protests and pleas did some good in the end.

I got myself some school exercise books and began to write down some of my story, beginning with my taking the Washington post under Bötticher. Apart from giving me something constructive to do I thought the document might be useful some day to the American immigration authorities when, as I firmly resolved to do, I should apply for admission to their country.

The food was poor. In the courtyard they had mushrooms from the prison farm spread out to dry. We were soon eating a lot of mushrooms as a substitute for meat of which there was very little. Three hundred grams of grey bread was issued each day, but there was nothing to put on it. If the cook was honest they put olive oil into the soup but if the cook could smuggle the oil to a customer outside the prison we got none. Some fresh fruit was available. Small baskets were sent in to the jail regularly if one could pay a little for them, which I did arrange to do. The climate of Casablanca was pleasant and if I could avoid fretting and worrying I could appreciate it. I was able to make contact with a local lawyer, Claude Shearer, who agreed that for a fee he would do what he could to bring my case forward, though he could make no promises. It all took time, time, time.

Many of the prisoners I met seemed to be sailors of various nationalities, thrown into jail for being drunk and doing stupid things. For example, a couple of Norwegians turned up and I was able to talk to them in Swedish. They had been drinking in town, needed a car to get back to their ship and stole one which they found with the keys in the ignition. Before very long they ran it into a tree. They could not remember very much about any of it after that and here they were.

Some prisoners were Spaniards who wanted to immigrate. They crossed first to Algiers on visitors' permits, were then caught at the railway station without a visa and got twenty or thirty days in prison. On release they were often allowed to stay. It was official policy to get more white settlers into Morocco. Other inmates were there for thefts, petty frauds, confidence trickery, occasionally more serious crimes such as assaults. They seemed for the most part very ordinary fellows and not at all stupid or brutal although many were illiterate and totally uneducated. One of the long-term prisoners had his own pet kitten which he took outside for exercise and obviously loved. Cats! There seemed to be far too many and at night their yowling and howling outside kept me awake. They were, the guards said, the best orchestra in Casablanca, which did not say much for the local human musicians.

A sad case was a Spanish fisherman, about forty years old, who had gone to a brothel in the Kasbah. He emerged afterwards into the dark, narrow alley outside to find himself immediately confronted by a gang of youths who attacked him. He had backed against the wall, drawn his knife and as the first of the gang came at him, he killed him. The others ran away and the women he had just left helped him to get away through the back of the house. Probably he could have escaped altogether but he had given himself up to the police voluntarily. He would claim he had acted in self-defence for the dead man had his own knife out too, as did the others. He supposed they had attacked him because he was white.

There was one brutal murderer among us, Aliadi, who seemed totally without moral understanding. He was handsome and moved like a cat, agile and strong. Without the slightest qualm he had killed two women, a wife and her young daughter, when they interrupted him during a petty burglary. When, after a long wait, his case came to court he was sentenced to death but he seemed totally indifferent. The other prisoners said he would never be executed because the political situation was so delicate that the government would not dare to do it.

An elderly Moroccan man, in appearance upright, tall and noble with a small carefully trimmed beard, came in. He spoke to no one but was clearly in great agony of mind. The story I heard from the guards was dreadful. He had, according to the custom of his people, married by arrangement a young girl in her teens but she and her young male cousin had gone away for a weekend on the boy's motorcycle. On the girl's return the old man had cut her throat immediately and now, obviously in the greatest mental torment, he was awaiting trial by the French who would never understand the imperatives that had driven him. After a few days he was moved to some other accommodation, perhaps to a mental hospital.

I met another extraordinary man by becoming ill. I began to lose weight rapidly. Lachmann insisted I should report sick at the prison surgery.

'The man you will meet is Monsieur Fleischel. He is from Alsace too, like me. He's excellent, very experienced, a first-rate fellow. He is also a prisoner. The official doctor hardly ever shows up. Fleischel is really good, the guards go to him too. He doesn't charge.'

'What is a doctor doing in this place?' I asked. 'Was he doing illegal abortions or something?'

'No, he is not a qualified doctor. He was a book-keeper. He falsified his employer's accounts and when he ended up in here he was, after a while, trusted and given the job of assisting the regular doctor. He discovered himself to be a natural at it, by instinct almost, and he was never happier in his life. There was a cholera epidemic in the prison. That was before I got here. The guards were scared even to enter the place and the doctor didn't come near. Fleischel took care of everybody! He did wonders, quite fearless. Afterwards he got a big remission of his sentence and they let him out with a very good recommendation but immediately he went off and did the same thing again! He came in here singing, happy as could be to get back inside! He never wants to leave. If they let him out he does something to get himself arrested again immediately.'

Fleischel, when I met him, looked like a sketch done by Dürer, a beautiful head full of character.

'You're German, aren't you?' he asked, in his Alsatian Deutsch.

'Yes Messieur.' I told him a little about myself and that I was feeling ill and losing weight rapidly. I had lost about six kilograms already. He examined me competently.

241

'Short of fats. I will give you a supplementary milk ration and cod liver oil.' It made a lot of difference to me.

I too was soon allowed a measure of freedom within the prison. There was a long hall with cell doors on each side and at the end a large door which opened onto a covered courtyard. Twice a day, from ten to eleven and from four to five we filed from our cells and out into the yard for exercise. A high roof on stilts above provided shade. On Thursdays we stood in line as we re-entered and a man in uniform issued each of us with our wine ration. Since he wore a uniform, at first I treated him as if he were a guard but I discovered he was a prisoner too! One day he appeared in the courtyard during the exercise period and said, 'Mr Riedel, would you like to work in the office? When we are there we can keep the lights on at night, we have plenty of wine and it's a different life.' I agreed at once.

I spoke German, Spanish, Swedish and English, which were useful when a prisoner came in speaking any of these. My French, which had been very basic, improved rapidly. I was literate and able to make myself generally useful. I was allowed to remain in the office writing or reading, or talking with two or three similarly privileged prisoners and the guards as long as I chose, or walk freely in the exercise courtyard. I had to tell the other 'trusties' all my story first, with as much humour as I could. They laughed.

Here was another collection of interesting men. Our office foreman acted as if he were still the boss of a proper business. He had been the manager of a company down town and money had gone astray so here he was. Very dignified, he reminded me of Lionel Barrymore, the film star. Another man looked like a scientist with big soulful eyes behind his glasses, very intelligent, smooth and polite. He showed us photographs of his family. He was a confidence trickster. He would offer to sell his 'mark' a small bar of gold at a bargain price, wrapping it in a packet and taking the money, departing quickly. The packet proved to contain a lump of lead or something so now he was 'inside'. If people were not so greedy and stupid, men like him would never be able to cheat them.

There was Viané, a corporal from the Foreign Legion. He still wore the Foreign Legion Uniform, kepi and all. A little man but little men are dangerous, they say.

'I shot my girl friend! You know, she deserved it! She was just a cheap tart. We had this argument and she kept teasing me about being so small, and not just here,' he touched the top of his head, 'but down here too! She kept on at me, and on, and I lost my temper. I took my revolver out and held it to her head and said "Belt up or I'll shoot you!" and she said "Go on, little prick! Do it! Do it!" So I did! All six bullets. *Voila!*'

'Good God. What happened in court?'

'I said it was a matter of honour. "Oh," the judge said, "M. Viané, do you expect to get the *Légion d'Honneur* now? I should give you ten years hard labour!"' In fact he got five years since it was recognised he had been provoked. His defence lawyer was a former professional soldier, a colonel, who must have done a brilliant job pleading for him.

Gomez had volunteered for the French division which fought on the German side. He was an older, stubble-faced peasant from Algeria, of Spanish descent. He was about forty years old but with his haggard face and stubble looked more. He was a devout Catholic and hated communism so he had volunteered to fight the Reds. In the terrible Russian winter his toes had been completely frozen. He showed us the stumps. He was taken to hospital in Breslau where he was well treated and since he was no longer fit for the army they sent him to work on a farm in Wurttemberg. The farmer had lost all four of his sons and allowed Gomez virtually to take over the entire place. When the Americans found this dark skinned, French-speaking man they were going to hand him over to the gendarmes but he escaped and made his way back to Algeria. The police caught him two years later. By that time tempers had cooled a little so he was not executed as he might have been otherwise. Instead, here he was in prison. He volunteered to take over the prison kitchen and as soon as he did so the food became better. A good deal of our rations had been sold by the previous cook on the black market.

It was now more than six months since I was taken off the *Elvie*. Helen wrote in June that she was going to leave Terre Haute and go to Fort Lauderdale in Florida. She had been in touch with an old school classmate who had been working there. They had the idea that the two of them could open classes as the nucleus of an art school which might grow into something bigger. It seemed an excellent idea to me when I heard of it, by which time their decision had been made anyway. They set themselves up in what had been a small office building and were soon joined by a third woman artist who had been in China. She had fled the communists that were taking over there. I was glad Helen was well enough to work now and even to earn her own living.

The *Juge d'Instruction*, Morriére, at last came to interview me. There was never any question of my innocence. I was told that my likely sentence for using the false passport would be six months, not three, after which I would be released under certain conditions. He would not let me out on bail because my identity was still not certain, despite my having been questioned so thoroughly. In civil terms, I was still a mystery man with no documentation and no nationality. Even when released I would be

243

regarded as an alien and required still to report regularly to the police just as I had been in Sweden. From my previous conduct they could not be sure I would not try to escape the country before my trial. Privately to myself I had to admit, that was true. I was apparently no nearer to having my case considered in court. Yes, I had been in jail already several months but as far as the civil authorities were concerned my imprisonment had not started until the date of my being formally charged before the Attorney-General. That was, of course, in early March! It was only June 1947 now.

I made the best of it. I used my time as well as I could but chafed constantly. A copy of the typescript of my story, which I had now written in English as far as the time of Walter Flinsch's death in the Heinkel 177, was sent secretly to Helen by way of Norwegian sailors, who, I learned later, kept their promise and did post it to her as soon as they had arrived at a port beyond French jurisdiction. I never managed to get any further with typing it but made some notes about my time in Sweden.

It was 10 October when I came to the court. I was immediately convicted, sentenced and released.

I was free! At least, free in a sense. What I had was a *Certificat d'Immatriculation* or foreigner's pass which allowed me to remain for a maximum of fifteen days in Morocco. In practice it was explained that I should be able to extend my time by reporting every fortnight to get the document date stamped and initialled by the police. If I failed to report then naturally I should be arrested again as an illegal immigrant and be back in jail awaiting a further interview with the *Juge d'Instruction*! I was given a ration book, a *Carte de Consommation pour Europeen* with coupons inside. What, I wondered, would the rations be for a non-European? There was also a *Récépissé de Demande d'Emploi*, duly stamped by the Immigration Department, which would allow me to seek paid work. Desameriq was there to see me released and took me in his Jeep into town. Where should I live now? Desameriq handed to me all the money that remained and helped me to open a proper bank account. I had little enough now, only a few hundred francs.

'Look, you fellows got me here,' I said to him, taking it as lightly as I could. I knew him well enough now to know that he would not be annoyed. 'Isn't it for you to get me out now? I never wanted to come to Morocco at all, remember! A dangerous character like me, don't you want to see the back of me? I heard there was a Norwegian oil tanker in Rabat,' I said. 'I could get a job on that and it would take me away.' He shook his head.

'No, you will have to stay, you are on probation, conditional liberty. We can't just let you go. But you can get a job and we need people like you in

Morocco. You could settle down here, you know. They would allow your wife to join you here. You must keep us informed of your whereabouts. Sorry, but that's how it is.' He had found me an hotel in the town centre and I stayed there for a few nights. It seemed remarkably cheap but my small reserves would soon melt away. I must live carefully until I could find work.

24

The Gracie Blue

I approached the American consulate but was told again that the rules had been laid down very firmly and there was nothing anyone could do for me in that direction. Almost insolently the consul said there was no chance whatever of my being allowed to enter the USA. I was disappointed but not surprised. Perhaps time would permit a change of attitude. Helen wrote that the art classes were not doing very well. They were only attracting the type of woman who wants a little hobby and a chat to enliven a dull day. Most of them had no talent and not much interest in developing what they had. The teachers made only just enough money to keep the three of them eating and paying the rent. If they had been prepared to make themselves better known in the local Country Clubs and had joined that suburban social set their classes might have become fashionable and done better but this kind of artificiality was not for them. Helen was waiting for me but I could not say when I should be able to join her and it certainly did not seem a good idea for her to come to Morocco.

I heard soon of an old American army camp, built at Ain Seba after their invasion in 1942, where very cheap hostel-type accommodation was available. It was only twenty minutes from Casablanca by road so I moved out there with my few belongings by bus. The main road to Rabat ran by the camp. What an enormous relief it was to be able to walk easily to the sea, do as I pleased and above all get decent food. In ten days my weight went from 67 to 72 kilograms.

Now I began seriously to look for work. I scanned newspaper advertisements, cards in shop windows and kept my ears open. There seemed to be some demand for people who could drive and maintain cars. I applied for a driving licence and went back to Desameriq to get his support with the documentation. The BST now were quite helpful. Desameriq even invited me to his home for a meal, which made a pleasant change from my solitary and frugal existence. Early in November I picked up a job as driver and mechanic for a wealthy widow who lived alone. I drove her at short notice to Marrakesh, Agadir and other places where she stayed in hotels or with relatives for a few hours or days at a time. She treated me as an ignorant servant and the pay was barely above subsistence level. I was constantly on call with neither defined working hours nor time off. Early in December when I asked for some improvement she dismissed me.

Through the many contacts with garages and service stations that had arisen through this job I heard of an American entrepreneur who had a road haulage business, employing local drivers and a fleet of trucks. At once I went to see this man, Mr Weckerlé, indeed an American but of French background. Here was a great stroke of luck for me. He was expanding into the tourist trade. The idea was to have a chauffeur and suitable luxury car to take visitors anywhere in Morocco they wished to go. The driver must be someone with languages who knew his way around and could look after the car too. It sounded just what I needed and as far as he was concerned I was the right man. The job was mine! I began on 9 December but first I must learn my way around Morocco. It would never do for me to get lost with a group of angry Americans or Englishmen. For several days I was carried to and fro as a sort of extra cargo on the trucks to Marrakesh, Rabat, Safi, Agadir, Fez, all over. The truck usually had a mechanic as well as me and at night the driver took the cab to sleep in, spreading himself across the seats. I and the mechanic had to lie where we could with a camel blanket for warmth. Sometimes we were on top of the cargo, which might be oranges, but more often we lay underneath the truck or wherever we could. At all hours of day and night, depending on our journey, we called in at roadside cafés and snack bars. No alcohol was sold at these places but the food was good enough and the drink was usually some kind of peppermint.

So after a few days I became a professional chauffeur with a cap! The car was a Fraser-Nash. I became very busy. To receive my first good, solid pay packet gave me an enormous lift and there were tips too. Things were not so bad now. My passengers were of all kinds, distinguished only by their having money to spend and either business to do or time to spare for a holiday. A party of high-ranking French air force officers were fascinated when they heard I had been in the *Luftwaffe* and beset me with questions. There was little I could tell them about air fighting from the German side. I had never done any. Three senior Englishmen who engaged me turned out to be on their way to see Winston Churchill, who was on holiday just then in Marrakesh. They were friendly when they found I knew English and had been something of a diplomat. They required first to go to Agadir, then to Mogador[1] for a day and a night, where I gazed out over the Atlantic and wished myself on the other side of it. Next day in Marrakesh I thought I might even see the great man Churchill but he was in bed when we arrived, suffering from some illness.

[1] Now called Essaouira.

I had other customers: South Africans, Swedish businessmen, officers on leave from ships in the various harbours, all kinds of people. I drove them here, there and everywhere, shuttling to and fro. All the while I kept a special eye on the ships. One day, I thought, I might be able to get myself away, legally or otherwise. I saved every franc I possibly could. Whatever happened, I should need money. I pestered the lawyer, called again at the US Consulate, wrote to Le Roy, all without positive result. Helen, I think was beginning to believe I should never see her again. Our marriage really had ceased to exist. We had parted on the Swiss border in 1944. Except for those few weeks when I had been in prison in Stockholm and for a week or two afterwards I had not seen her and now it was almost Christmas 1947. Neither of us could pretend things were well between us.

In Casablanca now I lived in a cheap boarding house in the Rue d'Horloge, sharing a room with a young Irishman, inevitably called Patrick. One afternoon in a café I glanced at a newspaper, *Le Petit Morroccain*, in which was a brief news item that set my pulses racing.

The British yacht, *Gracie Blue*, entered the harbour yesterday. Captain William Edward T. Nicholson and his wife are on their way to Florida, USA. They expect to stay a few days in Casablanca.

To get into the harbour area from the landward side required a *Laisser passer* to be made out at the dockyard gate. Records were kept there so everyone who checked in had to be checked out again before midnight. If one of the passes was not handed in there would be an uproar and a search to prevent anyone leaving the port without proper papers, inspection and permission. I knew the procedure.

Soon, with my scrap of paper in my pocket I was talking to Mrs Nicholson on the deck of the yacht. She told me they had come from the Irish port of Cork but her husband was English. He was not there just now but I could wait for him. Soon a youthful-looking man, brown bearded and with brown eyes behind his glasses, came along the quay from some errand in town, and jumped down to the deck. This was William Nicholson. I told him my situation and begged him to take me with him. He nodded. I should have to pay a fare, but if I could help him with the boat it would not be very much. He had no money to buy fuel or other supplies, in fact he had been forced to sell his sextant in Spain just to get as far as this. He was looking for paying passengers. He did not want to hang about, either. If he waited too long here they might decide to send him back to Ireland and I gained the impression that he did not want that under any circumstances. I made no secret of the fact that for me to leave Morocco without permssion would be illegal, but he didn't care.

'Once we are at sea, I could put you down as a member of the crew. This boat is registered in Ireland so once out of territorial waters the French can't touch us.' Two young Irishmen who had joined him in Cork had proved useless, seasick most of the time, ignorant about boats and not very ready to learn. He meant to dismiss them in Casablanca. He had picked up two Spanish fishermen in Vigo, Carlos and Bautista, as crew. They were working their passage to the Americas but he could speak no Spanish. I told him I knew the language and could be useful to him in translating orders.

Would I like to look over the yacht? The *Gracie Blue* was an altogether different proposition from the *Elvie*. She had been a pilot boat built for the British Admiralty in 1885 but still in first-class condition, 25 metres (82 ft) long, very robust and seaworthy. Nicholson explained the sails. She was a yawl with jib, staysail and quadrangular mainsail on the main mast with a gaff, a mizzen mast and small sail at the extreme stern. Crossing the Atlantic in her was not a silly idea. He would aim first for Las Palmas in the Canary Islands, then the Cape Verde Islands to take the shortest route possible to reach the Brazilian coast. He would perhaps turn south for the Argentine or north for Florida, he had not decided.

His enthusiasm for his yacht was delightful and understandable. He showed me the two-cylinder engine in the tiny engine room immediately under the companion way. This motor, he assured me, would push the boat along at five knots if the wind did not blow. That speed seemed unlikely to me but I dared not challenge him. Here too was a proper toilet and some wardrobes. The saloon, ahead of the engine room, with a skylight above, was astonishingly large with fine mahogany panelling all round, leather padded bench seats on either side and a substantial table for six persons in the middle. The fittings were all gleaming brass, Victorian style. Forward of the saloon on the starboard side was a small cabin which, Nicholson said, would be mine. The main mast, solid timber about 30 cm in diameter, came down through here. There was a bunk built against the inward-curving hull, with cupboard and drawers beneath, a table and wash basin, luxury indeed compared with the *Elvie*. Further forward again was a large cabin in the bows, lit only by portholes, where there were bunks for two crewmen.

'She's a super ship!' said Nicholson. 'You know, a pilot boat had to be really good, seaworthy to meet the big ships in rough weather, handy so that it could get alongside without fuss to put the pilot on, and capable of being sailed single-handed. That's the advantage of the yawl rig. It's well balanced, a single man at the wheel is all you need.'

Aft of the engine room was another single cabin, better appointed than the one that would be, or might be, mine. Anyone taking this would have to pay full fare! Aft of this again was the Captain's own cabin where he and his wife would sleep. This was the best appointed of all the accommodation, fine timber panelling, two bunks, a bench seat, cupboards, and a dressing table with mirror across the whole width of the boat at the stern end. Here we sat to talk. Mrs Nicholson produced some food and a cup of tea.

How much would it cost for him to take me, as a working passenger, I asked.

'Thirty thousand francs.' I did a quick calculation. (Roughly the equivalent of $300 American.) It was impossible for me.

'I can't find so much.' Nicholson looked very disappointed.

'I am practically stuck here,' he said. 'Can't move without money!'

'I can sell my typewriter!' I reckoned after some thought that if I scraped everything together I could raise Fr 8500, cash, but would be able to pay more later. 'When we reach Las Palmas I can get money from my wife in America, she will send some. I shall be able to give you the whole sum. I have a camera, a good Leica. That must be worth Fr 6000. I could give you that to hold for the time being, as security.' Taking it all together I could find about half what he asked. He could see I was in desperate straits and so was he.

'I'll take you! We'll square up in Las Palmas.' he said. 'If we can get you onto the boat without being arrested, you can come.'

If I was caught I should never get out of Morocco again! The very thought made me shiver. I decided to go to see Desameriq, ask him formally for permission to leave, and perhaps he would give me clearance. Subterfuge would then be unnecessary. I called on him in the office. He greeted me in friendly fashion and, when I explained that I had the chance to go with Nicholson, he telephoned his superiors at Rabat on my behalf. The answer was immediate, and negative. Why must the French hold me in Morocco? If I had a visa allowing me to enter the USA or some other country they would release me, they said, not otherwise. They knew I had tried and failed to get such a visa and if I landed there without it I should simply be sent back here, or to Germany! I should consider myself lucky not to have been deported to Germany already. After leaving Desameriq I felt I had done all I could to keep on the right side of these strange laws. I would escape, one way or another, and feel no guilt.

I went to the yacht and explained. Nicholson thought, with a little ingenuity we ought to be able to manage my escape. We must work out a safe way for me to get on board. I already began to feel tense and guilty. every person I saw might be waiting to report me if I did anything suspicious. The dockyard was well guarded. There were checkpoints for trucks and goods vehicles, Customs men looking for contraband, immigration authorities and always, the BST in the shadows. An American destroyer was moored in one basin.

Could I stay on the *Gracie Blue*, hiding until Nicholson sailed this very night? No, that would not do. He had things that must be done before leaving, supplies to buy, would be staying for a few days yet and I would certainly be discovered by the most casual inspection. I must hand in my pass at the gates this evening as usual. It would be safest for me to continue living ashore until the time came for departure. Anyway, I had to sell the typewriter, get my small amount of money out of the bank, draw the last of my wages and tell my boss I was leaving. I should sign in as usual with the police, keeping myself legal as long as possible. Meanwhile I could visit the boat when I liked, each time getting my *laissez passer* on entry to the docks and handing it in as I left. Nicholson would be glad to have some help on shore, he spoke no French and I could accompany him to help with shopping. Our excuse, if questioned, would be that I was acting as interpreter for the captain.

It would never do for me to be seen walking through the dock gates with baggage.

'How much baggage?'

'Only a single suitcase.'

'Well, we can attend to the suitcase at once, tonight!' said Nicholson. 'Then it will be safe and ready.' We would take advantage of the American destroyer's presence. The harbour was in three main sections, the commercial shipping quay, the basin for yachts and small craft, and the naval dockyard. The French guards at the naval gate would think nothing of it if a couple of Yankees in a taxi with some bags came in to join their ship late at night. When it was fully dark we would use the dinghy to move ourselves around the harbour without being noticed. Nicholson, as excited as a schoolboy, put on his cap and jacket with epaulets and gold stripes on the cuffs, rowed me across to the main quay and left me there to climb the stone steps and leave by the gate. I would get a taxi in the evening and wait for him outside the naval gates. He proposed to row round there and after tying up the cockle-shell would join me in the street outside. This went smoothly and we drove to my boarding house where, while the Captain waited in a nearby café, I quickly crammed everything, except the precious, saleable typewriter, my alarm clock and a few toiletries, into my case. Patrick was not there so I did not need to explain anything to him.

The taxi took us back to the dockyard, Nicholson's uniform with its gold striped cuffs and cap disguising us as we passed through the gates towards the American ship, saluted by the guard as we went through. Near the bows of the ship we got out and dismissed the cab. Nicholson left me standing while he went to get the rowing boat. The destroyer with its lights on hummed with the sound of generators and ventilators as ships do when tied up at the wharf. A few sailors moved about on board, talking in their American accents. No one walked up or down the gangway. I stood there, alone, exposed, for an age. It should have been a matter of a few minutes but after twenty I was still waiting with my suitcase, feeling sure that I was being watched from the gatehouse. Something had gone wrong! 'What is that fellow doing,' they would say to one another 'standing on the quayside in the dim light with a suitcase, in civilian dress, obviously no American sailor.' I took a few paces along the quay, turned on my heel and strolled back, pretending that I was merely stretching my legs, taking a breath of air. Someone official in uniform and an officer's cap, approached along the quay on a bicycle. What should I say when he stopped and questioned me, as he was sure to do? I tried to take a nonchalant pose.

'Bonsoir,' he said, and rode by. It wasn't a uniform. My imagination was confusing me.

He was quite scruffy and his cap was just a workman's headgear.

At last, Nicholson reappeared.

'Damnation. They've closed the section where I left the dinghy. The stupid old bugger there wouldn't let me through I had to sneak round and scramble over a ten foot wall to reach it! Never mind, here we are now.' He took me to some steps further along the quay, we got the case down into the dinghy and rowed round to the yacht, stowed my bag in the cabin. Nicholson, it seemed to me, was highly delighted with the whole exploit, he had enjoyed himself with this little game. His wife again produced tea and a snack. While I sat below the two Irish boys came back. Nicholson went on deck to talk to them. Voices were raised, and, after a few minutes, they departed. He had, as he said he would, given them the sack.

Now I must leave. I strolled back as casually as I could to the gates, handed in my pass and slipped out of the docks again. December 29th; first part of the exercise completed.

On New Year's day, 1948, I visited the *Gracie Blue* again and again, taking a bottle of wine to celebrate. The Captain and his wife were teetotallers so my proposed party was a dull affair.

We began to make more plans. It would be safest if the *Gracie Blue* could leave harbour quite openly without me on board. If the BST suspected anything they could inspect the boat and find it perfectly innocent. Then the Captain would anchor off a deserted part of the shore a few kilometres to the north where I had sometimes been swimming when living in the old camp at Ain Seba. Carlos would row ashore to pick me up in the dinghy. It seemed feasible. Carlos, when approached, had no objection. He and I went by bus to look at the place.

'What do you think?' I asked him.

'It shouldn't be any problem!' he said, although I realised the surf was worse than I remembered and there were rocks which I had scarcely noticed before. When the time came I would go at night to the beach and shine a torch out to sea. Carlos would come for me. Would a simple electric torch light be visible from the yacht?

'No problem!' said Carlos. Was he only trying to please me, giving me the answer he thought I wanted to hear? The surf looked bad to me, but he was the sailor.

I sold the typewriter, collected my last entitlement of wages, drew all my money together and paid Nicholson as much as I could. I retained only enough cash to feed myself for the remaining few days and to pay the rent on my room for a week more in advance. For two or three days Nicholson shopped, stocking the boat, and he visited the British Consulate.

The date Nicholson decided on arrived. I was to meet Carlos in town, hand over anything remaining that I wanted to keep and he would take it to the yacht. Nicholson would sail in the afternoon, move a few kilometres along the coast and wait off Ain Seba. I should get myself there by bus and flash my light out to sea at 9 p.m. and the dinghy would come. If anything should go wrong, Nicholson said, I must make my own way to Las Palmas. He intended to give the *Gracie Blue* a thorough scraping and painting when he got there and would have to pick up some paying passengers too. He would be there for a week or two at least.

Pat, with whom I shared the room, had no idea I was going. After he left in the morning I made a small bundle to give to Carlos, leaving behind a few almost worthless items, my battered alarm clock, a pair of slippers and a dressing gown which Pat could keep for himself. I did not wish to take the key of the room, nor did I want to draw attention to my departure by leaving it with the landlady. As I left I hid it out of sight on the ledge over the door. I would send a postcard from Las Palmas, to explain and tell Pat where the key was hidden. Carlos was waiting at the agreed place and grinned as he scurried off with my little parcel. The rest of the day was ahead of me. I decided to have a last walk round the town and the market, and perhaps go to a cinema to fill in time before dusk when I should have to catch the bus. I had no intention of returning to the boarding house again but, long before the appointed time, the emotional strain of these last few days suddenly overwhelmed me with weariness. I would need all my strength for the night pick-up off the beach. I could still go back to the room for a couple of hours' rest. I climbed the dark, ill-kept stairs, went up to the flat roof for a last look at the lights of the city and the harbour beneath the stars. Then down again to the room.

To my horror, I found the door of our room standing open, the key I had hidden in the lock and everything in chaos. The place had been turned upside down, drawers pulled out, Patrick's property scattered on the floor. Shocked, I thought 'The BST have guessed my secret and have been here looking for me!' For a few moments I could do nothing but sit on the bed, trembling. Then I fled down the stairs, thinking to rush to the harbour to warn Nicholson that I was about to be arrested! I came within distant sight of the quay before the folly of this dawned on me. The yacht sails were partly up, people were moving about on deck. The BST, I decided, having missed me at home would be down there waiting. To arrive there in a sweat would give the whole game away whereas, if I did nothing, they could prove nothing. I turned back, went this way and that in the streets until, quite exhausted, I decided there was nothing to be done but to return to the boarding house.

I sorted things out, put Pat's things away again. I could do what I had intended, sleep for a while. I looked for the alarm clock I had left behind. It was missing. Why should the BST take an old, cheap clock? How ridiculous! What use would it be to them? All they wanted was me, not the clock. And why should they have made such a mess? I couldn't find my old dressing gown either! Had the BST taken that too? It made no sense.

Could this have been an ordinary robbery, not the BST after all? If they meant to arrest me, why didn't they come? Lie down and try to relax.

I was woken abruptly when Patrick came back, switching on the light.

'Pat,' I said, 'someone's been here. The room has been searched, they've taken the clock and some other things. You'd better check to see what else is missing!'

He looked around, counted his few things.

'Nothing's gone!' he said, before long. 'But we must report this. I bet it was that guy across the passage. I never liked the look of him!' I realised, the man who had moved into the room opposite could have seen me hiding the key and taken his chance. It had been a simple robbery after all. I had panicked needlessly.

'Oh my God! Pat, what time is it?'

'Half past midnight! Why, what's the rush? Hey, where are you off to?'

I was already hours late for the rendezvous. By the time I arrived at the beach and flashed my torch out to sea, it was after 1 a.m. Nicholson surely would not have waited so long. He would have sailed without me. Or, possibly, he was still out there. Carlos at this very moment, might be rowing in, about to beach the dinghy. I stared, but saw nothing. I flashed the torch. Such a feeble light! Would it be visible out there? There was something, moving in the distance! Disappointment. It was a big ship, a steamer far out to sea. It vanished. No dinghy, no Carlos. The surf, it seemed to me, was heavier than I had seen it before. Probably it would be impossible to get the little boat safely ashore. Had Carlos tried, had he failed, had he drowned?

I stood there, cold, depressed. The whole plan had been a nonsense from beginning to end. Picking up a man off a beach in the night with a dinghy!

Totally impractical, like something out of a childish adventure story. I had been a fool ever to agree. Nicholson, with his immature sense of adventure had trapped me into a silly game.

It must have been about 4 a m when I finally gave up, trudged back to the main road and was picked up by a truck driver who took pity on the solitary, exhausted man he saw walking back towards the city. He dropped me in the totally deserted streets. I had never seen Casablanca like this before. I wandered about aimlessly. When daylight came I had recovered spirits enough to go to the harbour. Having failed to find me at Ain Seba, I thought, Nicholson, who seemed always very sympathetic, might have come back to look for me. Down to the docks. No sign of *Gracie Blue*. She had gone without me, carrying every solitary thing I owned and all my money except the few coins still in my pocket. The only hope was if, somehow, I could get to Las Palmas.

Back to the room where Patrick was awake.

'We must report the robbery!' he said. Well, why not? We roused the landlady who was annoyed but agreed the fellow who had the room near ours must have been to blame, but we had no proof. The police came and took notes but there didn't seem much chance of their doing anything about such a trivial theft. I wondered what to do. I decided to try to catch a lift down the coast. If I could hitch a truck to Agadir and then get into Ifni, a tiny postage stamp piece of Spanish territory on the African coast, I might find someone who would let me work my passage to the Canaries. How I should get through the border post beyond Agadir I had no idea for I knew it was well guarded by troops of the Foreign Legion. I would face that problem when it came. I thought I knew from my chauffering days where to go to cadge a ride with a truck driver but this failed. The truck drivers were prepared to help fellow Arabs but they expected to be paid if the passenger was European. After a fruitless day waiting at the roadside I had to go back to the boarding house. At least I still had somewhere to sleep. Despair.

Next morning the landlady called me and took me busily up to the roof. Here was a laundry room. Some children had been playing up there and had found my alarm clock and dressing gown hidden away in a dark corner. Whoever the thief was, he had evidently secreted them there until such time as he could take them away without being seen. The recovery of this property meant less than nothing to me. From this position on the roof, I took a casual look in the direction of the harbour. Anchored close to the entrance of the harbour was a yacht. It was a yawl, the hull was faintly blue. The *Gracie Blue*! From the street, it was impossible to see it. Only the accident of my being on the roof had revealed it to me. Nicholson had, after all, come back.

Caution forgotten I rushed down to the docks, hired a ferry man and persuaded him to take me to the yacht. It was a long row. Arrived, I called to Nicholson and out on deck they all came, the Captain, his wife, Carlos and Bautista. As I clambered on board I swore not to go ashore again until we could leave Casablanca for good. Nicholson, affable as ever, agreed and as darkness fell we let the ferryman take his boat back to the dock, hauled up the anchor and departed. I should be missed, no doubt, but by midnight when the guards checked their bits of paper at the dock gates, we should be far away. So now, on 6th January 1948, the voyage began.

The two Spanish crew were Bautista Haz Olveira, 35 years old and Carlos Servino Cobas, 30. Bautista came originally from Vigo and spoke a dialect, Gallego, very like Portuguese. I soon discovered that he was illiterate. He and I could communicate only with difficulty. Carlos was a better educated man but less experienced with boats and fishing than Bautista. Nicholson knew no Spanish and had no intention of learning any. To hear and see him giving orders to his crew was highly entertaining. He would shout, with much arm waving and gesturing, '*La ropa, La ropa,*' meaning them to grab a rope and tie it or untie it or pull it. In Spanish '*La ropa*' means *clothing* so Carlos and Bautista would stare in total incomprehension. They began to learn Nicholson's ways and I was able to interpret, so between us we managed the boat well enough.

Our first night at sea was fine and we made good progress under sail with Nicholson and the Spaniards taking turns at the wheel as I slept. When the dawn came I was troubled to see that the coast of French Morocco was still very near. To make for the Canary Islands we had been sailing south-west, almost exactly parallel to the shore. Just over there was Mogador where I had been quite recently with my English trippers, staring out to sea. Now here I was gazing the other way. There were fishing boats around but they were all heading for port. The steady breeze that had helped us on our way in the night was strengthening and it was obvious that a storm was coming. The very last thing I wanted was for Nicholson to decide we too, should run into Mogador or Agadir for shelter. Fortunately he took pity on me. We were battered and thrown about for the whole of that day and the next night, always aware of the coast on our lee side, which was worrying. He set a course to give us more sea room. When daylight came the weather had improved and there was nothing whatever in sight, no shore, no ships, only the sea. We were all exhausted and Nicholson simply heaved to and let us drift while we slept. If a big ship had come and hit us that would have been the end of us but he reckoned the chances were very slight since we were not in a main shipping lane. Sure enough, when we woke we were still completely alone.

We reached Lanzarote, the first of the Canary Islands, and moored in Arecife for a few days' rest. We attracted some attention, people in boats hailing us and asking where we were going. I wrote at once to Helen, telling her where I was and asking her to send money to Las Palmas, drawing on the small reserve I had left in our bank account before the war. She should address her letters not to me directly but to Nicholson care of the British Consulate. I needed at least $200 and suggested she could split it into three separate letters, with some postcards or something in each envelope to disguise the currency. We left Lanzarote on 20 January. At the next island, Fuerteventura, in the harbour of Puerto del Rosario, Juan Pedro Domingues a local man rowed out and asked in Spanish 'Do you have any foreign stamps? I'm a collector, I'll buy them from you!' I had all my letters from Helen so I quickly emptied the envelopes and sold them. The money wasn't much but it was all I had now. On we went to Las Palmas on Gran Canaria. Here Nicholson planned to stay about four weeks to beach the ship, scrape and paint the hull, and above all find passengers with money.

The money from Helen had not arrived yet and did not come, which upset Nicholson because he had been relying on it. I had promised to pay my full fare and reassured him. He would get it eventually. Meanwhile, he had the Leica but he insisted he would not sell it. It was mine and I should keep it until we were absolutely desperate. I did not know then that the Leica had been affected by the humidity of my long sea voyage but it still worked.

Nicholson had contracted malaria at some time in the past and was suffering from a recurrence of the fever. He had to take to his bed. For a time we could not move. We were now all truly at our wits end with barely a few pesetas between the five of us. On shore, as I walked around, a man approached me and said 'Would you sell that coat?' It was my good Swedish overcoat which had been very necessary earlier. I thought in warmer climates I did not need it. He gave me the equivalent of $10 in Spanish money and now I could buy myself a meal. The next day the remaining money was stolen out of my locker on the boat! I suspected Bautista but it was Carlos who suddenly had enough to take us all to a restaurant that evening. Now there was nothing left at all. We found a clear stretch of beach and at high tide moored there close in so at low tide the ship rested on the mud. Carlos and Bautista began the scraping operation, which was tiring and hard. Helen wrote to say that she had sent $100 and it had actually arrived at the British Consulate. Since Nicholson was ill and had not called for it they had simply sent it back to her, unopened. I suggested she should try again, addressing the envelope now to me at the Real Club Nautico. Before it arrived Nicholson, slowly recovering, actually sold some of our fresh water casks leaving us with capacity of only half what we had before but at least allowing us to eat.

In the harbour there was a steady traffic of large ships: tankers stopping briefly, a few passenger liners, some cargo vessels remaining for longer periods to load and unload. I remembered I had fifty Swedish crowns still and when a Swedish ship came in I rowed to it and exchanged the money for pesetas. It really was the last I had. While on the ship I was treated to a splendid meal. I had not seen real butter for longer than I could recall. The sailors were throwing away scraps that would have kept us going for a whole day. I decided to try begging. Next day I took the dinghy and rowed over to a British tanker, the *Alexia*, moored in the deep water and clambered up the ladder. I was taken at once to the Captain, Mr Norris, who came from Ayr in Scotland, and his first officer Mr Blyth, who was a retired Royal Navy Captain. I explained our situation. They called one of the cooks from below and I was allowed to help myself to canned goods, fresh meat and vegetables. They gave me water too, for we had almost emptied our tanks. They seemed anxious to have a new person to talk to, exchanged stories with me about the war years, showed me over the ship. When I got back to the yacht I had provisions for everyone.

I tried again a few days later and once again came back well laden. I offered to pay a few cents for the food. The cook gave me such large quantities of potatoes and rice that I could hardly carry them. As long as we were in Las Palmas my dinghy trips had to continue. I became expert at talking people into giving us stuff or selling it at very low prices. So it went on. I visited the tankers *Thelidomus* and *Saconnet* (an American ship), the *Empire Kinsman*, the *Alcoa*, the *Umtali*, the *Umgani* and other vessels, finding the British and Americans always welcoming and generous, the Swedish, Danes and French were less so, but no one turned me down altogether. As Nicholson said one day 'You could bum your way round the world indefinitely like this!' I was afraid we should acquire a bad reputation.

Bautista received some mail, a letter from his wife. I had to read it to him as best I could for it was in the dialect and probably not correctly spelled even so. He seemed to follow, all the same, nodding and smiling enthusiastically. Now the problem that preoccupied us was finding passengers with money. We made it known that there were places available and there were many enquiries. But most of the people who came along were penniless or could not find anything like the amount Nicholson was obliged to ask. Soon after arriving in Las Palmas I had written to the address Helge Rosvaenger had given me before he left the *Elvie* in Vigo. His idea had always been if possible to reach the Americas and now there would be a place for him and his lady on the *Gracie Blue* if he could get to Las Palmas and find the fee. Early in February there came a friendly reply from him, addressed correctly now to Peter Riedel at the Club Nautico, instead of Stig Nilsson which, all along, he had known was not my real name. He had evidently not had many singing engagements and was back in his old trade of chemical engineering, developing some new kinds of underwater protective paint for ships. I understood he was reluctant to chance everything again on a risky voyage with an uncertain reception at the end of it.

Behold, one day, coming in from the ocean with fishing nets hanging up on the little mast, was the *Elvie*! Some work had been done on those rotten bow timbers and she had been painted but there could be no doubt. I hailed her and went aboard. Incredible, I thought, as I stared and remembered that this little wooden walnut shell had brought sixteen people from Sweden to Africa. What had happened to them? The fishermen told me the group had split up. They had been held in Safi by the French for some days but had been released and sailed to Las Palmas where the boat had been sold. Some of the party, they thought, might even be in Las Palmas still but the others had dispersed, some to South Africa, some to Venezuela and Brazil, one had gone back to France, they believed.

At last *Gracie Blue* acquired passengers who could pay. Ernst Heine was the first, a tall, very fair, freckle skinned, red curly haired German. He agreed at once to pay 3,000 pesetas and, to my delight, he had it in mind to go to Venezuela too. Although it was good to have someone to speak to in my own language, he was not a very easy man to like, claiming to have a superior family and education behind him and requiring everyone on board to address him as Herr Heine while I and the others were just Peter, Carlos and Bautista. But Heine had money so he could state his own terms. He took the best of the two small cabins.

A Spaniard on the quay side wanted to buy a passage to South Africa. I talked to him, explained why Latin America was better. After all, people spoke Spanish there and there would be less difficulty with visas. Why not Venezuela? He went away and came back next day with four friends.

'We'll pay! We hear a man can earn five or six times as much in Venezuela for the same work as we are doing here. Take us to Venezuela!' His friends all seemed respectable working men although they were not sailors and would not be able to help much on the ship. They were Ezequiel, Adolfo, Eligio, Paco and Manuel. So with Nicholson, Mrs Nicholson, me, Bautista, Carlo, Heine and five Spanish, we were eleven. It was crowded but compared with seventeen on the *Elvie* it seemed spacious to me. Nicholson was now feeling better and rested. I made a few last trips with the dinghy and some food was bought on shore with our good Spanish money. At last we were away. It was the end of March.

We sailed well and made good time at first but soon ran into calms and had to use the motor sparingly. The lack of a sextant was a nuisance now. Nicholson said he did not need it. We were bound for America and that continent was too big for us to miss! Fortunately, after another lesser storm, the weather was excellent and the air perfectly clear so that we could see great distances. Flying fish appeared, one of them landing on deck at Mrs Nicholson's feet. There were no severe storms, indeed we would have welcomed more wind. Nicholson had not taken a route that would catch the trade winds so we ran a serious risk of being totally becalmed for a long time but fortunately we did manage to keep moving, reaching our best speed of about 8 knots according to the log when things were going well.

After two weeks we had not seen a single ship of any kind. We were far from sure of our position. I took my turn at the wheel with Nicholson, Bautista and Carlos and we steered south-west, hoping to strike the coast of Brazil. Our food and water began to get low again and there were eleven of us now all eating and drinking. For all we knew we had several more weeks to go. On and on, nothing seemed to change except the fitful breeze and the level of water in our casks.

In the middle of the night Carlos, at the wheel, yelled. He saw the lights of a ship coming towards us. Nicholson, in his pyjamas, came on deck and signalled 'We need help,' with a light. Had they seen us? Their foaming phosphorescent wake lessened quickly but the ship still kept moving, taking a long, long time to stop entirely in the water. When it did stop it seemed far away, almost over the horizon from where we were, the lights barely visible and disappearing each time we dipped below the wave tops. Nicholson dressed quickly and got into the dinghy, alone, and simply rowed off into the darkness. 'Wait here till I get back!' he said. We waited and waited. An hour went by. We became anxious. Had he reached the ship? Had he found her and lost us on the way back, just rowed and rowed and into nothing? We were in the middle of the Atlantic, our captain had vanished, what should we do? If he did not return at all, who would be in charge of the boat? Me? The only one who knew anything at all about navigation, but no sailor. I talked to Mrs Nicholson.

'Should we start the engine, go looking for him?'

'He said to wait. He said, never start the engine without his permission.'

'Yes, yes . . . but, this is different. He could so easily miss us. We can't just sit here doing nothing! We should look for him.'

'Try shouting!'

We shouted. No reply. Nothing. Lap, lap, lap, went the waves. Otherwise, silence. Another hour. Nothing.

'I'm going to start the engine!' I said.

No one had any better idea. I went to the primer, pumped it, pressed the starter, Chuff, chuff . . . the engine fired once. I was about to press again.

'Ahoy!' Nicholson's voice, far away in the distance! In a few minutes he was back with us. He had rowed to the ship, gone on board, met the captain, explained, and had rowed back to this tiny little speck of a boat in the darkness. He seemed to think nothing of it! Now we did start the engine and sailed over to the ship. It was an American Liberty ship, one of those which were welded together by Kaiser in thousands during the war. It was on its way from Bordeaux in France to Dutch Guiana, for aluminium ore, bauxite. In no time we had filled up with fresh water, food and fuel. Nicholson marked our exact position on the chart. We were more than half way across but there was a depressingly long stretch of ocean still ahead of us. The ship started her engines again and disappeared. We sailed on alone.

When the Spaniards were steering I noticed that they often took their hand from the wheel for a few moments to light a cigarette. Each time they did so the *Gracie Blue* swung her head round to starboard, making a little progress northwards before the wheel was back under control again. Since Carlos and Bautista both smoked constantly, these unintended changes made nonsense of our intended course. Well, as Nicholson said, the Americas were too large for us to miss altogether and it didn't matter much where we sighted land. Unlike Columbus we knew it was there!

Mrs Nicholson announced one morning that she was pregnant. On the instant, she was in total command of the *Gracie Blue*, anything she wanted us to do was done without question. Nicholson seemed almost beside himself with pride.

Twelve days later in the night I was taking my turn at the wheel and saw, very faintly, a light directly ahead, flashing. I called Nicholson.

'Splendid, splendid! It must be the entrance to the Caribbean!'

'We should heave to. It could be a rock.'

'No, no, keep on, straight ahead. We shall pass between the islands.'

Half an hour later the light was distinctly closer.

'Captain, I really think we should heave to until daylight. It is too dangerous. It could be anything, rocks, a reef, shallows, who knows.'

'Keep on, keep on, don't worry!'

A little later, 'Look, Captain, I believe I can see clouds.'

'What of it?'

'When there are clouds like that, cumulus clouds, it means there is an upcurrent beneath. I know it from my gliding experience. There is land there, warm land surrounded by cool sea. We are heading directly for the coast. That light could be marking a reef. We must heave to and wait for the dawn.'

'Hmm. Are you sure of this?' There was no doubt in my mind. He could see the clouds too, now, catching the moonlight, and they stretched a long way on either side.

'I insist. We must heave to!'

'Very well, very well. Heave to.'

When the boat came to rest in the water, I listened hard and was sure I could hear waves breaking and even imagined I could see surf. We sat out the rest of the night. As always in equatorial latitudes, when the sun rose it came up quickly. Within minutes of first light we saw, directly ahead of us, a desolate, rock-strewn barren coastline with only a single, insignificant buoy and the light on a rusty tower to signal its presence. We had been heading directly for a certain wreck on an uninhabited shore. We had crossed the Atlantic but where were we? Certainly not where we had expected. The cigarette smokers had ensured that we could be almost anywhere.

Underway again we rounded a headland. At the first opportunity we put into a quiet bay, took a stroll on shore and rested before getting the *Gracie Blue* sailing again. It turned out we had arrived on the island of Tobago, north of Trinidad, and when all is said and done that was an astonishingly accurate landfall although more by sheer luck than navigation.

We were short of provisions once more and Nicholson thought to stop another passing ship, for there were plenty now. It did not work. After all that time alone now we were merely one sailing vessel among many and no one was inclined to take any notice of us. Another yacht came up to us eventually. It proved to be a fishing schooner from Trinidad with an all black crew grinning and shouting. We heaved to and they did too. Nicholson rowed over and returned minutes later with a huge fish for us. Mrs Nicholson cooked it and we ate well.

Venezuela was our destination and we sailed easily along the coast. One of our Spanish passengers yelled in terror. A human corpse floated by. There was nothing we could do. There was a flurry of genuflecting and muttered prayers among our mainly Catholic group. Who was he? A drunken sailor who had fallen overboard in the night? Someone killed in a fight, a murder victim dumped at sea, who knows? We sailed on through the sunshine with the mainland coast becoming visible on our port side. Heine and I were leaning against the rail on deck, admiring the view. There was a sandy island off our port bow about two miles away, a smooth sea but suddenly white capped waves appeared in a sort of patch. I thought even that I could see fishes being dragged to the surface. It was curious and puzzling but I did not recognise what I saw. Suddenly a violent wind struck us. The yacht heeled over. Bautista at the wheel was caught unprepared. He had been almost born and bred on fishing boats but they were not yachts, they all had engines. He did not know what to do. I looked at Heine, startled as the deck tilted further beneath me and I grabbed something to stop my feet sliding.

The *Gracie Blue* heeled more, hesitated.

'It's OK,' I said, expecting her to roll back again.

'No it isn't!' Heine yelled. Nicholson, who had been in the cabin, dashed out on deck, grabbed the wheel, turned the yacht's bows to the wind, and slowly she came upright. In no time things were under control again, the wind died as suddenly as it had risen and we were again in calm water on a sunny day, peaceful and beautiful, but Nicholson was white and shaking. Belatedly, I realised it had been a small tornado or whirlwind, it could have developed into a water spout.

'In Spain, you know, I had to sell some of the lead ballast weights out of the keel. Can you imagine it? We crossed the Atlantic, weathered two storms with no trouble whatsoever and then we bloody nearly capsized on a clear blue sunny day in the Caribbean!'

So we came to La Guaira, Venezuela, the port for Caracas. It had taken us a month from Las Palmas. We moored in the yacht basin with other small vessels, some engaged in the coastal trade. The anchorage was quite crowded. Our Spanish passengers and Heine who had documents in order, said their farewells and were gone. The Nicholsons had decided to go on to Florida, after a few days rest and restocking. They would keep Carlos and Bautista with them as crew for the present. Mrs Nicholson must go ashore here to find a doctor to check her condition. Nicholson and the two crewmen would stay on the boat.

My own position was still doubtful. Without any kind of papers at all the immigration authorities even here were doubtful. For the time being at least I must stay with the *Gracie Blue*. I wrote to Helen again for cash.

On the fifth of May, Nicholson, Carlos, Bautista and I, lying and sitting around on deck, heard some kind of disturbance on a small sailing ship that was moored nearby. Angry voices were raised, there were thumps.

'Drunks having a row!' said Nicholson, as we looked across the water to the other vessel, the *Maria de Lourdes*. She was loaded with coffee and cocoa and we had seen the Captain going ashore earlier to complete the paperwork ready for sailing next day. As we looked the voices grew louder and became alarmed rather than angry. There was a reddish glow through the skylight of what was probably the galley.

'Those idiots have set their ship on fire! We must help. Get into the dinghy!'

We rowed quickly across to the other ship from which flames now were shooting up with two men visible in silhouette, trying frantically to fight the blaze. The flames now were reaching the rigging and sails of the vessel.

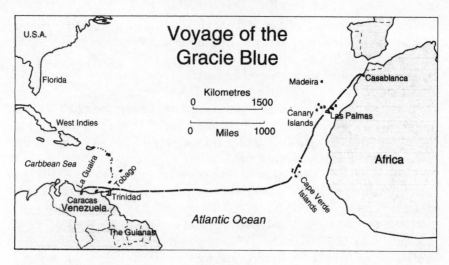

We pulled alongside and scrambled onto to the deck but just as we did so we ourselves were suddenly engulfed in a fireball and a searing rush of unbearable heat. I had a momentary glimpse of a man blazing like a candle and another on fire thrown into the air and then I was on fire too, in the water, struggling to get away, realising that the fuel tanks on the ship had exploded.

Spluttering, swimming, I turned to look back, in pain. The ship was ablaze from stem to stern, other men nearby were in the water coughing and spluttering, someone screaming. Boats came, I was dragged out of the water and was soon in a vehicle, being carried along a bumpy road, in hospital, receiving treatment, dimly aware that Nicholson, Carlos and Bautista were there too.

Next morning, bandaged and tended by nursing sisters the four of us discovered we were in the Hospital of San Juan de Dios. We were all badly burned but despite the pain, not in serious danger. The two crewmen of the *Maria de Lourdes* were very much worse. They were in the casualty unit of the social security hospital and one at least, we were told, was unlikely to survive. Nineteen years old, he had suffered burns to most of his body and been blown off the ship into the water. The other, a fifty-five year old, had severe burns to his face, chest and arms. His situation was doubtful. We had all been rescued by the Port Fire Brigade but they had not been able to save the *Maria de Lourdes* which was reduced to a burnt out hulk and would not be salvageable. We read all about ourselves in the newspaper *EL UNIVERSAL* of 6 May, where the fire and explosion made the front page.

So, at last, I came to port.

Epilogue

Peter recovered from his burns and was allowed to remain in Venezuela. The country was full of refugees, sleeping in shacks and garages, anywhere they could, some even without shelter in the streets. Helen gave up the art school and joined him.

From this low point they began to rebuild their lives. Peter found work as an engineer and they were able to move into a better apartment in the suburbs of Caracas. Helen knew no Spanish but began to learn, found friends who spoke German and who took her to the market and showed her the way around. Much of what they saw in Venezuela distressed them, not only the serious poverty of many of the people but also the needless cruelty to animals.

They had been in Venezuela nearly three years when, having a little money to spare at last, Helen decided she should visit her family in Terre Haute. Peter was still not allowed to enter the USA but heard of a gliding meeting in Canada and decided he would go to it although it was many years since he had flown a sailplane. He flew by a round about route via Trinidad and the Bahamas. Through a glider pilot friend, Ron Claudi, Peter found work in Canada with a construction company and believed he would be allowed to remain there. Helen went briefly back to Venezuela, disposed of their property there, picked up their pet cat and dog and joined him. They remained in Canada two years, living near Ottawa. Helen returned to her painting but in the end Peter's application for residence was rejected and he was expelled at short notice.

They went then to South West Africa and lived in Windhoek. Peter was employed as an engineer to help with designing and supervising the construction of railroad sidings. He was able to do some gliding and became chief instructor at the Windhoek gliding club, flying a British Slingsby T-21 two-seat training sailplane.

Helen was able to earn some money by painting and selling her work through a local camera shop. She developed quite a thriving cottage industry producing coloured greetings cards with African themes.

When the railway work was finished Peter's job also came to an end. They moved to Pretoria and Peter worked in civil engineering while re-training to qualify again for a commercial pilot's licence.

When the Eisenhower administration came into government in the USA, the immigration laws were relaxed, allowing Peter to live in the USA. He and Helen moved in 1955 first to Terre Haute, where he worked for a time as a pilot for a local businessman, then he obtained a job as an engineer with TWA in Kansas City, where they bought a house and Peter was at last admitted to full US Citizenship. He was sent by the firm to Seattle as a member of a group observing some of the first Boeing 707 airliners being constructed there for TWA. He was able to bring about some important improvements in the methods of construction used. Later he worked as an engineer for Pan American Airlines, being sent by the company with Helen to Pakistan and later Vietnam.

After retiring from Pan Am Peter visited Australia in 1971, the only continent to which he had not previously been. (There, among other things, he flew some modern glass-fibre reinforced plastic sailplanes including Martin Simons' Kestrel 17.)

One reason for this visit was to prospect the route for a proposed round the world trip he wished to make in a self-launching sailplane. This was an extension of his idea of 1939, to fly in stages across the North American continent. Subsequently he worked for the flying doctor service in East Africa as a pilot, returning to the USA to live for a time in Florida.

In 1974 there was a meeting of old time glider pilots and vintage sailplanes at the Wasserkuppe. Peter brought to this rally a full-sized replica of the PR 2 glider he had built as a schoolboy and which he had flown in 1920. The replica also flew. It subsequently was hung on display in the entrance hall of Frankfurt Airport. Peter began to write a history of gliding on the Wasserkuppe during the twenties and thirties, which was intended to be a single volume but grew into a large three volume work, published in German during 1977–85. He returned temporarily to Germany to interview many of the survivors of the early German gliding movement and during this time he made a 500 km (300 miles) cross-country soaring flight into France which qualified him for a second diamond added to the Gold badge originally won in 1939. Finally settling in Ardmore, Oklahoma, he managed a small gliding school there for a few years.

His idea of a soaring trip around the world continued to occupy him and he made great efforts to organise it and find sponsorship. Progress has been slow. Approaching the age of 92 years he has been forced to concede that he himself might not be able to do the flying. Instead he hopes to arrange a relay of pilots of different nationalities to fly the many stages. Helen remains with him.

266

Of the many other persons mentioned in his story, a little is known about some of them.

General Von Bötticher survived the war, was interrogated by the Allied authorities and released to live in retirement in Germany. Of him it has been written (by D. Kahn) that he was the most interesting and important of all the German Military Attachés who reported to Berlin during the years preceding World War Two. The views he expressed coincided exactly with those that Hitler most wanted to hear. He was convinced that the USA was in the hands of international Jewry, constantly underestimated the military potential of the US forces, ignored or mocked at facts such as Lend-Lease and discounted arguments that were of vital importance but which contradicted his views. After the Pearl Harbor attack he believed the Americans would concentrate first on Japan. The contradiction between the General's personal statements and the stream of factual data of expanded aircraft production which accompanied his reports, was sufficient to draw comment from post-war analysts.

'Wild Bill' Donovan played a central role in creating the Central Intelligence Agency but to his disappointment was not appointed to lead it once it was established (this honour went to Allen W. Dulles). He remained influential in the USA and was appointed as ambassador to Thailand during 1953-54. After this he returned to practice law in the USA but began to suffer from ill health and died in Washington DC in February 1959. (There is a full biography by A. Cave Brown entitled *The Last Hero*, Michael Joseph, 1982.)

Admiral Canaris, according to Alfred Jodl one of the German Army's leading Generals, 'served the enemy for years'. Otto Skorzeny declared 'Canaris betrayed his country's military secrets directly and wittingly from the beginning of his career to its end'. These statements are probably incorrect but the fact that Canaris was centrally involved in an anti-Hitler conspiracy beginning in 1938, is well documented. He seems to have been a highly complex and inconsistent character. While plotting against the Führer he apparently supported most of the eastward expansionist moves which the Führer made and turned against him only when it became clear that war would result. 'This,' Canaris is reported to have said in September 1939, 'is the end of Germany.' Yet he put considerable effort into moves by the *Abwehr* that helped to precipitate the war and while the conflict lasted there is little to suggest that he ever betrayed secrets to the Allies. He did, eventually, contribute to various schemes to assassinate Hitler, all of which failed. (See Chapter 9 in A. Cave Brown, *op cit* and Chapters 8-13 in H. Höhne, *Canaris*, Doubleday & Co, 1979.)

Paul Leverkühn, born in 1893, served in the German army during World War One and was chosen by Canaris to go as Consul to Tabriz in 1940 because he had military experience in that region. It is apparently correct that Paul Leverkühn and William Donovan were involved in pre-war attempts to retrieve the Tsar's fortunes on behalf of Anna Anderson, the Anastasia claimant and her supporter, Botkin. Leverkühn set up a company in New York in connection with the claim and Donovan did some work on this. Leverkühn's friendship with Canaris suggests this Anastasia business might have been a cover for more clandestine activities. It is probable that he introduced Donovan to Canaris in Berlin and Leverkühn was possibly involved from the beginning in the (ineffective) Canaris conspiracy against Hitler.

On visits to New York, Leverkühn stayed at the home of the German Consul-General in New York, Otto Kiep and his wife. A close friend of the Donovans, Kiep may also have been one of Canaris' men. Leverkühn certainly acted as a go-between in tentative peace moves by Canaris and Donovan at a late stage in the war. After the defection of his assistant from Istanbul, Leverkühn was recalled to Germany and interrogated by the *Gestapo* but survived. He represented Field Marshal von Mannheim at the Nuremburg war criminal trials. He subsequently returned to a distinguished career in law and banking in a rebuilt Germany. Leverkühn's own book, *German Military Intelligence* (Weidenfeld & Nicolson, 1954), is an anthology of stories rather than an autobiography.

Hanna Reitsch, despite volunteering to form and lead a suicide pilots' squadron and being one of the last people to visit Hitler in the Berlin bunker, also survived. She was interrogated by the British and Americans and imprisoned for some time. She returned as soon as possible to the sport of soaring and became National Champion and a member of the German International team in the fifties, spent some years in Ghana training glider pilots for Kwame Nkrumah, and continued actively glider flying and even breaking records until her sudden death from a heart attack in August 1979. As well as her own books, a biography by Judy Lomax (John Murray, 1988) is readily available.

Helge Rosvaenger eventually was able to return to professional singing and remained at the height of his powers for years, making many recordings which are still occasionally played on radio. He has an entry in *Groves Dictionary of Music*.

William Nicholson sold his yacht, the *Gracie Blue*, probably in Florida. He then made his way with Mrs Nicholson via the USA to Canada, briefly staying in British Columbia and Saskatchewan to arrive in Chauvin, Alberta, Canada, a very small town where he set up as a garage operator. Unfortunately by 1950 things had gone badly wrong and he departed, heavily in debt and actively sought by the Canadian police who appealed also for help to the Irish constabulary. He was never found.

The FBI agent to whom Peter Riedel spoke at White Sulphur Springs, Morgan, got in touch with the Riedels years later. Morgan at this time was living comfortably in retirement in Miami.

Index

Åalborg, Danish port, 222
Abwehr, German Military Intelligence Department, 16, 19, 22–3, 98–100, *passim*.
Ain Seba, French Morocco, 246 *et seq*
Air Ministry, German, RLM, *Reichsluftfahrtministerium*, 13, 15, 18, 127
Akaflieg Darmstadt, engineer student flying group, 66
Akaflieg Dresden, student flying group, 162
Alaska Highway, 113
Aliadi, murderer, 240–1
Allen, C B, journalist, USA, 29
America, Soaring Society of, SSA, 7
Amsee, sanatorium, 165–6
Anschluss, Austrian, 16
Anzio landings, Italy, 177
Apelbol, farm, Sweden, 212
Ardmore, Oklahoma, 266
Argentina, 11, 13
armament aid, Japan, 151
armaments exports from USA, 72
Arnold, General, US Army, 75, 78
arrest, Safi, 232
arrest, Sweden, 214
Aschenbrenner, General, *Luftwaffe*, 147
Aschersleben, town, Saxony, 138, 210
assassination plot by army generals against Hilter, 180
Attaché, Military, duties & legality, 16
Attaché Gruppe, German Air Ministry, 20, 127
Australia, 7, 266
Australian Gliding magazine, 7
Austria, 16, 209

Ball-bearing trade, Sweden, 176, 182–3, 196

Bayer, Alfred, soaring pilot, USA, 29
Beresin, Major, USSR, 83, 98, 101–2 *et seq*
Berlin, bombing, 128n, 168n
Berlin, life in wartime, 127, 128–9
Belgium, invasion of, 86
Bergwall, Hans, absconder, 220 *et seq*
Berjois, Paul, sailor & mechanic, 220 *et seq*
Birch-Jensen, Charles, Swedish soaring pilot & author, 210, 212 *et seq*
Birch-Jensen, Elisabeth, Charles' sister, 213, 232, 237
BMW, *Bayeriche Motorenwerke*, 23
BOAC, British Overseas Airlines Corpn., 176
Bolling Air Base, USA, 84–5
Boord, Richard, RAF Officer, 208
Bötticher, General, German Military Attaché to USA, 9 & *passim*, 267
Brazil, soaring expedition, 12
Breakfast Club meeting, California, 60–2
BST, French *Bureau de Securité du Territoire*, 233 *et seq*
Buenos Aires, City, Argentina, 12
Burberry, Joan & family, 24, 175
Busch, Major Fritz, *Abwehr* officer, 170 *et seq*

Canada, 265
Canadian aircraft industry, 74
Canadian flight training programme, 74, 114
Canaris, Rear-Admiral Wilhelm, Head of *Abwehr*, 16, 22, 166, 173, 177, 180, 267
Canary islands, 231, 256 *et seq*
Caribbean Sea, 261 *et seq*
Carlsson, William T, US diplomat, 208
carpet weaving, Saxony, 159

Casablanca, French N. Africa, 7, 233 *et seq*
Casablanca civil prison, 238 *et seq*
Cedeira, Spanish fishing village, 227
Certifcat d'Immatriculation, 244
Chamberlain, Neville, British Prime Minister, 43, 89
Christian Scientists, banned organisation, arrests, 161
Churchill, Winston, British Prime Minster, 43, 89–90, 247
Claudi, Ron, soaring pilot, 265
Cleveland Air Races, USA, 18, 39
cloud flying in sailplane, 33–4
Cobas, Carlos Servino, Spanish sailor, 249 *et seq*
Colombia, S. America, 9, 12
Committee of the Union of Free German Officers in USSR, 183
concerts, 228 *et seq*
concentration camp, Majdanek, 183 *et seq*
concentration camp, Oranienburg, 136
Consuls, conference of, 77
Consulates, German, closure of, 100
Copenhagen, Denmark, 167–8
Courageous, HMS, sinking, 71
Croneiss, engineer, Messerschmitt factory, 144, 155
Curtiss, Glenn L, Aircraft manufacturing Company, 19n
Czechoslovakia, occupation of, 52–3

Daimler-Benz, engine manufacturers, 183
Danish resistance movement, 168
Danzig corridor, 49, 69
Darmstadt, city, Germany, 10, 13, 66
Davos, sanatorium, 166, 173 *et seq*, 206
death camp, Majdanek, 183 *et seq*
Decker, Chet, soaring pilot, 14

Dehlitz village, Saxony, 11, 211
Denmark, invasion of, 86
Desameriq, G, *Inspecteur Chef*, BST, 233 *et seq*
DFS, *Deutsche Versuchsanstalt für Segelflug*, 12n
Dittmar, Heini, soaring pilot, 12n, 123, 142–3
dive bombing, 19n
Donovan, William, New York lawyer, head of OSS, 28–30, 45–6, 169, 179–180, 184 *et seq*, 206, 208, 232, 239, 267
Donovan, Patricia, William's daughter, 45, 85–6
Doris, friend & lover, 12–13, 175
Dornier, Professor Claude, aircraft designer, 141–2
Dover, British port, 225–6
Dresden, city, Saxony, 158–9
Drottningholm, Swedish ship, 122
Dunkirk, evacuation, 88
Du Pont, Allaire, Richard's wife, 14
Du Pont, Richard, soaring pilot, President of SSA, 14, 30
Du Pont, Stephen, Richard's brother, 37–9
DVS, *Deutsche Verkehrsfliegerschule*, 10, 20

Eden, Anthony, British politician 43
Elbe, River, 209
Elmira, town, New York State, 9
Elmira, Harris Hill, soaring site, 10
Elvie, converted fishing boat, 219 *et seq*, 259
Enköping, town, Sweden, 207 *et seq*
Espenlaub, Gottlob, craftsman & pilot, 124
espionage, illegality, 16
Europa ship, spy scandal, 27–8, 40

FBI, Federal Bureau of Investigation, 99–100, 104–112, 119
ferrying, bombers, 160
Fincke, *Gestapo* man in Sweden, 199
Finland, Winter War, 72–3
Finnish contacts, 177 *et seq*
Fleischel, prisoner, 241–2
Flinsch, Walter, pilot, 160–3
flight training programme, Allied, 74, 114
Ford, Henry, automobile manufacturer, 71, 92–3
Foreigners' Commission, *Utmännisches Kommission*, 204–5, 210–11
Frankfurt on Main, arrival, 123
Fritsch, German Army Colonel-General Werner von, 48

Gablenz, Karl August Freiherr von, Head of Lufthansa, 12–13, 134–5, 154

Gaeta, Colonel, Italian military attaché, 118, 122
gas chambers, Majdanek, 184
Geheime Kommandosache, Commanders' secret reports, 171
Georgii, Professor Dr Walter, meteorologist, 10, 12
Gerdes, Captain, *Luftwaffe* pilot, 198 *et seq*
Gestapo, 137, 161, 188
GL-7, *Luftwaffe* Dept of Foreign Armaments, 127–8, 131
Glendale Airport, California, 59–60
Gluhareff, Michael, engineer, 37
Goebbels, Dr, German propaganda chief, 11, *et seq*
Göering, *Reichsmarshall* Hermann, Head of *Luftwaffe*, 19n, *& passim*
Goddard, rocket experiments, 13n
Golcher, Major, German Attaché Gruppe, 180, 183, 198, 205
Gold badge for soaring, Gold C, 37, 62, 266
Gomez, prisoner, 243
Göteborg, Swedish port, 221
gliders in battle, 86, 143
Gracie Blue, yacht, 248 *et seq*
Graf Spee, scuttling of, 71
Grand Canyon, 109
Grancourt Belair, French town, 232
Greenbriar Hotel, White Sulphur Springs, Virginia, 119
Grosskopf, Fritz, *Abwehr* officer, 20–2, 166 *et seq*

Halle, city, 11, 210
Hamburg, fire raids, 176, 183
Hansen, Georg, *Abwehr* officer, 166, 173, 177
Hardison, US Air Attaché, Sweden, 206
Harris Hill, Elmira soaring site, 10, 29–32
Harth, Wilhelm, meteorologist, 12n
Haus der Flieger (Pilots' House, German Acro Club), 196
Heinkel, Ernst, aircraft designer & manufacturer, 155–6, 144–5
Heimann, Colonel von, Military Attaché, Sweden, 168, *et seq*
helicopter, Focke Achgelis, 39
Hess, Rudolf, German Deputy *Führer*, 57
Hebb, German Press Attaché, 204–5
Henje, Sonja, ice skater, 15
Heydrich, Reinhard, *Gestapo*, assassination 1942, 125
Hindenburg Cup for soaring, 10
Himmler, Heinrich, SS chief, 45, 177, 180, 184, 197
Hirth, Wolf, soaring pilot, 12n
Hitler, Adolf, German *Führer*, 11 & *passim*
Holland, invasion of, 86
Hoover Airport, 32

Hoover, Edgar, Head of FBI, 99
hostage, threat to Helen, 205
Hühnerberg, *Luftwaffe* Colonel, *Attaché Gruppe*, 127

illness, Helen, 164–5, 235
information, sources, 77–79, 100
information, collection and filing methods, 79–82
interrogation, Casablanca, 232 *et seq*
Ingrid, Bergwall's girl-friend, 220 *et seq*

Japanese, relations with, 116, 117–8, 147, 151–154, 156
Japan, war with USA, 118
jews & anti-semitism, 24–5, 129, 192
jewish executions, early reports, 122, 126–7, 129, 159–160
jewish extermination camps, reports, 183–4, 191
Juge d'Instruction, 239, 243
Jungfraujoch soaring expedition, 15

Kalkreuth, Bertha von, sculptor, 28
Karlis, refugee, 220 *et seq*
Kasparsson, Ragnar, Swedish journalist, 204–5
Kattegat strait, storm, 221–2
Keams Canyon, Arizona, 111
Klegenstüber *Abwehr* Lt-Colonel, 172
Klemperer, Dr Wolfgang von, engineer, soaring pilot, 60–1
Klug, Helen (*see* Riedel), 44–6 & *passim*
Knudsen, William, American commentator, 189
Kotzenberg, Dr, merchant, philanthropist, 24
Krämer, Dr, *Abwehr* agent, 171 *et seq*
Kristallnacht, 25, 129
Krumitsch, singer, 220 *et seq*
Kyffhäuser myth, 193

Lachmann, prisoner, 238 *et seq*
La Coruña, Spanish port, 227, *et seq*
La Guaira, Port for Caracas, Venezuela, 263 *et seq*
Långholmen prison, Stockholm, 215 *et seq*
Lauterback, Richard, *Time* Magazine reporter, 184
Le Bris, Captain, pioneer aviator, 227
Lehecka, Emil, soaring pilot, 30
Leila, refugee, 221 *et seq*
Le Roy, Howard, Washington lawyer, 89, 186, 239, 248
Leube family, Malmö, Sweden, 174, 209, 219
Leverkühn, Paul, lawyer, banker, *Abwehr* agent, 27n, 45–6, 113n, 234–5, 268
Leverkühn, Renate (cousin), 28, 45–6, 234

Lichtenstein radar SN-2, 199 *et seq*
Lidice, village, Czechoslovakia, 125
Limfjorden, strait, 222
Lindbergh, Charles pilot, 91
Linz, Frau, Jewish landlady, 24, 128–9
Lipetsk, German secret air base in
   USSR, 67, 149
Lippisch, Alexander, aircraft designer,
   123–5, 142–3
Lisbon, Portugal, 123, 230
Løgstar, Danish port, 223
Lublin, Polish city, 179
Lublin, death camp Majdanek, 183,
   188
Lucht, Rulof, *Luftwaffe* Engineer
   Officer, 19–20, 131
Lufthansa, German National Airline,
   10, 13
Luftwaffe, German Air Force, *Passim*
Lund, Larry, garage proprietor,
   Enköping, Sweden, 207
Lund, Else, Larry's wife, 209
Lya, refugee, 221 *et seq*

Magi, refugee, 220 *et seq*
Manhattan, soaring flight over, 9
Maria de Lourdes, trading ship, 263–4
Maritsa, Finnish girl, 209
Marrakesh, Morocco, 247
Majdanek, Mahdan Tatarski, Death
   Camp, 183, 191
marriage to Helen, 102–5
Marshal, General, US Army, 75
Märte K, friend of Ninnie, 176 *et seq*
Messerschmitt, Willi, aircraft designer
   & manufacturer, 143
Mihm, Richard, pilot, 12n
Milch, Erhard, *Luftwaffe* Field
   Marshal, 21, 131, 134, 135, 159
Morgan, FBI Agent, 234, 269
Morocco, N. Africa, 231
Morongo Indians, 62
Morriére, *Juge d'Instruction*, 243
Moses, Senhor, Brazilian newspaper
   proprietor, 24
Munich crisis, 43–6
Myrland, Arthur, New Mexico
   rancher, 65

Nazi Party, *Nationalsocialistische
   Deutsche Arbeiterpartei*, 11–12,
   67–8
Nansen Pass, 205
Nicholson, William Edward T, owner
   of *Gracie Blue*, 248 *et seq*, 268
Nicholson, Mrs, wife of William, 248
   et seq
Nelson, Donald F, President, General
   Motors, 92
New York, proposed bombing raid,
   135
Nietzsche, misinterpreted ideas, 191
Ninnie, (Caroline) R, friend, 176 *et
   seq*
Nilsson, Stig, Swedish sailor, 219

Nordernschørt, General, Swedish Air
   Force, 204
Normandy, Allied landings, 178
Norway, invasion of, 86, 189

Oliveira, Baucista Haz, Spanish sailor,
   249 *et seq*
OSS, USA, *Office of Strategic
   Services*, 169, 179, 205
Oranienburg, town & concentration
   camp, 136, 152
Oskarshamn, town, Sweden, 198–200
Ostermann, Hans, Swedish garage
   chain company, 207
Ovchinnikov, Major, USSR Army,
   83, 98, 101–2

Paky, Hungarian refugee, 220 *et seq*
Palm Springs Airport, California, 62
Pan American Airlines, 10, 266
Patrick, Irishman, co lodger, 248, 253
   et seq
Pearl Harbor, attack on, 118
Poland, invasion of, 70–1
Plate, River, battle of, 71
Pneumothorax treatment for TB, 165
promotion, Riedel's, 85

Quislings, 187, 194, 234

Rancho Montoso, New Mexico, 65
radar, Lichtenstein SN-2, 198 *et seq*
Rechlin, *Luftwaffe* test centre, 19, 23,
   154, 156–7
Reitsch, Hanna, pilot, 12n, 15, 39–40,
   88–90, 128, 142, 197–8, 268
refugees, 210, 215 *et seq*
Resenberg, Dr, German diplomat, 75
Rhön Mountains, Germany, 7–10, 124
Ribbentrop – Molotov Pact, 66
Riedel family
   Mother, suicide, December 1913,
      11
   Annchen (sister), 11, 167
   Beats (sister) died in car accident,
      1932, 11, 86
   Felix (father), 11
   Felix (brother), 11, 125–7
   Helen née Klug, (wife), 7, 44 &
      passim
Riefenstahl, Leni, film director, 18
RLM, Air Ministry,
   Reichsluftfahrtministerium, 13, 15,
   18–21, 127
Rock Creek Park, Riding School, 43
Rome, fall of, 178
Roosevelt, Franklin D, US President,
   72, 90
Rostock, town, Baltic coast, 157–8
Ross, Colln, German author, 145–6,
   150
Rosvaenge, Helge, singer, 220 *et seq*,
   258–9, 268
Rowehl, Theodor, *Luftwaffe* pilot,
   153–4

sailboat, *Sturmvogel*, 164, 182
Saint Louis, city, USA, 111–2
Safe, port, French Morocco, 231
Saxony, German province, 11, 158–9
SCADTA, *Sociedad Colombo-
   Alemana de Transport Aeros*, 10, 13,
   91
Schact, Hjalmar H G, German
   financier, 25
Schindeler family, Stockholm, 215
Schnizelbank song, 41–2
Schwarze Kapelle (Black Orchestra),
   16n
Schulenburg, Frederic Werner Graf
   von, German diplomat, 149 50
Schweningen, Dutch port, 224
Schwenke, Colonel, *Luftwaffe*
   Engineer Officer, 127, *passim*
Second World War, outbreak of, 70
Sefeldt, Captain Swedish Air Force,
   200, 207
Sell, Dr, German News Service
   Representative, USA, 75
Siberian prison camps, 215
Siberts, Valja von, singer, 224 *et seq*
Sikorsky, Igor, aircraft pioneer &
   designer, 37
slave workers, 159–60
Smirnoff Derby, transcontinental
   soaring race, 53n
Slussen, district of Stockholm, 212
Soaring Society of America, SSA, 7,
   30
South Africa, 265
SSA, Soaring Society of America, 7,
   30
Stanley, Robert, soaring pilot, 30
Stockholm, city, 166–173
Strandvägen, Stockholm street, 169
Strempl, Herbert von, German
   diplomat, 75
Sudetenland crisis, 40–3
suicide, mother's, 11
suicide, statistics, 11–12, 193
Suzuki, Major, Japanese Army, 116
Svensen, OSS Agent, 179 *et seq*
Swedish Air Force, 202
Swiss Air Force, 201
Sweden, 86
Swastika, embarrassment caused by,
   25, 29

Tannenberg, Dr, German economist
   & diplomat, 74–6
Toas, town, New Mexico, 90, 107–9
telegrams, recall, 203
Terre Haute, city, Indiana, 46–7,
   103–4
Tempelhof Airport, Berlin, 12
Thompson, Dorothy, American
   journalist, 87
Thomsen, German Ambassador, 74,
   133, 155, 169, 212
Thomsen, Ilmar & Edgar, refugees,
   220 *et seq*

Time magazine, Death Camp report, 184, 188n
Tobago, Caribbean island, 262
Tocumwal, NSW, Australia, 7
Todtmoos, sanatorium, Black Forest, 166
Todt organisation, 159
Towers, US Navy Admiral, 78
Tschersich, Günther, *Luftwaffe* Officer, 148–50
TWA, Trans World Airlines, 266

Udet, Ernst, pilot, *Luftwaffe* Officer, 15, 18–21, 88–9, 115, 128, 132–3
Ukraine, USSR, 149
unconditional surrender, 182
Ursinus, Oscar, editor of *Flugsport* magazine, 124
USSR, 69–71, 148–50
USSR, invasion of, 101–2, 115–6
Uthmann, General von, German Military Attaché, 207

Valentina, Rosvaenge's *de facto* wife, 220
Vansittart, Robert Gilbert, Baron of Denham, 185, 187
Vassila, Arnold, Estonian resident in Sweden, 218
Vassila, Valter, Arnold's nephew, 218
Venezuela, 218, 262 *et seq*
Versailles Treaty, 26–7
Viané, murderer, 242–3
Vigo, Spanish port, 229
Vihlein, Cor, Schlitz Brewery Director, 26–7

Waikerie, town, S Australia, 7
war declared by Germany on USA, December 1941, 118
war outbreak in Europe, September 1939, 70
war ended May 1945, 210
Warnemünde, town, Germany, 155, 161, 167
Washington Monument, 7–10
Wasserkuppe, German gliding & soaring centre, 7–10, 124–5, 266
Weckerlé, French-American entrepreneur, 247
Werewolves, Nazi resistance movement, 181
Werra, Hans von, pilot, escaped German prisoner, 95–8
Weskimeister, Voldemar, sailor, 219 *et seq*
White Sulphur Springs, Virginia, 88, 119, 165
Wiedemann, Fritz, German Consul, California, 56–7

Wiman, Ulva, owner of Apelbol farm, 212–3
Windhoek, S. Africa, 202, 265
Winslow, town, Arizona, 62
Winter War, Finland, 72–3
Witthoeft-Einden, German Vice-Admiral, 75
Wladislaw, refugee, 220 *et seq*
Wolfram, Hans, German Press Agency, California, 53–7

Yalta, three power conference, decisions, 209
Yoshikawa, Japanese officer, 116–7
Yugoslavia, invasion of, 94

Zossen, *Abwehr* HQ, 170, 209

Aeroplane types

Aeronca, 73
Bell P-39 Airacobra, 114
Boeing 'Clipper', 13, 54
Boeing B-17 Flying Fortress, 54, 73, 91–2
Boeing Stratoliner, 54
Boeing 707, 266
Bucker Jungmeister, 39
Consolidated PBY Catalina, 94
Consolidated B-24 Liberator, 91–3
Curtiss CW-20, 65
Curtiss P-36, 56, 86, 87
Curtiss P-40, 87, 114
Curtiss SB2C-1 Helldiver, 80
de Havilland Mosquito, 176
Douglas B-18, 54
Douglas DC-3, 54, 114
Fieseler Storch, 39
Fieseler Fi 103 V-1 flying bomb, 178
Focke Wulf FW 200 Condor, 135, 160
Ford Trimotor, 10, 21
Focke Achgelis, 39
Hawker Hurricane, 56n
Heinkel 111, 86
Heinkel 177, 132, 152–3, 156–163
Junkers 52-3M, 167
Junkers 88, 86, 138–9, 198–201
Lockheed C-69 Constellation, 54n
Lockheed Hudson (Electra), 55, 78
Martin 167 Maryland, 56, 78, 87
Martin B-26 Marander, 114
Messerschmitt M-23, 12n
Messerschmitt 109, 86, 201
Messerschmitt 163 Komet, 123, 142–3
Messerschmitt 110, 132
Messerschmitt 210, 132, 144
Messerschmitt 262, 201

Messerschmitt 321 & 323, 143
North American AT-6 Harvard, 56, 78
North American P-51 Mustang (NA-73), 54
Piper Cub, 73
Republic P-43, 98
Republic P-47 Thunderbolt, 98n
Short Stirling, 157
Supermarine Spitfire, 56

Aircraft factories (Various locations)

Beech, 65
Boeing, 54
Brewster, 27
Cessna, 65
Consolidated, 54
Convair-Vultee, 54
Curtiss, 65
Dornier, 23, 141–142
Douglas, 54
Fieseler, 23
Focke Wulf, 152
Ford, Willow Run, 93, 139, 152
Glenn L. Martin, 50–1, 77–9, 113
Grumman, 84
Heinkel, 152, 155–163
Henschel 130, 153
Junkers, 23, 138–40
Klemm, 23
Lockheed, 52n, 54
Messerschmitt, 23, 123, 142–3
North American, 54
Northrop, 77
Ryan, 77
Stearman, 65

Sailplane types

Condor, 12n
Fafnir, 12n
Grunau Baby, 12n
Habicht, 39
Kranich, 15, 29–32, 53, 59–65, 84–5
Minimoa, 30
Moazagotl, 12n
PR-2, 61, 266
Rhönsperber, 30
Ross Stevens RS-1, 30
Slingsby T-21, 265
Sperber Senior, 9
Weihe, 125